Bibliotheca
Classica
B. H. Johnsonis

The Critical Method in Historical Research and Writing

THE MACMILLAN COMPANY
NEW YORK • CHICAGO
DALLAS • ATLANTA • SAN FRANCISCO
LONDON • MANILA

IN CANADA
BRETT-MACMILLAN LTD.
GALT, ONTARIO

THE *Critical Method* IN *Historical Research* AND *Writing*

HOMER CAREY HOCKETT
EMERITUS PROFESSOR OF HISTORY IN
THE OHIO STATE UNIVERSITY

A REWRITTEN AND EXPANDED EDITION
OF THE AUTHOR'S
INTRODUCTION TO RESEARCH IN AMERICAN HISTORY

NEW YORK: *The Macmillan Company*

PUBLISHED SIMULTANEOUSLY IN CANADA

PRINTED IN THE UNITED STATES OF AMERICA

FIFTH PRINTING, 1961

To F. B. H.

For Constant Aid and Inspiration

PREFACE

The original edition of this Manual was the child of necessity: it grew out of the author's experience and needs. A generation ago it fell to him to advise graduate students who were writing essays for advanced degrees in American history at The Ohio State University. Since each candidate had a subject of his own the adviser dealt with them separately until their increasing numbers made individual conferences a serious burden for him. Relief was found for a time in the fact that there is a methodology common to all topics which can be presented in a course in which candidates meet in a group.

This plan in turn proved unsatisfactory because it depended too much on lectures and student notetaking. There was need of a suitable book to place in each candidate's hands. The chief existing works were unsuitable for one reason or another: They were in French, German, or some other foreign language; or they applied primarily to the history of foreign countries, especially those of Europe; or they dealt with all of the social sciences and sometimes even included literature. They were more helpful to the adviser than to the student whose project was restricted to the field of American history.

It was this situation which led to the preparation of a thin volume entitled *Introduction to Research in American History*. It was intended to lighten the task of supervisors charged with duties similar to those of the author, and on occasion to guide the study of capable beginners who lacked other instruction. The Macmillan Company was persuaded, with some misgivings on their part, to publish the book. This was in 1931. Its reception seemed to prove that it met a felt want.

There have been many reprintings of the volume with minor revisions. The time seems ripe for bringing it up to date by adding bibliographical data and other pertinent matter which has appeared since the first issue. The text has been reorganized and largely rewritten and much new material has been incorporated. As candidates for advanced degrees are likely to become teachers, emphasis has been placed on their orientation for the teaching profession and the relation of history to the mental discipline and sound citizenship of youth in the world society of our times. The Manual takes the novice and attempts to lead him step by step until he attains the master's degree. The latter part of the book contains matter which the author hopes may be helpful to candidates for the doctorate, or those who wish to become professional writers of history or to utilize their historical training in related fields. These changes are so considerable that they warrant giving the present revision the new title: *The Critical Method in Historical Research and Writing.*

A treatise of this character hardly lends itself to an engaging literary style; but the author is consoled by the reflection that the kind of student for whom it is written knows that lively interest in a subject may enliven a dull presentation.

HOMER CAREY HOCKETT

Santa Barbara, California

CONTENTS

ABBREVIATIONS

With a few exceptions the abbreviations in this list follow the rules set out in *The Authors' Book* (New York: The Macmillan Company, 1944) and *Webster's New International Dictionary* (2d edn., Springfield, Mass.: G. and C. Merriam Company, 1946). These works are standard authorities on spelling, capitalization, italicization, and syllabification. Usage in such matters is not absolutely fixed; writers and publishers vary somewhat in their practices.

It is a general rule that words and phrases from foreign languages are to be italicized unless long-continued use has made them virtually a part of the vocabulary of English. An example of a phrase which has thus been Anglicized is the French *chargé des affaires,* which is no longer printed in italics because it has been for centuries a part of the international language of diplomacy. The same rule applies to the abbreviated form of a foreign term, but its application varies because one person may conceive that the term requires italics while another thinks it does not. An example is *ibid.,* the abbreviation for the Latin *ibidem.* Webster indicates that it should be italicized, while some publishers print it in roman type.

Abbreviations and words of foreign derivation used in the present Manual are given here for ready reference. With the exception of "etc." every foreign derivative should be italicized; but in the list the italics are omitted as unnecessary because of this general statement. When any of these abbreviations begins a footnote the first letter should be a capital. However, not all publishers follow this practice. English abbreviations are not italicized, but the same rule applies as to capitalization.

Latin Derivatives

ante (before): Used with page numbers to call attention to some preceding matter in the same chapter.

cf. (*confer* - compare): Used to direct attention to another passage or discussion in the same book or elsewhere.

et al. (*et alii* - and others): Used following name of author, editor, or compiler to indicate that others have assisted in the work.

e.g. (*exempli gratia* - for example).

etc. (*et cetera* - and so forth).

et passim (and here and there): Used to indicate that matter referred to is not found within definite page limits but is scattered.

et seq. (*et sequentes* - and following): Used to indicate that the matter referred to is found on pages beginning with the one cited and those following. The form ff. is sometimes used for the same purpose.

ibid. (*ibidem* - the same): Used to refer to the work last cited.

i.e. (*id est* - that is).

infra (below): Used with page citation to call attention to matter in a subsequent chapter.

loc. cit. (*loco citato* - in the place cited): Best used with writer's name in citing any writing (not a book) such as a magazine article or letter already referred to if other citations have intervened.

op. cit. (*opere citato* - in the work cited): Best used like *loc. cit.* but in citing a book.

post (after): Used like *ante* but referring to subsequent matter in same chapter.

q.v. (*quod vide* - which see): Used to direct attention to something to be found at a place cited.

sic (thus): Used in brackets after an error found in a quotation to indicate that the error is part of the quoted matter.

supra (above): Used like *infra* but referring to matter in a previous chapter.

vide (see): Used like *q.v.* or *cf.*

viz. (*videlicet* - namely).

v. (*versus* - against): Used in citing law cases, as Smith *v.* Jones.

English Abbreviations

ch. - chapter.

chs. - chapters.

comp. - compiler.

ed. - editor.

edn. - edition.

f. - and following. See p., below.

ff. - and following.
f.n. - footnote.
n.d. - no date.
n.p. - no place of publication given.
no. (or No.) - number.
p. - page. (P. 50f. means pages 50 and 51; pp. 50ff. means page 50 and the next two or three.)
pp. - pages.
rev. - revised, revision.
ser. - series.
sess. - session.
tr. - translator.
vol., vols. - volume, volumes (may be omitted and volume number alone given, as X, XVI, etc.)

Additional abbreviations are explained where first used in text or footnotes. For use of foreign terms, abbreviations of English words, and guidance in the use of italics consult any good dictionary.

PART I

The Principles of Historical Criticism

A. Introductory: The Historian's Task

1. History in Today's Culture

The term "history" as used here means the written record of past or current events. By this definition all the ages before mankind learned how to write are prehistoric. Of course those early times were not without events, and modern man may write about them. In one sense such writings are history, but they rest on materials quite unlike those used by the historian. The sources of his knowledge are primarily written documents, although he may sometimes supplement these by utilizing various kinds of unwritten matter, such as structures, utensils, weapons, artifacts, drawings, fragments of bone, and other evidences of human life antedating the invention of writing. These, however, are properly the materials for writers who deal with the prehistoric period. We distinguish them from the historians by calling them archeologists, anthropologists, or ethnologists. Others who write about the phases through which the earth's crust has passed, changes which are also past events, are called geologists or geophysicists, while those who study the origins or behavior of the celestial bodies are astronomers or astrophysicists.

All of these writers are attempting to find out what has happened in the past or is occurring now by examining such evidences as are available in their respective fields of research; and the attempts of all spring from a characteristic of human beings which impels them to learn all they can about the past, present, and future place of the race in the cosmic scheme of things.

This sweeping statement goes beyond the usual thinking of most of us. Unless one is something of a philosopher one's interest is likely to be centered about some one phase of this vast sphere of inquiry. Any aspect of it is extensive enough to enlist all one's powers; if the chosen phase is history its subject matter embraces all man's acts and thoughts throughout the historic period. This inclusive scope dooms written history to be forever fragmentary. Much of the material needed for telling the complete story has been lost or destroyed; much of it has existed only in men's unrecorded thought. Although research is continually uncovering material which adds to the historian's available resources, the task of using all of it exceeds human capacity. Such being the case, the writer of history—and his readers—are entitled to ask what justification there is for pursuing the subject at all.

2. The Uses of History

History is not the only subject that is pursued under difficulties. All human knowledge is fragmentary and it is inconceivable that it can ever be complete. It does not follow that the pursuit of any branch of knowledge is fruitless. Each step forward brings an exhilarating sense of achievement and often yields results of immediate utility. The fruits of growing scientific knowledge are the most conspicuous evidences of this fact. One has only to think of the progress of medicine, the invention of the airplane, automobile, television, or the mastery of atomic energy to realize that science has wrought wonders in recent years. Yet it has certainly only made a beginning in the discovery of nature's secrets.

Worthy contributions to man's life may be claimed for history. The social sciences have aided man to adjust his life to a changing world; the study of history in particular affords a mental discipline that helps him meet new problems soberly and intelligently instead of emotionally and superficially. Many of our most thoughtful leaders are convinced that wisely selected portions of our history, competently taught by well-trained teachers, would not only make the subject interesting to young people but be one of the best means of training them for citizenship. They believe also that the history of our country can be taught as part of that of a world community, bringing into view the worth of other cultures and the evils in our own, and at the same time inculcating wholesome understanding of our national ideals and traditions and devotion to them.

Last but not least of the uses of history is the intellectual honesty which should be developed by the quest for truth in any field of knowledge, in defiance of all temptations to wander from the strait and narrow path which alone can lead to it.

3. The Development of Historical Method

a. *A Page from an Ancient Historian*

The forerunner of the modern school of historians was the Greek Thucydides who wrote his *History of the Peloponnesian War* in the fifth century B.C. (471–396?). Explaining his method he said that he supplemented his own observations by the reports of other eyewitnesses. Perceiving that the accounts of the witnesses varied more or less, he decided that the discrepancies were due to lapses of memory or partisan bias, and that they should be subjected to the "most severe and detailed tests possible." He realized also that his efforts to be exact deprived his style of color, but hoped that the want of an engaging manner was offset by "an exact knowledge of the past" which might aid "in the interpretation of the future." It would be difficult for a modern historian to justify his calling more fittingly in as few words.

b. *A Period of Confusion*

For many centuries few writers profited by Thucydides's example. During the Middle Ages *authority* (statements in the writings of Aristotle, the Church Fathers, the Scriptures, the dogmas of the Church) stifled the spirit of inquiry. This attitude is not even now wholly abandoned, but it has given way generally among scholars to the belief that facts can be ascertained and the truth established only on the basis of *evidence*. A sign of this change appeared when Renaissance scholars developed the principles of textual criticism in the effort to restore the original reading of ancient writings of which they had only faulty copies. The clearest evidence of the new intellectual orientation came, however, in the field of natural science.

Much Greek thought had been *a priori*; that is, it started with propositions which were thought to be self-evident (axiomatic), needing only to be stated or set forth in a definition. Thus it was self-evident that a straight line did not change direction. From this axiom it was deduced that parallel lines in the same plane are equidistant throughout their mutual extent. From this deduction another was drawn, *viz.*, that the opposite sides of a parallelogram are equal. Thus by successive deductions, each based on those which preceded, Euclidean geometry was evolved.

In other fields the results of this style of thinking were less happy. Aristotle taught that heavy bodies have a "natural tendency" to fall to the earth, while very light ones go upward because that is *their* "natural tendency." From these "axioms" he deduced that of two falling bodies the heavier falls the faster. A characteristic of such reasoning was its blindness to the necessity or even possibility of testing conclusions experimentally.

The Middle Ages inherited this manner of reasoning and went even further by regarding the classical heritage of "knowledge" as a body of ultimate truth. The theologians of the era thought it self-evident that man was the crowning work of the Creator and deduced the belief that the earth as his abode must be the center of the created universe. They were not ignorant of the illusion of transferred motion, but it seems not to have entered their heads that the earth was a sphere rotating on its axis, which would have explained the apparent movement of the celestial bodies around it. Anyway they preferred a deduction based on their theology.

c. *The Impact of Science*

The intellectual reorientation which resulted from the adoption of the experimental method was nothing short of revolutionary. The new spirit of investigation aroused the stagnant intellect of Western Europe; the minds of leaders became dynamic. The Copernican hypothesis that the sun is the center of the planetary system, published in 1543, was a fruit of the new way of reasoning. That way doomed *a priori* logic to a slow death. Each step led to another. Copernicus had assumed that the orbits of the planets were circular. This error was rectified a few years later by Johann Kepler (1571–1630) by the use of the new technique. Employing Tycho Brahe's tables recording his observations of planetary movements, Kepler discovered that they did not support the theory of circular orbits, and after much experimenting with alternative assumptions found that slightly elliptical orbits tallied with Brahe's tabulations.

Galileo (1564–1642), another convert to the new way of thinking, disproved by experiment Aristotle's teaching that bodies of different weight fall at different speeds, and by other experiments worked out the "laws" of falling bodies. Sir Isaac Newton (1642–1727) in his turn utilized the findings of his predecessors and the recent advances in mathematics to formulate the law of universal gravitation.

Thus gradually men turned from authority to evidence based on observation and experiment, and the former notions about nature and its ways were superseded.

The story of the advance of science discloses a simple procedure. It has three stages: observation, hypothesis, and experiment. As the result of observation the scientist forms a guess or hypothesis, which is a tentative conclusion about the facts observed. The truth of the hypothesis must be tested by further observation, which takes the form of experimentation. The experiment is in fact controlled observation, purposely including the examination of additional phenomena to test the tenability of the hypothesis. Thus all three processes are actually phases of intelligently directed observation. The scientist does not proceed, as one might suppose, with his feet constantly on the ground of ascertained fact. He must be continually formulating and testing hypotheses or he could not progress at all. As Lord Kelvin put it, the thinking of the scientist is always at least two jumps ahead of knowledge. Scientific *thinking* is thus the advance guard of knowledge, exploring paths which may lead to truth previously unknown.

This excursion into the history of science is not really a digression, for the methods of research in all fields are related. Modern historians share the spirit of the scientist and use scientific procedures to gather dependable information. Especially for a century or so historians have sought to adapt the methods of science to their special problems. Some, indeed, have made efforts to discover and formulate the laws governing human conduct, assuming that as natural phenomena men's acts are ruled by natural laws. Most, however, have decided that their tools are not suited to dealing with problems of that type and have accepted the more modest role of narrators and interpreters of men's doings, leaving to the newer sciences of sociology and psychology the investigation and formulation of the laws which govern them. Nevertheless they do not hesitate to appropriate the results obtained by these sciences, and in future will undoubtedly draw upon them more and more.

History is not a science of *direct* observation, like chemistry and physics. The historian like the geologist interprets past events by the traces they have left; he deals with the evidences of man's past acts and thoughts. *But the historian, no less than the scientist, must utilize evidence resting on reliable observation.* The difference in procedure is due to the fact that the historian usually does not make his own observations, and that those upon whose observations he must depend are, or were, often if not usually untrained observers. Historical method is, strictly speaking, a process *supplementary* to observations, a process by which the historian attempts to test the truthfulness of the reports of observations made by others. Like the scientist he examines his data and formulates hypotheses, *i.e.*, tentative conclusions. These conjectures he must test by seeking fresh evidence or re-examining the old, and this process he must continue until, in the light of all available evidence, the hypotheses are abandoned as untenable or modified until they are brought into conformity with the available evidence. Time was when it was thought that the proper application of the rules of evidence could establish the truth beyond question, but historians have learned that they can hope at best only to establish facts beyond reasonable doubt. It is virtually impossible ever to be sure that no further evidence will be brought to light to modify conclusions.[1]

The historian's task is a dignified and worthy part of man's unceasing effort to discover whatever may be discoverable concerning the cosmos and his place in it, and to perpetuate the knowledge gained. As Thucydides suggested so long ago, "an exact knowledge of the past" may aid in "the interpretation of the future." More than that should now be said, for the link between past and future is even closer than he thought. History makes the deeds of men live after them. Its function is to transmit knowledge of the past. It is a nation's memory, perpetuating its deeds, its traditions, and even its mistakes, but also its aspirations and ideals. It makes the past a part of us, shapes our deeds in many ways, and links past and present with the future, making all one.

[1] For a good presentation of the use of hypothesis in historical work see Allen Johnson, *The Historian and Historical Evidence* (New York: Charles Scribner's Sons, 1926), ch. 7. (Hereafter this book will be cited as Johnson, *Historical Evidence.*)

This citation of Johnson's book illustrates the form used in articles published in periodicals or elsewhere when it is not feasible to give bibliographical data except in footnotes. Some subsequent footnotes will further illustrate this practice while others will illustrate the somewhat different practice followed where there is a formal bibliography.

4. The Training of the Historian

One who has given the matter no thought might suppose that writing history is an easy undertaking, a mere gathering of facts and assembling them in an orderly way. Even a child may indeed be assigned a story to be retold in its own words, and such an exercise might well be the first step in training a future historian. Further steps may be taken in the secondary school, where students may be led to form sound judgments in simple cases of conflicting evidence—or of suspending judgment where a conclusion is not warranted. The full value of training in historical method, however, is hardly to be realized by students with less preparation than a good college course affords.

a. *Three Essential Processes*

There are three essential steps in the production of any written historical work: the gathering of the data; the criticism of the data; and the presentation of facts, interpretations, and conclusions in readable form. None of these processes is simple; each has its own technique, and in its advanced form each requires superior mentality and special training.

It must be realized at the outset that the process of collecting data does not yield material ready for use in historical composition. Such material is in the raw state and cannot be used until it has been subjected to critical examination. The principles of criticism are what is most commonly meant when the term "historical science" is used. They require careful study; yet there is no part of the historian's task that the beginner is so likely to slight. He usually has to be taught to cultivate an attitude of skepticism—to understand that his material is made up in large part of statements by more or less ignorant, partisan, unscrupulous, careless, or incompetent persons. The principles by which all statements are tested and sifted are in reality little more than common-sense rules carefully formulated, but a mastery of them will help the beginner to avoid blunders which are inevitable if he learns his lessons from his own unguided efforts and experience.

The culminating effort of the historian for which everything else is preparatory is of course the synthesis of his sifted material into an accurate and readable account of the subject investigated. The undertaking will be judged by the finished product, and the competent critic will not fail to look into the writer's use of the three essential techniques.

Difficulties beset the writer at every stage of his work. In the first place his search for material must be adequate. Then throughout the study his "eye must be single." Even though he cannot hope to tell the whole truth he must strive to tell nothing but the truth. With the most honest intentions he will find it difficult to be impartial because of his own preconceptions, party, sectarian, racial, national, or other group associations and resulting bias. It is not given to man to escape bias altogether.

When he has done his best in these respects there is still a technique of presentation to be followed, for in order to be professionally orthodox a historical production must include bibliographies and footnotes drawn up in the form prescribed by recognized usage. Finally the effectiveness of the study will be proportionate to the skill with which the writer can use the English language.

b. *Auxiliary Sciences*

The gathering of the data pertinent to any topic one may undertake to investigate requires a considerable technical equipment even when all of the material is available in printed form in one's own language. Many researches require much more, for example the examination of documents in foreign languages, modern or ancient; the reading of medieval Latin chronicles, or the deciphering of ancient Roman or Greek monuments, Egyptian hieroglyphics, or Assyrian cuneiform tablets. The requisite equipment varies of course with the field in which the research lies, as does the knowledge which may be required of such "auxiliary sciences" as epigraphy, paleography, diplomatics, chronology, etc.

The auxiliary sciences, indispensable for work in some fields, are tools employed by the historian as occasion requires rather than essentials of all historical work, but every investigation which eventuates in written history involves all three of the essential processes described above. Since it is simpler to master these processes before undertaking to study the auxiliaries, the present Manual is confined, except for certain illustrative matter, to the field of American history. Its treatment of the principles of criticism and historical composition may nevertheless serve as an introduction to these essential processes for the student whose contemplated research lies outside the field of American history.

c. *The Preparatory Training*

In addition to the essential techniques there are certain prerequisites which must be met by any one who undertakes even as modest a contribution to history as a master's essay. The curriculum of a good college of liberal arts offers an adequate general education, and an undergraduate major in the social sciences should yield a sufficient acquaintance with subject matter and point of view in the field of history. If the student is in the graduate school he should take one or more "background" courses during the first year of graduate study in order to gain solidity of content and breadth of information in the particular field in which his research falls. One who is working independently must make up for the lack of such courses by extensive reading.

If institutions offering work leading to the master's degree in history would make a course in method available to undergraduate seniors, it would enable them to do vastly better work as candidates for the degree at the end of one year of graduate work. To crowd instruction in method, the necessary courses, research, and the writing of the essay into one academic year practically insures an inferior production. In fact more time is almost always required, and some universities frankly announce that two years must be devoted to the task.

Any one who attacks a historical theme should have learned certain fundamental lessons from his general studies. From the natural sciences he should have gained some insight into scientific method in general—the functions of observation, experiment, and hypothesis in the reasoning process, and the relations of cause and effect; from biology and the social sciences he should have learned that there is a continuity which runs through all changes, and that this continuity holds in the history of human institutions and relations; from the languages he should have learned to express his ideas effectively, at least in English, as well as how to read the languages needed in his research. If these lessons remain to be learned along with the historical techniques, the path to achievement will be long and hard.

5. The Rewards

The writing of a good study even for the master's degree will bring a practical reward by opening doors for employment, especially in teaching, which otherwise would remain closed. In addition, a master's essay may make a real even if minor contribution to historical knowledge and thus become a source of justifiable pride on the part of the author. More important than either of these rewards for hard work is the discipline which should result from the use of the critical method. The candidate will have been required to make a painstaking effort to find evidence and weigh it without prejudice with truth as his sole objective. He will have gained a supreme value if he has learned to distinguish between *assertion* and *fact.*[2] If this discipline helps him to form permanent habits in reaching judgments it will be a factor in shaping his character. Such training is vital for sound citizenship but is all too rare. It is no exaggeration to say that the perpetuity of our free institutions depends as much on the sound judgment of our citizens as upon their honor.

Many of the users of this Manual will never write more history than is required in the essay for the master's degree. Some may follow with a doctoral dissertation or even more ambitious undertaking. Increasing opportunities are opening for trained workers in the field of history and related work. Whether historical training leads into these or not, one will still be a citizen, and the training should make him a good one.

[2] The *New York Times* recently warned its readers that they must make this distinction for themselves. Having made some statements in October, 1953, about Communism at Fort Monmouth on the strength of certain assertions by a United States senator, the *Times* had to confess editorially three months later that no evidence had been found to support them. The newspapers have learned a lesson, ran the comment, "that will not quickly be forgotten . . . but the reading public should understand that it is difficult to ignore charges" that may turn out to be false. "The remedy lies with the reader." (Quoted by *Time*, January 25, 1954, p. 79. See also issue of February, 1954, p. 72, under caption "Reader Beware.")

B. The Principles of Historical Criticism

The first step in the production of a historical work is naturally the gathering of the data pertinent to the topic. In the beginner's case, however, it is desirable that he be first introduced to the critical method. He will then be better prepared to handle his data and more able to select it with discrimination.

The aim of the historian is to ascertain *facts,* as they must be made the basis of all conclusions or generalizations. Conclusions, interpretations, and generalizations are themselves facts of a higher order, serving to give history its meaning and value. *Statements* are the raw materials with which the historian works, and the first lesson he must learn is that they must not be mistaken for *facts.* They may be facts but that cannot be taken for granted. His task is, if possible, to make such a use of statements that through them he will arrive at facts.

A statement is nothing more than what some one has said about a matter, and there are many reasons why statements may not be wholly or even partially true. The maker may or may not have witnessed the event; he may have lied deliberately; he may have colored his report more or less unconsciously because of his own interests, sympathies, or prejudices; he may through ignorance or some other form of incompetence have been incapable of making an accurate observation and report.

In view of all these possibilities of error it becomes the duty of the historian to *doubt every statement until it has been critically tested.* A proper examination will reveal the falsity of some statements and the dubious character of others. Still others will emerge indorsed as probably true or true beyond reasonable doubt.

The critical examination of statements involves two separate processes, although the critic may learn to carry them on simultaneously. The first is preliminary and preparatory in that it affords the data which the second employs. It is known as External (or Lower) Criticism. It examines *documents*—a comprehensive term which here includes not only manuscripts but books, pamphlets, maps, and even ancient inscriptions and monuments—with the aim of obtaining all possible information of any significance about their origin, and if need be, of restoring the original form or wording. External criticism begins with the collection of material if one gathers data about origins at the same time. If it is clear that a document is authentic that part of its external criticism is already done.

Equipped with the results of external criticism, the historian next applies Internal (or Higher) Criticism to determine the *meaning* and *trustworthiness* of *statements*—not *documents.* This branch of criticism is designed to yield a sifted body of statements appraised according to the degree of probability each possesses—a mass of information in which *facts* and probabilities are made ready for use in a discriminating essay.

It should be noted that examination of a document may reveal internal *evidence* of its origin, etc., which belongs under the head of *external* criticism, while internal *criticism* often utilizes external *evidence.* Internal evidence, in other words, supplies facts for use in external criticism and vice versa.

1. External Criticism

The investigation of the origin of a document requires the discovery of all that can be learned as to where, when, why, and by whom it was written. The inquiry seeks the author's name, party, sect, race, and other group affiliations; it asks whether the document is what it purports to be, and whether it is the original or a copy; in the latter case it asks whether it is a correct copy, and if it is not, it inquires whether its errors can be detected and eliminated and the original reading restored.

In one way or another documents often come to be mistaken for something which they are not. Sometimes forgeries gain acceptance; spurious documents of other kinds become current in various ways.

It is obvious that the historian can hardly judge of the trustworthiness of *statements* unless he knows that the *document* containing them is really what is seems to be. The investigation of its origin may reveal its real character. Without adequate information supplied by external criticism, internal criticism has little to work with. An anonymous document may, indeed, reveal the bias of the author and even his purpose and by its general tone give some hint of its date and other circumstances attending its production, but the identification of the author by name may be of importance in evaluating the document.

a. *Determination of Authorship*

i. USE OF INTERNAL EVIDENCE

The Bible has been a fertile field for external criticism. For a long time devout people deprecated the application of critical principles to Holy Writ as sacrilegious, but the method must be judged by its fruits. It was quite possible for pious Bible readers of two or three generations ago, interested in the Book of Isaiah, for example, for its spiritual values, to pass unnoticed the internal evidence that not all of it was written by the same man. It might seem that little if any critical training would be needed to show a reader that this was the case, for the first chapter dates the period of the prophet's activity by referring to the contemporary kings of Judah, while chapter forty-five mentions Cyrus as king of Persia at the time of the writing of that later chapter. It was only necessary to know that Cyrus reigned about two centuries later than the kings named in chapter one. Given that bit of information the conclusion was easy that Isaiah "son of Amoz" (ch. i: verse 1) could not have written the entire book as it appears in our modern Bible. But many readers of former generations lacked even that modicum of extra-Biblical education. The evidence scholars have today proves that the book was the work of at least three prophets, Isaiah being the first. Because the names of the others are unknown they are for convenience designated respectively the second ("deutero") Isaiah and the third ("trito") Isaiah.

ii. USE OF SUPPLEMENTARY DATA

By checking all the internal clues with the history of Judah's neighboring kingdoms the critics determined that the activity of the real Isaiah fell in the years between about 740 and 700 B.C., while the deutero Isaiah delivered his messages to the Jewish exiles in Babylon around 540 B.C. The third Isaiah came still later. Internal evidence tells something about these other Isaiahs although their names will probably never be known.

The story of the results obtained by the external criticism of this book of the Bible can be told in these few words, but they make the process seem simpler than it was in fact. It is instructive to know a little about the problems the critics had to solve and the data which made the solution possible. It was not the work of a single scholar; many made some contribution to it. To begin with, the dates of events as given in ancient documents had to be restated for modern use in terms of the Christian calendar. This was a difficult task. Much Old Testament chronology is given in terms of the reigns of kings, and the length of their rule is stated in years disregarding fractions. That is, a king who ruled for a year and three months was said to have reigned "two years." Events were dated by referring to the year of the king in whose reign they occurred. (For examples see Isaiah vi:1; vii:1; xxxvi:1; xxxix:1; II Kings xviii:1, 9–10; xxi:1, 19; xxii:1; and numerous other places.) [1]

There are frequent references in the Book of Isaiah to contemporary events in neighboring kingdoms, but their chronology was also baffling to students until events common to Hebrew history and these other countries could be dated. Dates thus ascertained gave clues making it possible to establish parallel chronologies.

The comparison of the history of two or more states requires a knowledge of the language of both. During the period covered by Isaiah the two Hebrew kingdoms had for neighbors Egypt, Assyria, Babylonia, Persia, and several smaller countries, making the linguistic equipment needed by modern critics formidable indeed. Some of these languages remained unknown until quite recently. Egyptian records were not deciphered by Europeans until early in the nineteenth century, and not until the middle of that century was the key found to the Persian of the time of Cyrus. Henry C. Rawlinson succeeded in deciphering part of an inscription on the Behistun Rock on which Darius I had recorded his conquests including that of Babylonia. The results of Rawlinson's work were published in 1846, and provided clues which enabled later scholars to decipher

[1] Citation of Bible passages in the text enclosed in parentheses is an alternative to giving references in footnotes. This alternative is followed in this Manual.

other parts of the inscription and recover two more ancient languages, Susian and Babylonian.[2]

Thus archeology, the knowledge of many languages, and the history of several nations were needed to interpret the internal evidence found in the Book of Isaiah and give it its proper—and intelligible—place in the general history of the eighth, seventh, and sixth centuries before Christ. The study of Isaiah illustrates the application of most of the principles of external criticism on a scale not likely to confront the worker in the field of American history. It begins with an analysis of internal evidence; draws data from the findings of archeologist and linguist; calls on the expert in chronology for his contribution; requires a comparison of events in several countries; and by combining the information brought together by all these means succeeds in answering rather fully most of the questions asked by this branch of criticism, *viz.*, when, why, where, and by whom the book was written. The student who reads Isaiah with this collateral information in mind can see something of the process by which these several questions were answered.

Two questions remain to be answered: Has the original of Isaiah been preserved? If not, do we possess correct copies of it? The answer to the first is No. As for the second, the restoration of a lost original requires a technique which will be discussed later. In the case of Isaiah, the oldest known copy is believed to have been made about the beginning of the Christian Era. The several parts which compose it are combined in this early copy substantially as they are in our modern Bible. Scholars can do little more than guess why and when they were brought together, and they have still less to go on in judging whether they reproduce the exact words of the lost original. It is probable that they do not.[3]

The application of external criticism to Isaiah proved to be both harmless and instructive. It did no injury to the influence of the book;

[2] Jack Finnegan, *Light from the Ancient Past* (Princeton, N. J.: Princeton University Press, 1949), 196–197.

[3] It is now possible to determine the age of organic remains of any kind with considerable accuracy by using carbon 14. It measures the time that was required for the remains to lose as much of their original radioactive character as they have lost. The papyrus of Isaiah was found in 1949, and at that time was the oldest known copy of any Old Testament book. In 1953, however, other manuscripts were found containing a large part of the Old Testament, some of them probably two hundred years older than the Isaiah papyrus. The brief study so far made indicates that a good deal of revision of the text of our present Bible may result.—*Time,* February 22, 1954, p. 57.

on the contrary, giving it its correct place in the history of the Jews and their neighbors aided in understanding it. Elaborate as external criticism is seen to be by this illustration, it leaves untouched the further story of the attempts of the *higher* criticism to interpret the *meaning* of its prophetic passages. The conclusions in this area are highly controversial.

iii. TONE OF A DOCUMENT

The Bible affords many other illustrations of the uses of historical criticism. The ancient Hebrews had no conception of critical principles. Nowhere in their writings is there apparent any such motivation as influenced Thucydides. Their aims were controlled by their religious purposes, and such of their writings as come nearest to being historical are made up of material selected to show God's dealings with his chosen people. They arranged the books of the Old Testament in the order best suited to this purpose. This order creates some problems for the modern Bible student. The Book of Ruth will illustrate how one of these was solved.

Although the English Bible in use today departs somewhat from the Hebrew arrangement of the Old Testament it retains the position of Ruth, *i.e.*, just after Judges. Its opening words are: "Now it came to pass in the days when the judges ruled . . .," that is, about the twelfth century B.C. This reference to the days of the judges may have led the naive scholars who gave Ruth its place to think that it fixed the time of its writing. To today's critic, fixing the date of a writing by the *events it recounts* is like assuming that a history of our War of Independence must have been produced at the time the war was fought.

From internal evidence and comparison with other Biblical writings critics have decided that Ruth was written after the return of the exiles to Jerusalem from Babylon, probably about 400 B.C. Although anonymous, the *tone* of the book indicates that it was written by a liberal-minded Jew or group of Jews as a protest against the teaching of Ezra, a scribe who led the returned exiles. This man believed that the Hebrews had been paganized through generations of intermarriage with their heathen neighbors; that this contaminating influence had led them away from the worship of their own God, and that all their misfortunes were God's punishment for this sin. Hence he demanded that those returned exiles who had brought their pagan wives with them give them up. (See Ezra, chs. ix and x.)

In the charming story of Ruth is found the counter argument. Ruth, of the land of Moab, widow of a Hebrew who had sojourned in that land, accompanies her widowed mother-in-law Naomi when she returns to her native Judah. In the beautiful words of verses sixteen and seventeen of chapter one she rejects Naomi's advice to remain in Moab. In Judah Ruth marries Boaz, and the story reaches its climax when it develops that their son Obed was the father of Jesse and grandfather of the great king David. Thus the Jews are reminded that pagan blood ran in the veins of their greatest king. Insofar as the story has any basis in fact it must be sought in the traditional genealogy of David, for the Jews were much given to genealogy; but it breathes the spirit of Isaiah who had long before declared that a "son" (descendant) of David was to be the hope of the Gentiles as well as of Israel (Isaiah xi:1–10 and elsewhere). The story is a remarkable tribute of the liberal Jew to the worth of the Gentile, and its tone establishes its postexilic date.

iv. ANONYMOUS WRITINGS

While in the case of the "other Isaiahs" and Ruth the lack of authors' names does not deprive us of any very important knowledge, a writer's name may bring in its train other useful facts, such as his character, connections, and trustworthiness. It may even prove his story to be fictitious. Hence external criticism properly seeks the authorship of anonymous documents. Of course anonymous writings share with those by known authors the need of the tests applicable to all statements.

A famous problem concerning the authorship of an anonymous document is posed by "The Diary of a Public Man." This document was published by *The North American Review* in 1879, and purported to have been written in Washington during the winter of 1860–1861.[4] It professed to include "Unpublished passages of the secret history of the Civil War," and was accepted as genuine by historian James Ford Rhodes, Lincoln's biographers Ida Tarbell and Carl Sandburg, and others. As late as 1926 Professor Allen Johnson wrote that the internal evidence indicated that the author "was a man of public distinction . . . had long been in residence in Washington. His contacts with the leading personalities at the

[4] It began in the August issue and ran through the monthly numbers ending with that for November (CXXIX, 125–140, 259–273, 375–388, 484–496). It has been reprinted with Prefatory Notes by F. Lauriston Bullard, and a Foreword by Carl Sandburg (New Brunswick, N. J.: Rutgers University Press, 1946).

Capitol were numerous. Though . . . a Northerner and a stanch Unionist he was in touch with Southern leaders . . . was recognized as a conservative and a lover of peace . . . had been a Whig; was probably now a Republican and . . . a member of the Senate."[5] Quite recently the "Diary" was described in a bookdealer's catalogue as an "enormously important day-by-day account . . . of great importance as source material on the Civil War."

Professor Johnson's interest lay in extracting from internal evidence all possible information concerning the anonymous author. Apparently none of the writers mentioned seriously questioned the accuracy of the diarist's statements, accepting them as reliable source material. Here then were two related problems: Who was the author? Are his statements truthful? Critics were intrigued by the puzzle of anonymity to such a degree that they seemed to forget the rule that no statement establishes a fact unless it is corroborated.

The authenticity of the "Diary" was discussed on a few occasions, as in *The American Historical Review* of January, 1937, but a serious and prolonged search for the secret of authorship was undertaken about 1913 by Professor Frank M. Anderson, who published the results in 1948.[6] After examining evidence pointing to various individuals as the possible author and finding in each case facts which disproved the supposition of his authorship, Anderson finally awarded the decision to a man named Sam Ward. He also concluded that the "Diary" was not written in 1860–1861, but later; and that while perhaps parts were based on a diary kept in the alleged years, the published version contained fictitious episodes added later. These conclusions should have warned historians that the "Diary" is *not* a valuable source of facts not to be found elsewhere, and by implication rebuked the writers who had so readily accepted its statements.

However, Anderson's findings have not been universally accepted as definitive. The problem has recently been revived, and there is no certainty that the time is near for writing Finis to the discussion.[7] The

[5] *Historical Evidence*, 59–60.

[6] *The Mystery of "A Public Man": A Historical Detective Story* (Minneapolis: University of Minnesota Press, 1948).

[7] Roy N. Lokken, "Has the Mystery of 'A Public Man' been Solved?" (*The Mississippi Valley Historical Review*, December, 1953, pp. 419–440. Hereafter this journal will be cited as *MVHR*). This article examines the evidence adduced by Anderson and holds it to be inconclusive at certain points. His citations of previous discussions are equivalent to an informal bibliography of the topic.

mystery, if and when it is solved, will have no great intrinsic importance, but as an example of the application of historical method will have value for students.

Another study of authorship concerns two letters over the signature of General Zachary Taylor written during the campaign of 1848 which resulted in his election to the presidency. These letters were addressed to his brother-in-law, Captain J. S. Allison. His Whig supporters knew that his availability as a candidate rested on his successes in the Mexican War, and were alarmed because both before and after his nomination he wrote letters attempting to explain his political attitude which were so uncertain in meaning that they injured rather than advanced his prospects. The Allison letters were written to offset the effects of Taylor's own communications, and probably had that effect, but that they were written by some one else was evident to keen observers because of the contrast between the incapacity of Taylor's own pen and the clear direct style of the letters.

The identity of the real writer or writers has been only partially determined. The authorship of the first has been established beyond reasonable doubt, but the evidence for the second is, up to this time, not conclusive.[8]

V. CLUES TO AUTHORSHIP

The clue to the authorship of an anonymous document is sometimes found in its relation to other documents. If a critic is familiar with a whole class of documents he is well prepared to determine the authorship of an anonymous one in the same class. He will find clues where the novice may see none. The moral is obvious: a writer should know the sources for his theme.

Among the documents recording the story of the early exploration and settlement of Virginia is one entitled "A Relatyon of the Discovery of our River, Made by Capt. Christopher Newport, and sincerely written and observed by a gentleman of the Colony." This document was first published in 1860, by the American Antiquarian

[8] These decisions are presented by Joseph G. Raybach after a careful survey of the evidence. See article entitled "Who Wrote the Allison Letters: A Study in Historical Detection," in *MVHR* for June, 1949, pp. 51–72. A similar problem is studied in *Abraham Lincoln and the Widow Bixby*, by F. Lauriston Bullard (New Brunswick, N. J.: Rutgers University Press, 1946). The problem is, Did Lincoln or John Hay write the letter. Bullard thinks Lincoln wrote it. The study is a good examples of the use of historical method.

Society.[9] The editor, Edward Everett Hale, did not identify the "gentleman of the Colony" who wrote it, but later scholars, more familiar with contemporary materials, think that the author was Captain Gabriel Archer, the recorder of the colony. The evidence is as follows:

The "Relatyon" informs us that Captain Newport took with him five "gentlemen, four maryners, and fourteen saylors," all of whose names appear in the roster of the expedition. As the "Relatyon" is by "a gentleman," "the maryners" and "saylors" may be disregarded, since in the early seventeenth century that title was not accorded to men of these classes. Of the "gentlemen" three call for attention. First is Gabriel Archer, the recorder. It might have been a part of his official duty to preserve an account of the expedition. Another of the gentlemen is John Smith; but in his "True Relation" he gives an account of the same journey which differs in so many ways from the "Relatyon" that they cannot be from the same hand. The third gentleman is George Percy, whose "Discourse," described below, is also clearly not the work of the anonymous author of the "Relatyon." Both Smith and Percy are thus eliminated, but the latter's "Discourse" contributes additional evidence pointing to Archer as the author of the "Relatyon."

When this party was in the neighborhood of the falls of James River, they discovered that the Indians in that neighborhood were hostile to those on Chesapeake Bay. This fact suggested a bid for their friendship on the basis of common enmity to the Chesapeake tribes. The passage in the "Relatyon" reads:

> Also we perceived the Chessipian to be an enemye generally to all thes kyngdomes; upon which I tooke occasion to signifye our displeasure with them also; making it knowne that we refused to plant in their countrys; that we had warres with them also, shewing hurts scarce whole, received by [from] them. . . .

The use of the pronoun "I" in this passage strongly suggests that the writer showed wounds which he had himself received. Yet a critic's attention would hardly be arrested by the passage unless his knowledge of other documents enabled him to correlate this statement with them. One of these other documents bears the title "Observations gathered out of a Discourse of the Plantation of the

[9] *Archaeologia Americana,* IV, 40–65.

Southerne Colonie in Virginia by the English, 1606." [10] The author was "that Honorable Gentleman, Master George Percy." In this document, commonly called "Percy's Discourse," occurs the following passage descriptive of events which took place several days before Newport's journey up the James River:

> April 26. About foure a clocke in the morning, wee descried the Land of Virginia. The same day wee entred into the Bay of Chesupioc. . . . There we landed and discovered a little way. . . . At night, when we were going aboard, there came the Savages creeping upon all foure, from the Hills, like Beares, with their Bowes in their mouthes, charged us very desperately in the faces, hurt Captaine Gabrill Archer in both his hands, and a sayler in two places of the body very dangerous. . . .

Smith, in the "True Relation," supplies the name of the wounded sailor—Mathew Morton—which does not appear in the roster of the up-river expedition. On the basis of the evidence derived from the three documents, then, the argument for Archer's authorship of the anonymous "Relatyon" runs thus: He was wounded in the first encounter with the Indians in the Chesapeake region, the only other person known to have been wounded being a common sailor; Archer was a member of Newport's expedition, the sailor was not; the writer of the "Relatyon" showed wounds which could have been none other than Archer's. There remains the bare possibility that one of the two other gentlemen wrote the account and showed Archer's wounds. Archer's authorship is not proved beyond possibility of doubt, but the hypothesis that he was the writer and showed his own wounds is more than plausible.

When the authorship of a document is attributable with certainty to one of a small group all members of which are known, there is a well-defined method of determining which of them is the author. It consists of a comparison of the tricks of style displayed by the document in question with those found in the indubitable writings of each member of the group in turn. The differences between Smith's "True Relation" and the "Relatyon" caused his dismissal as the possible author of the letter. Another and better case in point is the question of the authorship of certain numbers of *The Federalist*,

[10] Reprinted by L. G. Tyler, ed., *Narratives of Early Virginia* (volume V of *Original Narratives of Early American History*, ed. by J. F. Jameson. 19 vols., New York: Charles Scribner's Sons, 1906–1914), 5–23. The *Original Narratives* have recently been reprinted by Barnes & Noble, New York.

the famous essays by Madison, Hamilton, and Jay advocating the ratification of the Federal Constitution.[11] Similarly, if the author of an anonymous writing can be plausibly conjectured, a comparison of the tricks of style found in the document with those in other writings known to be those of the conjectural author will reveal either a convincing similarity or a dissimilarity which will send the critic in pursuit of other clues. The habitual use of unusual words, such as "except" for "unless," the consistent use of any synonym where there is a choice as "moreover" instead of "furthermore" (or vice versa), and repeated misspellings of a word, may be convincing evidence of authorship. Percy's "Discourse" is an illustration. Compare his spelling of "we," "Chesapeake," and "sailor" with the spellings in the "Relatyon." It must be remembered, however, that orthography had not yet been standardized in the seventeenth century and the same author often varied his spellings. Percy spelled "we" differently in the short passage quoted.

VI. GHOSTWRITERS

Not infrequently a problem of authorship arises in the case of documents ascribed to public men who employ advisers or other assistants in the preparation of their papers. President Washington consulted James Madison when he began to plan his Farewell Address, and Madison drafted a portion of it, embodying the President's suggestions. Later, at Washington's request, Alexander Hamilton extended and completed the draft, incorporating other suggestions by Washington. For the critical historian the question emerges, which of the three men was the real author of the Address, or what was the share of each in producing it? By the method described it may be concluded that the language is not Washington's. In that case the deeper problem remains whether the Address embodies Washington's ideas and views expressed in the language of another.[12]

[11] See the essay by Edward Gaylord Bourne on "The Authorship of the Federalist," in his *Essays in Historical Criticism* (New York: Charles Scribner's Sons, 1901).

[12] Miss Olivia Gander made a study of the authorship of the Farewell Address and presented it as the thesis required for the master's degree at the Ohio State University. Her conclusion does not bear out the theory advanced by some writers that Hamilton cleverly shaped the Address into a campaign document for the Federalist party. Miss Gander found that while Hamilton suggested some softening of phraseology at points where Washington seemed to him to have betrayed undue emotion, the President read the successive drafts so carefully that every sentiment in the finished paper was essentially his.

A similar problem is connected with the presidential messages of Andrew Johnson. There is good reason for attributing some of them to George Bancroft, so far as the literary form is concerned. Whether they faithfully reflect Johnson's views is of much more fundamental importance. If the putative author is the responsible source of the ideas set forth, he is the real author, even if the literary form is that of another.[13]

At the other extreme is the product of the "ghostwriter" who supplies the facts and ideas as well as the form, leaving a putative author nothing to do save to sign his name, pay the "ghost," and enjoy his unearned reputation. Most speeches of recent Presidents have been ghostwritten, but there is no secrecy about the fact or the person of the ghostwriter. The use of such an assistant is a necessity for a person as busy as a President of the United States. He cannot take the time to look up the data he needs and put it in form for a speech. He must nevertheless bear the responsibility for such custom-made speeches and it behooves him to see to it that they voice his own sentiments. An interesting study could be made of presidential ghostwriters.[14]

Still, a different problem is created by the plagiarist, who borrows both words and ideas of others without using quotation marks or giving credit. This form of spurious document will be discussed presently. Problems of authorship present all degrees of complexity.

b. *Evidences of Date*

A different phase of criticism relates to the *time* of the production of a document. We have examined some books of the Bible as illustrations. Nowadays publication dates, copyright dates, or other definite indications usually leave no uncertainty on this point, but

[13] William A. Dunning, "More Light on Andrew Johnson," in *The American Historical Review* for April, 1906, pp. 574–594. (Hereafter this journal will be cited as *AHR.*) *Cf.* communication of Carl Russell Fish on same subject, *ibid.*, July, 1906, pp. 951–952, and article by Dunning in Massachusetts Historical Society *Proceedings*, 2 ser., XIX (Boston: 1906). Problems of this kind are innumerable. Among them may be mentioned the authorship of President Jackson's Proclamation against Nullification, the words of which are those of Edward Livingston, the Secretary of State; and John Quincy Adams's relation to the so-called Monroe Doctrine.

[14] Ghost writing "autobiographies" is a favorite occupation of Robert B. Considine. He is quoted as saying "There are lots of guys with a story to tell, and there's nothing dishonorable in their not being able to tell it." See article in *Time*, January 24, 1948.

sometimes it is necessary to seek other evidence. Suppose that a fragment of an old atlas comes to hand, minus title page and all indications of date of publication save those afforded by the maps themselves. One of these shows Texas as a state of Mexico, proving that publication of the atlas preceded 1836. Another shows Missouri as a state, fixing the date of publication (if one possesses some knowledge of historical geography) as later than 1821. Careful scrutiny, aided by a knowledge of local history, narrows the gap between these dates still more, for the maps show the towns of Ann Arbor, Mich., and Fayette, Mo., both of which were founded about the mid-twenties. By continuing this process the date limits within which a document was written or published may sometimes be determined with approximate accuracy.

In the case of documents, the language used, the events alluded to, and even the spirit or temper may be made to betray the time of origin, if the critic is adequately equipped for interpreting the clues he finds. A recent example of misdating due to unskillful use of evidence concerns an old musical piece known from its opening words as *Sumer is icumen*. Nineteenth-century historians thought it was written about 1240 because that was the date of another piece on the same manuscript. Not until the 1940's was the error discovered when a professor from an American university pointed out that the handwriting of the two pieces was not the same, and that the musical notation of the *Sumer* did not come into use until long after 1240, making the probable date of *Sumer* about 1310.[15]

c Detection of Spurious Documents

i. FORGERIES

The tests employed in determining authorship and time of origin are often effective in detecting spurious documents. Forgers attempt to disguise their deception by counterfeiting the language and temper of the times and persons represented, but they are quite likely to betray themselves by anachronisms or errors of other kinds. One of the most famous forgeries ever exposed by external criticism is that of the "False Decretals." As early as the ninth century the papal archives contained certain alleged decrees of early popes, as well as

[15] See *Time,* January 15, 1945.

a document purporting to be a donation in the fourth century by the Emperor Constantine to Pope Sylvester of the right to govern Italy and the rest of the Roman Empire in the West. Both decretals and donation were accepted as genuine during the Middle Ages, but modern critics have proved their falsity.

> Their form does not correspond to the official form of such documents in the particular papal reigns to which the compiler assigned them. This diplomatics has shown. They use a method of dating which chronology has proved to be unhistorical. Although they supposedly belong to different centuries, their Latin style remains the same, and this the Frankish Latin of the ninth century. Philology has contributed this. It has also been found that their quotations from the scriptures were from the version of Jerome, amended during the time of Charlemagne, and that they contain passages taken bodily from a Frankish council of 829. Finally, they imply the view that the theology of the ninth century was the theology of the second, and that the early bishops of Rome exercised the same wide jurisdiction as the ninth-century popes. . . . It is probable that the collection originated in the diocese of Rheims between 847 and 865. . . .[16]

That American historians need to be on guard against spurious documents could be shown by many illustrations. Some years ago one of the leading monthly magazines suspended publication of alleged letters of Abraham Lincoln because their genuineness was found to be open to serious question. Errors of which Lincoln could hardly have been guilty figure prominently in the case against them. Thus in one dated May 9, 1834 he is made to allude to "that North East quarter of Section 40." Since the system of land surveys established by Congress in 1785 provided for townships of thirty-six sections each, a "section 40" would have been unthinkable to Lincoln, who was himself an experienced surveyor.

Again in the same letter Lincoln is made to say that a family named Bixby is "leaving this week for Kansas." As the territory of Kansas was not organized and opened for settlement until 1854, the passage seems clearly to be an anachronism, especially as it is very

[16] Henry E. Bourne, *The Teaching of History and Civics* (New York: Longmans, Green and Company, 1903), 35, f.n. 1. "Probably the authors believed that by representing the priesthood as an institution going back to the very beginning of the church, they were doing the very best thing they could to make it effective in its holy work."—Ephraim Emerton, *Mediaeval Europe, 814–1300* (Boston: Ginn & Company, 1895), 79.

doubtful whether even the name "Kansas" was ever used for the region as early as 1834.[17]

In 1945 a three-volume work was published under the title of *The Horn Papers: Early Westward Movement on the Monongahela and Ohio, 1765–1795.* Doubts of the genuineness of this production led to the appointment of a committee of experts who subjected the documentary materials—diaries, maps, court records, lead plates, etc.,—to numerous tests and reported that they were spurious.[18]

ii. PLAGIARISMS

Plagiarisms can be detected readily when the work containing them can be compared with the document from which they are taken; but if the original is not well known the plagiarism may escape detection for a long time. As in the case of anonymous documents, the discovery of the facts is most likely to be made by some one conversant with all of the documents in the class to which the questionable item belongs, although sometimes the detection comes about through pure accident. Dr. Reuben G. Thwaites included in the series of reprints known as *Early Western Travels* one which was later shown by Dr. Milo M. Quaife to be in large part plagiarized.[19]

iii. ERRONEOUS IDENTIFICATION

In its utility to the historian it makes little difference whether a spurious document originated in fraud or error. One which obtained wide currency through error is the instrument which was for a long time supposed to be the plan for the Federal Constitution which Charles Pinckney of South Carolina offered in the Convention of 1787. The story runs thus:

In 1819 John Quincy Adams, Secretary of State, in accordance with a resolution of Congress, prepared for publication the records of the Convention which had reposed in the files of the State Department since 1796. In the manuscript of the official journal he found a

[17] For a critique of these letters employing many principles of criticism see Paul M. Angle, "The Minor Collection: A Criticism," in *Atlantic Monthly* for April, 1929, pp. 516–525.

[18] Quotations from the report showing the evidence on which this conclusion was based are given in *MVHR* for December, 1947, pp. 528–530. The adverse judgment applied to volumes I and II.

[19] "Critical Evaluation of the Sources for Western History," *MVHR* for September, 1914, pp. 167–184. For another exposé of plagiarism see O. G. Libby, "A Critical Examination of Gordon's *History of the American Revolution,*" in *AHR* I (1899), 365 *et seq.*

minute showing that Pinckney had submitted a plan, but there was no copy of it among the papers. Thereupon he wrote to Pinckney asking for a copy of the missing document. In reply Pinckney sent a paper which he said he thought was a copy of the plan he had submitted. He found among his papers, he said, "several rough drafts of the Constitution I proposed to the Convention," and he was uncertain which was the exact form submitted. Without attempting to check the accuracy of Pinckney's selection, the Secretary of State inserted the paper in the proper place in the volume which he had prepared for publication (the *Journal*). The document which he thus labeled the Pinckney plan proved to be spurious.

James Madison, who had taken very full notes of the discussions in Convention, noticed, as soon as the *Journal* came to his attention, that the alleged Pinckney plan did not harmonize with his notes. In contemporary letters he declared that the published document could not possibly be the plan which Pinckney had submitted. The public, however, heard little or nothing of his doubts; and there was irony in the fact that when his own papers were published, a few years after his death, the editor borrowed the spurious Pinckney plan from the *Journal* and gave it new currency by inserting it in Madison's notes on the debates of the Convention just as if it were a part of Madison's own record.[20]

In this way writers were led to use the spurious document. Its marked similarity to the completed Constitution led many persons to hail Pinckney as the real father of the basic law, although the record of the Convention's proceedings in Madison's notes showed that the basis of discussion was the Randolph Resolutions, and that Pinckney's plan was referred to the Committee of Detail and not at any time considered in the Convention.

At length special students of the Constitution began to suspect that the original Pinckney plan had been lost, and that the alleged plan was a copy of one of the preliminary drafts of the Constitution which the Committee of Detail had drawn up.[21] This conjecture aroused fresh interest in the Pinckney plan, and critics set themselves to examine all available evidence as to its provisions. The pro-

[20] Henry D. Gilpin, ed., *The Papers of James Madison*. Washington: 1840.

[21] Max Farrand, ed., *The Records of the Federal Convention of 1787* (4 vols. New Haven: Yale University Press, 1911–1937), III, Appendix D, 595–609, and references in footnotes. (Hereafter this work will be cited as Farrand, *Records*.) The work done on the Pinckney plan is a good piece of criticism for beginners to study.

cedure was a very interesting example of constructive criticism, involving the careful comparison of all existing documents containing hints of Pinckney's views on the Constitution, especially his own utterances before, in, and after the Convention. The findings thus reached were dramatically confirmed by the discovery of a fragmentary copy of the lost original.[22]

One result is that Pinckney's original proposals are now known in essence. Another is that when one encounters references to the provisions of his plan one must know whether the writer has used the spurious document or the restored one. Unfortunately, knowledge of the latter was for a long time confined to a small group of specialists, and citations of the unauthentic instrument vitiated much otherwise intelligent writing. No constitutional discussion prior to the present century can be trusted if it turns upon provisions of the Pinckney plan.[23]

d. *Question of Original Form: Textual Criticism*

The foregoing description of the methods of detecting spurious documents might logically have been introduced as a phase of the question of original form. However, even a genuine document may contain text corruptions, which are essentially spurious elements, misleading to the historian unless they can be eliminated and the original reading restored. The process by which this is done is known as textual criticism, and is so intricate that in some fields of history it has given rise to experts who devote themselves almost exclusively to such tasks, each working in a field sufficiently restricted to permit a very wide acquaintance with the texts which must be compared as well as a mastery of the appropriate auxiliary sciences.[24]

[22] *Ibid.*

[23] The dangers attending the citation of documents which have not been proved genuine are illustrated by the numerous references to the pseudo-Pinckney plan. The Supreme Court cited it in the income-tax decision of 1895 (157 U.S. 429); Chief Justice Charles Evans Hughes referred to it in a lecture delivered at Columbia University in 1927 (see *The Supreme Court of the United States,* New York: Columbia University Press, 1936, p. 10); and an article on "Congress and the Appellate Jurisdiction of the Supreme Court," in the *Michigan Law Review,* XXXIV, 655, footnote 11, cites it.

[24] Textual criticism is just as necessary in the case of literary texts as in those relating to history, and the procedure is essentially the same for both classes of documents. The efforts to reproduce the original readings of Biblical texts, the works of ancient Greek and Latin writers, the plays of Shakespeare, etc., rest upon the same principles.

Strictly speaking such specialists are not historians unless they write history as well as criticize documents. Their function is to provide the writer with authentic documents and pure readings, and this is, of course, an essential preliminary of sound historical composition, yet not a part of it even when performed by the historian himself. Textual criticism is at most the handmaid of the historian, who should ever regard composition as his proper task. Yet, although great collections of carefully edited documents now exist in all civilized countries, the historian must on occasion criticize texts for himself, and must always be on guard lest he be misled by the use of impure ones.

i. ORIGIN OF CORRUPTIONS: COLLATION

Corruptions, by which are meant any kind of deviation from the original forms, creep into documents in many ways, but chiefly through careless copying by scribe, typist, or printer. Where the original is preserved the only safe course for the writer is to compare the copy which he intends to use with this original—a process called collation. John Quincy Adams records in his diary that on one occasion he was charged with publishing an incorrect version of the Constitution. The critic, however, had not compared the Adams version with the original manuscript, and when Adams inspected the original he found that both his version and that consulted by the critic were incorrect! [25]

Many errors creep into the work of historians through failure to compare documents with the originals. One great advantage of photostat and microfilm copies lies in the absolute elimination of copyists' errors. Of course this means that these reproductions must use the originals; and of course they reproduce any errors in them. Where written, typed, or printed copies are used, collation with the originals should always be resorted to if practicable. One can seldom go behind the official printed forms in government publications, although even these cannot be accepted as certainly exact. It is always advisable to check them.[26]

[25] *Memoirs,* ed. by Charles Francis Adams (12 vols. Philadelphia: J. B. Lippincott & Co., 1874–1887), VI, 124–127. *See post* (for page see Index under Punctuation).

[26] This rule of collation holds throughout the process of composition and publication. Copy for the printer should be carefully collated, and printer's proof should likewise be compared with the original or collated copy. *Careless proofreading is all too common.*

When documents are published they are often printed in such a form that corruptions and interpolations become indistinguishable from the original text. Gilpin's edition of Madison's papers is an example. If the historian has access to the original manuscript, his advantage over the user of the printed version is obvious. When the diary of Gideon Welles, a member of President Johnson's cabinet, was first published (1911), it was rightly hailed as a valuable addition to the contemporary evidence bearing on various problems of Johnson's troubled administration. Some time afterwards a scholar examined the manuscript and called attention to the fact that interpolations had been incorporated in the published diary as if a part of the original entries. Pending accurate discrimination between the two elements its value was distinctly lessened.[27] An excellent example of the way in which corruptions occur is found in the history of Madison's notes of the debates in the Constitutional Convention. When the *Journal*,[28] edited by Adams, was published, more than thirty years after the Convention, Madison compared his notes with it and detected certain errors in it. Yet he changed his notes in numerous places where it seemed to him that the *Journal* was correct and his notes wrong. In other words, he trusted his *memory*, after the lapse of a generation, as a safe judge between the two records where they differed, and unfortunately, as critics have been able to demonstrate, in nearly every instance he substituted an erroneous reading for his own originally correct record. By this and other attempts at revision previous to his death in 1836, Madison succeeded in corrupting his notes to a lamentable extent. When they were published in 1840 these changes were incorporated with the original text and the whole printed in uniform type, without a hint that Madison's original notes were not reproduced exactly.[29]

This corrupt edition of Madison's notes was the chief source for the proceedings in Convention during the remainder of the nineteenth century. Near its close the Government printed an edition reproducing Madison's manuscript and other records of the Convention, showing by the use of different styles of type both the

[27] Howard K. Beale, "Is the Printed Diary of Gideon Welles Reliable?", *AHR* for April, 1925, pp. 547 *et seq*. See the use made of the *Diary* by George Fort Milton, in *The Age of Hate*, reviewed in *AHR* for July, 1931, pp. 837–838.

[28] See *ante*, p. 29.

[29] Gilpin, ed., *op. cit.*

original text and all changes, thus giving the historical fraternity for the first time a trustworthy reprint.[30]

ii. RESTORATION OF ORIGINAL READING

American history is of such brief duration that the loss of important originals, although too frequent, has been slight in comparison with the losses which Europe has sustained. The scholarship of the Old World has frequently found it necessary to try to recover the reading of lost originals from impure copies. Where extant copies differ it is impossible, of course, for all of them to be correct. It may be that none is like the original. Identity of wording may mean only that all reproduce the same corrupt archetype. In that case they have merely perpetuated any corruptions it contained. The problem here centers around the archetype, which may be lost like the original, the question being, Did it accurately preserve the original, or did it contain corruptions? This is the question raised by the archetype of the Book of Isaiah (see *ante*, page 17, and note 3). It has been noted already that later copies show few variations from the oldest form extant.

a) *Variant Readings*

When dealing with copies which do not read alike the critic's first step is to determine as far as possible the interrelation of the copies in which the variations occur. If A is the lost original, B and C may be independent copies of it, and D may be a copy of B. Or D may be copied in part from A and in part from C, reproducing some of C's corruptions and introducing others of its own. A great variety of interrelationships is possible; but whenever the critic seeking to restore an original reading discovers that one copy is exactly like another (*e.g.*, if D is a copy of B), one of the identical copies is eliminated. This process of elimination is continued until there remain only independent copies.

The divergent readings of these independent copies are then compared, and any available evidence is brought to bear in the effort to determine the original reading. One must beware of accepting a reading merely because it occurs oftener than any other, for one may

[30] Department of State: Bureau of Rolls and Library, *Documentary History of the Constitution* (5 vols. Washington: Government Printing Office, 1894–1905). Superseded by Farrand's *Records*.

have the original reading while a dozen which agree in a different reading may be incorrect because all are copies of the same faulty one. Certainty of conclusion is often impossible, and one must be content with what one finally judges, in the light of all the evidence, to be the most plausible reading.

The late Max Farrand attempted to restore the original reading of Benjamin Franklin's celebrated *Autobiography*. The original is known to have been composed of four parts written respectively in 1771, 1784, 1788, and 1790. Franklin himself revised the first three parts and made two copies both of which have been lost. However, a French translation, never printed, was made from one of these copies by Le Veillard, and the manuscript of this translation is now in the Library of Congress. Franklin's grandson, Temple Franklin, published an English version in 1818 which Dr. Farrand believes was based on the copy used in Le Veillard's translation. In 1868 Joseph Bigelow edited Le Veillard's copy and thought he had corrected errors made by Temple Franklin. Dr. Farrand concluded that the Temple Franklin version did not reproduce Le Veillard's exactly yet is the "best obtainable" form of the *Autobiography*.[31]

Bible scholars have applied this type of textual criticism to the study of the gospels of Matthew, Mark, and Luke. Internal evidence shows that Mark's gospel is the oldest of the three but that he drew on a still older writing now lost; in turn Matthew and Luke follow Mark closely in many passages although both contain material not found in either of the others. The important conclusion is that these three gospels do not give three independent accounts of the life of Jesus but for much of it only one (Mark's). This makes it difficult to determine exactly what the Great Teacher did and said and the actual order of the events recorded. The difficulty is increased by the fact that we do not have the original of any of the gospels, nor do we know how many copyings intervened between the originals and the oldest copies which have been preserved. What matters most is that despite all changes which may have been made in the course of repeated copying the gospels still portray the luminous personality of the Christ.

The restoration of the original reading of a document is difficult

[31] Max Farrand, ed., *The Autobiography of Benjamin Franklin*; and *Benjamin Franklin's Memoirs* (Berkeley and Los Angeles: University of California Press, 1949). In the *Memoirs* Farrand prints the four texts which he used in the attempt to recover the original reading of the *Autobiography*. *Cf.* review by Stanley Pargellis in *MVHR* for December, 1949, pp. 504–505.

even in a field as recent as the history of the United States. A convenient illustration from American history is found in the story of the resolutions introduced at an early session of the Federal Convention of 1787 and made the basis of its discussions. The original draft, introduced by Edmund Randolph, long since disappeared. The delegates seem to have made copies for their individual use, and a few of these copies, or copies of these copies, are still in existence. On them are based the efforts to restore the original reading.[32] There are reasons for thinking that none is without corruptions. The extant copies are in some cases at least three removes from the original: first, the delegates copied the original more or less accurately; next they made changes to correspond to decisions in the course of debate; finally they sometimes recopied embodying these and other changes. The desirability of restoring the original reading of the resolutions is evident, if one wishes to make a critical study of the Convention's progress.

For convenience the copies, in the form in which they have come down to us, may be designated as follows: One made by Madison will be called A. It is reproduced in the *Documentary History of the Constitution* [33] and in Farrand's *Records.*[34] Another, by Brearly, will be called B. It also is to be found in the *Documentary History.*[35] A third, by Paterson, is in the New York Public Library and has never been printed. It will be called C. D designates the form found in the *Journal* edited by Adams and published in 1819. E denotes the form printed in Gilpin's edition of the Madison papers. F is the form given in Yates's *Secret Proceedings and Debates*, published in 1821. G is a form printed in the third edition of Elliot's *Debates.*

[32] *Cf.* John Franklin Jameson, "Studies in the History of the Federal Convention," in American Historical Association *Annual Report* for 1902, I, 89–167. (Hereafter these reports will be referred to as AHA *Report.*) Availability of additional materials has made it possible to carry some of these studies further than Jameson did. In a master's thesis written at The Ohio State University George Woolfolk cast additional light on the original reading of the Randolph Resolutions. His conclusion agrees with that of Dr. Max Farrand that copy A is correct with the exception of the ninth resolution, the original reading of which is still in doubt. *Cf.* Farrand, *Records,* III, 593–594. Woolfolk presents the evidence on which his conclusion is based but Farrand does not.

The supposition that delegates made their own copies of the resolutions was strengthened by finding Charles Pinckney's among the Pinckney papers acquired by the Library of Congress in 1939. This copy was in Pinckney's handwriting with pencilled annotations. The discovery illustrates how new evidence turns up from time to time tending to confirm or refute tentative conclusions.

[33] III, 17–20. [34] I, 20–22. [35] I, 332–335.

Critical comparison of these seven forms reveals their interrelationships and reduces the number of independent copies to three—A, B, and C. Copy D is found to be taken from B. Brearly's papers, including his copy of the resolutions, were deposited in the State Department by his executor. Adams used them in preparing the *Journal,* and there was then no other source from which he could readily have obtained a copy. Slight discrepancies between D and B are attributable to Adams's efforts to "restore" the original reading. E is professedly a copy of A, with an addition made by the editor on the warrant of a statement by Madison in a letter written in 1833. F is a copy of D. Yates records that he made a copy and preserved it with his notes, but when the latter were prepared for publication, the copy had disappeared and the form in the *Journal* was substituted. G reproduces B plus a "resolution 16." This resolution was in fact a motion made immediately after the reading of the Randolph Resolutions (as the *Journal* shows); Elliot mistook it for one of the resolutions. D, E, F, and G are thus all found to be copies derived directly or indirectly from A or B, most of them with additional corruptions.

The variations in the wording of the three independent copies A, B, and C, occur in resolutions 4, 5, 6, 7, 9, 11, and 13. Resolutions 1, 2, 3, 8, 10, 12, 14, and 15 agree, and are not under suspicion, because, the copies *being independent,* the identity of these portions could not be accounted for if the reading was impure. If there were corruptions in these resolutions, identity of reading would prove that the copies were not independent. *Identity of error proves interdependence.*

Resolution 4, the first in which a variant reading occurs, is as follows in A:

> Res.[d] that the members of the first branch of the National Legislature ought to be elected by the people of the several States every [1] for the term of [2]; to be of the age of [3] years at least, to receive liberal stipends by which they may be compensated for the devotion of their time to public service; to be ineligible to any office established by a particular State, or under the authority of the United States, except those peculiarly belonging to the functions of the first branch, during the term of service, and for the space of [4] after its expiration; to be incapable of re-election for the space of [5] after the expiration of their term of service, and to be subject to recall.

B varies from A at the following points: (1) instead of the second blank, the words "three years" occur; (2) instead of the fourth blank, the words "one year" appear; (3) instead of the fifth blank the words "one year" appear again.

C agrees with A in having a blank space where B reads "three years"; and varies from both A and B in omitting entirely the words beginning with "to be incapable of" and ending with "term of service."

It would be a plausible guess that the original resolution contained all of the blanks which appear in A, and that the words which appear at three of these points in B are due to interpolations by Brearly representing later decisions of the Convention. This conjecture is confirmed by external evidence. Fortunately the published records of the Convention are now quite full; not only is the official journal accessible in printed form, but also the notes of a number of the delegates.[36] These records are very useful in determining the original form of the resolutions. Madison's notes of the debate on June 12 show that the second and fourth blanks were filled on that day with the words found in B, and the notes of Yates and the record in the *Journal* confirm Madison. The *Journal*, in addition, shows that the last blank was filled, as in B, on that date.

This leaves the omission in C to be accounted for. It has been conjectured that Paterson simply overlooked these words when making his final copy.[37] A glance at the full resolution will show how easily he might have done so. The repetition of almost identical phraseology in adjacent lines, as here, is a common source of error on the part of copyists, since the eye is likely to light upon the phrase where it *recurs*, after it has been once copied, thus missing the intermediate words.

In the present instance there is another possibility, for the *Journal* of June 12 shows that the omitted clause was struck out on that day. If Paterson struck it out of his first copy in conformity with this action, the omission from his final copy, like the additions in Brearly's, was because he followed the changes made in the Convention. In either case the evidence indicates that the reading of A is correct.

Applying this method to resolutions 5, 6, 7, 11, and 13, in which

[36] Farrand, *Records*, I and II.
[37] Jameson, *loc. cit.*, 111.

variant readings occur, the critic arrives at the conclusion that A is correct. Madison doubtless made a deliberate effort to preserve the original form in his copy, and avoided using it to record changes made in the course of discussion. Yet even Madison's copy comes under suspicion in the reading of the ninth resolution, and up to date all efforts of the critics have failed to give a reading for this resolution which can be certified as the original. The reading of A is as follows:

> Res.[d] that a National Judiciary be established to consist of one or more supreme tribunals, and of inferior tribunals to be chosen by the National Legislature, to hold their offices during good behaviour; and to receive punctually at stated times fixed compensation for their services, in which no increase or diminution shall be made so as to affect the persons actually in office at the time of such increase or diminution. that [*sic*] the jurisdiction of the inferior tribunals shall be to hear & determine in the first instance, and of the supreme tribunal to hear and determine in the dernier resort, all piracies & felonies on the high seas, captures from an enemy; cases in which foreigners or citizens of other States applying to such jurisdictions may be interested, or which respect the collection of the National revenue; impeachments of any National officers, and questions which may involve the national peace and harmony.

The reading of B agrees with that of A after the first sentence, but this sentence is quite different:

> That a National Judiciary be established to consist of one Supreme Tribunal, to hold their Offices during good behavior, and to receive punctually at stated times fixed compensation for their services . . . etc.

C is like A except in having a blank before the words "inferior tribunals" in the first sentence.

None of these versions is satisfactory. A is questionable because it is not easy to think of more than one *supreme* tribunal, and because the phraseology at this point is inconsistent with that of the latter part of the resolution, where the jurisdiction of "*the* supreme tribunal" is defined.[38] B is likewise inconsistent, for the definition of the jurisdiction of the inferior tribunals, which it shares with A, requires a mention of them in the first sentence. C is open to the same criticism as A, although the blank before "inferior tribunals" sug-

[38] Italics author's.

gests that the words "one or more" may have been later additions, intended to fill the blank, instead of going before "supreme tribunal."

Madison's notes for June 4 strengthen this conjecture, for on that day the resolution "that a National Judiciary be established" was adopted, after which the words were "added": "to consist of one supreme tribunal and of one or more inferior tribunals." Whether these words appeared now for the first time, or whether they were in the original resolution and were now "added" in the sense of being *also adopted*, is not clear. That the latter may have been the case appears from an entry in Paterson's notes for May 29, which indicates that the original resolution contained a clause providing for both supreme and inferior tribunals. Whether such a clause was in the original resolution or not, it is safe to conclude that the words "one or more" are misplaced in A and C.

As for B, on June 5, according to the *Journal*, Madison moved to strike out of the resolution the provision for "appointment by the Legislature." These words, then, must have been in the original, and Brearly must have struck them out because of this action. The *Journal* shows further that the words "and of one or more inferior tribunals" were struck out on June 5, thus giving further evidence that the words "one or more" accompanied the reference to the inferior tribunals instead of the supreme tribunal, and accounting also for a part of Brearly's omission.

The jurisdiction clauses of the resolution present additional perplexities, but enough has been said to illustrate the procedure in attempts to restore original readings.

b) *Conjectural Emendation*

When there are no variant readings and the extant reading is questionable the critic's only recourse is to the method of conjectural emendation. Minor corrections are sometimes easily made by this method, as in the case of words which are repeated through the inadvertence of the scribe. The meaningless repetition of such words as "and," "the," or "that" is clearly the result of careless copying. Of course it is not impossible for an original to contain such errors, in which case emendation would not restore its form, but would improve upon it.

A meaningless passage indicates a corruption, and context may suggest a plausible correction. A certain textbook quotes President

Hayes as saying in a message to Congress that an isthmian canal "would be vitally a part of our coast line." The word "vitally" is evidently a slip for "virtually." Probably the similar appearance of the two words misled a careless compositor and the proofreader failed to catch the error. Collation is needed to determine the word used by the President. Comparison with the original manuscript would be difficult, but can at least be made with the version printed in Richardson's *Messages of the Presidents* (see Index).

An interesting example of successful emendation is that which J. N. Madvig performed in the matter of a passage in one of Seneca's letters. All extant readings at the point of difficulty ran thus:

> Philosophia unde dicta sit, apparet; ipso enim nomine fatetur. Quidam et sapientiam ita quidam finierunt, ut dicerent divinorum et humanorum sapientiam. . . .

The better the critic's knowledge of classical Latin the clearer it was that these words did not make sense, and that the reading must be corrupt. For a long time the conjecture of scholars was that words had been omitted between *ita* and *quidam.* Madvig, whose Latin was supplemented by a knowledge of paleography, pictured to himself the passage as it must have appeared in the original or lost archetype, written in capitals without space between words or sentences and without marks of punctuation, thus (in part): NOMINEFATETURQUIDAMETSAPIENTIAM. . . . It was then easy to surmise that some careless copyist whose manuscript had since been followed had wrongly separated the words. Madvig's final step was to make sentence and word divisions at two new points suggested by the context, thus bringing out the meaning. His emendation consisted solely in making these divisions: nomine fatetur quid amet.[39] (Thus corrected the entire passage may be translated into English as: Why philosophy [Greek for the love of wisdom] is so named is apparent; for the name itself expresses what it signifies. Accordingly some men have defined wisdom as the understanding of things of gods and men.)

Greek and Hebrew writings present similar difficulties. Ancient Hebrew used only consonants; the reader supplied the vowels. Paleography—old styles of writing—is a formidable subject in its own right. The reader may test his skill by attempting to decide how the following words should be divided to give the writer's

[39] Charles V. Langlois and Charles Seignobos, *Introduction to the Study of History,* 78–79.

meaning: HEISNOWHERE. Only the context can indicate whether these letters mean: He is now here, or He is nowhere.

There is grave danger that conjectural emendation may introduce new corruptions if the correct reading is not obvious. Undoubtedly many Shakespearean critics have violated the great dramatist's texts by well-meant efforts to correct passages which they assumed to be corrupt because the meaning was obscure to them. The wise critic will be slow to attempt emendation. In the case of President Hayes's message, if it were impossible to check the word in doubt, the safe procedure for the critic who wished to correct the textbook would be to insert his conjectural reading in brackets, thus: "would be vitally [virtually?] a part of our coast line." The question mark would indicate his own uncertainty.

2. Internal Criticism

When it has been decided that a document is genuine, when all that is possible has been done to make sure that its reading is true to the original, and when everything that can be learned about the time, place, and other circumstances connected with its origin is at the disposal of the historian, he is ready for the work of internal criticism.

The inquiry now shifts from *document* to *statement*, and it becomes the investigator's duty to make sure that he *understands* each statement which he intends to use. This phase of criticism is known as Positive Criticism.

a. *Positive Criticism*

It is important to avoid reading into a statement a meaning which the maker did not intend to convey. There is a great temptation to make this mistake when one *wishes* or *hopes* to find a particular meaning in a statement, and great care is required to avoid this form of intellectual dishonesty. Taking words out of context is a common form of this transgression. The partisan is prone to misrepresent his opponents in this way, and even the impartial historian who maintains an attitude of detached indifference toward partisan controversies is in danger of becoming so enamored with his theories or hypotheses that he will support them by twisting meanings. The quest must be for facts, even if they upset one's pet notions.

i. LITERAL MEANING OF STATEMENTS

The first question to be asked is, What does the statement say? The question may seem foolish until one reflects that statements are often made in a foreign language, or in unfamiliar terms, or in unusual senses of familiar words. Technical terms, obsolete words, references to customs or institutions which existed in distant places or at remote times, even when in one's own language may convey as little meaning to the mind of the novice as if they were in an unknown tongue. This is the sort of difficulty the young student encounters when he begins to read the plays of Shakespeare. When the immature person is set to study the first charter of Virginia and reads that the lands granted to the Company are "To be holden of Us, our Heirs, and Successors, as of our Manor at *East-Greenwich* in the County of Kent, in free and common soccage only, and not in Capite," the teacher should not be surprised to learn that the passage is "Greek" to the youngster. The King James version of the Bible records that "Jacob sod pottage" (Gen. xxv:29), a statement which means little or nothing to one who does not know the modern equivalents of the words "sod" and "pottage."

Much history turns on the correct understanding of words and phrases. In some cases, where these have taken on new meanings, the recovery of the original connotation is difficult if not impossible. A notable instance is the phrase "law of the land," found in Magna Carta. There has been much study of its meaning and there is still disagreement. Many students see in it the "ancestor" of "due process" which has played a stellar role in the constitutional history of the United States, especially since the Civil War. The words have undoubtedly acquired a meaning quite different from their original sense.

Even dissimilarities of spelling from period to period are disconcerting. Such a passage as that quoted from Percy's "Discourse" on page 23 may prove to be difficult reading for twentieth-century students. The native name of one of the Indian villages near the English settlement at Jamestown in the early seventeenth century, variously rendered by the settlers as "Kiskyack" and "Cheesecake," led one acquaintance of the author of this Manual to surmise that there were Czechs among the early immigrants to Virginia. Plainly the historian must have a wide knowledge of the language, laws, customs, and institutions of the countries and periods in which his work lies, or he cannot interpret the documents with which he must work. One of the chief reasons for the recent translation of the Bible, published as *The Revised Standard Version*, was to aid readers by using twentieth-century English. This version renders the statement in the King James translation (see above) thus: "Jacob was boiling pottage."

ii. REAL MEANING OF STATEMENTS

Having determined what a statement literally says, the critic must try to ascertain whether it *means* what it says, for there is often a difference between the literal and real meanings. The critic is not here concerned with the truthfulness of the statement. Rather he seeks to discover whether the statement is intended to be taken literally or in an oblique sense. To take an ironical saying, for example, as the expression of the maker's real opinion is to miss the intent. The necessity of perceiving the intent may apply to the entire document. If it is fable, parable, or allegory its purpose should be understood. The Scriptures abound in figurative language the real meaning of which is not always easily grasped. It is not always as obvious as in the verse "Wisdom crieth . . . in the streets" (Proverbs, i:20).

Misunderstandings are not easy to avoid. It is nearly always difficult to determine exactly what meaning figurative language is intended to convey, and often, indeed, not even easy to recognize a figure of speech. Preceding the House election of 1825 John Quincy Adams, as his diary records, received an anonymous letter from a partisan of a rival candidate threatening to "raise the standard of revolt and civil war" if his favorite was defeated. These words might have expressed the actual intent of the writer or merely threatened persistent political opposition such as, in fact, followed Adams's election.

The historian is not infallible, but if he fortunately possesses sobriety of judgment he will be saved from many a misinterpretation. Too often writers display the naïveté of the student who wrote in a test paper that in a certain presidential campaign the Whigs did not frame a platform until the night before the election. The surprised teacher found that the student had construed literally a statement in the textbook that the Whigs framed no platform until the *eve of the election!*

This phase of criticism is called "positive" because it sometimes obtains affirmative results; that is, it may determine just what statements say and mean. It does not attempt more than this, leaving the determination of truthfulness and reliability to later tests.

b. *Negative Criticism*

Nor is it the purpose of *negative* criticism to establish the dependability of statements. Indeed, it seeks to discover every possible reason for *doubting* them. It is the rule that every statement must be doubted as long as any reasonable ground for doubt can be found.

When external criticism has supplied data concerning the author of a statement and the circumstances under which it was made, and positive criticism has ascertained what it intends to say, the critic is in position to test it in still other ways. It may be untrustworthy either because of some kind of incompetence on the part of the author which prevents him from knowing the facts, or because of some form of untruthfulness which prevents him from telling the truth even when he knows it.

i. TESTS OF COMPETENCE

In testing competence the first concern of the critic is to ascertain what opportunity the maker of a statement had to know the facts. If he was an eyewitness the presumption is, other things being equal, that he has given a more accurate account of what occurred than a person not present could give. But eyewitnesses are not equally good observers, and the critic must try to judge them with due discrimination. It must be remembered that in history as in science truth is established only upon the foundation of *reliable* observation. Any statement which deserves the credence of the historian must be found to rest ultimately upon such observation.

In recent years experimental psychology has aided the historian by revealing how the human mind reacts in certain situations. One result has been an enhanced sense of the difference between competent and incompetent eyewitnesses and a new emphasis on the importance of *trained* observation. "If a witness should testify in court that he had seen a red cap at dusk but not a blue coat, his testimony would be discounted at once," for experimental psychology has proved that in a dim light blue is more visible than red.[40] "The

[40] Johnson, *op. cit.*, 33, citing Hans Gross, *Criminal Psychology*, 206.

tendency of the mind to fill in the gaps of sense impressions is a highly significant fact for the historian." [41]

Some years ago a bomb exploded in Wall Street, New York City. Eight eyewitnesses testified that at the time there were a number of vehicles within a block of the spot and that the bomb was carried on a red motor truck. Another eyewitness testified that the bomb was in a horse-drawn truck and that only one other vehicle was in sight. It was eventually proved that the eight witnesses were wrong and the one right. The advantage enjoyed by this one was due to the excited state of mind of the eight and the fact that he was an army officer whose experience had taught him to keep his wits under fire.[42]

How can eight eyewitnesses agree and yet be wrong? Their agreement proves that their observations were not independent. The statement of one heard by the other seven led them by suggestion to "recall" what they had not actually seen. Psychiatrists are beginning to criticize the failure of courts to take cognizance of the mental condition of witnesses. Writes one: "It is astonishing that so much justice is dispensed on the basis of persons whose emotional and intellectual capacity has not been determined." [43] (The press reports a recent ruling that Indiana law does not require that a juror be sane.)

Unusual emotional stress of any kind is likely to render observers incompetent. So, of course, is ignorance. The critic must determine whether any influences of these kinds affected the eyewitnesses. The rustic who prayed that the Lord would give him a visible sign that his sins were forgiven by causing one of the stars to move, and who then believed that he actually saw a star move, may have experienced spiritual satisfaction, but is disqualified as a witness on astronomy.

Some eyewitnesses may have been in very unfavorable positions for observing what went on, even though actually present. Theoretically the peace negotiations at Versailles at the close of World War I were conducted openly, in the presence of representatives of the press; but the room was so crowded that reporters generally stood in the adjacent halls, almost out of sight and sound of the speakers. A knowledge of this fact has an important bearing upon

[41] Johnson, 31. See discussion *ibid.*, 25 *et seq.*
[42] *Ibid.*, 24, 25.
[43] *Science Digest*, August, 1953, p. 28.

the historian's attitude toward their accounts of what was said and done.

An unfavorable position for observation may be due to the sheer negligence of a potentially competent observer. Edward W. Bok recounts that while a youthful reporter on a New York daily he was sent to cover a play. Having already seen it once he felt certain that he could make a write-up *in absentia*, and yielded to the temptation to keep another appointment. In due time he turned in his copy but learned too late that the performance had been called off because of the illness of the leading lady![44]

When James Madison took his notes on the debates in the Federal Convention of 1787 conditions for accurate reporting were almost perfect. He describes them thus:

> In pursuance of the task I had assumed I chose a seat in front of the presiding member with the other members, on my right & left hands. In this favorable position for hearing all that passed, I noted in terms legible & in abbreviations & marks intelligible to myself what was read from the Chair or spoken by the members; and losing not a moment unnecessarily between the adjournment & reassembling of the Convention I was enabled to write out my daily notes during the session or within a few finishing days after its close in the extent and form preserved in my own hand on my files.
>
> In the labor and correctness of this I was not a little aided by practice, and by a familiarity with the style and train of observation and reasoning which characterized the principal speakers. It happened also that I was not absent a single day, nor more than a casual fraction of an hour in any day, so that I could not have lost a single speech, unless a very short one. . . .
>
> With a very few exceptions, the speeches were neither furnished, nor revised, nor sanctioned, by the speakers, but written out from my notes, aided by the freshness of my recollections.[45]

Here we have an intelligent, dispassionate, painstaking man, favorably placed for seeing and hearing. Careful comparison of his report with the fragmentary notes of other delegates reveals few important omissions or errors of other kinds, except those due to this unfortunate efforts at revision many years after the original notes were taken.

[44] *The Americanization of Edward Bok* (8th edn., New York: Charles Scribner's Sons, 1921), 61–62.

[45] Farrand, *Records*, III, 550.

Madison as a reporter contrasts significantly with Major William Jackson, whom the Convention employed as its official secretary. He seems to have owed his appointment to influence rather than fitness.[46] Adams found that his minutes were hardly more than the notes from which full minutes should have been, but were not, written up.[47] Jackson, whom Adams consulted in 1819 when preparing the papers of the Convention for publication, had no recollections which could aid Adams in rescuing them from their "disorderly state," although he said that he had taken extensive minutes with a view to publication.[48] When he delivered the records of the proceedings to Washington as directed by the Convention, he first burned all the loose scraps of paper in his possession.[49] Among these quite possibly may have been copies of Pinckney's plan and the Randolph Resolutions, neither of which was copied into his minutes nor otherwise preserved by him. Such facts are significant to the historian who wishes to judge between Jackson and Madison as "eyewitnesses" and reporters of the Convention's doings.

The testimony of eyewitnesses, however subject to suspicion it may seem to be, must be made the starting point of investigation. But an absentee who has been trained to reason accurately from complex and imperfect data may be able to make a statement by way of conclusion that is even more reliable than that of the ordinary eyewitness. This possibility is what justifies trials in court, inquests, and official investigations of all kinds; and it affords ground for believing that the trained historian can tell a more truthful tale than any single source he uses.

At its best, the work of writers for the public press approximates that of the critical historian. Special correspondents are often highly trained men who take great pains to make statements which may be relied upon. For the most part, however, it is unfair to hold newspaper reporters to the same standards of accuracy which are required of the historian. Bok's negligence, to be sure, was extreme, and almost cost him his position; yet the conditions under which a reporter ordinarily works excuse him from any prolonged effort to sift evidence and ascertain facts in detail. In the few minutes which he can spend upon the spot where a "news event" has occurred, especially if it is of an unforeseen kind, and has taken place before his arrival, he cannot do much more than interview such persons as

[46] *Ibid.*, I, xii, footnote 6.
[47] *Ibid.*, III, 433.
[48] *Ibid.*, 426.
[49] *Ibid.*, 82.

may be within reach. They may or may not have been eyewitnesses; they may or may not be intelligent. What he hears he sends in, interlarded with such phrases as "it is said," and "it is alleged." Thus he neither assumes responsibility for the truth of the assertions nor fixes it upon anyone else. If the accident or other event which he reports actually occurred, he is not held to a very strict accountability for details, such as, who was at fault or what the damage amounted to in dollars.

Something more may be expected where the reporter has covered a public meeting, such as a political convention, and was therefore an eye- and earwitness; but the accuracy of statements will vary with the personal qualities of the individual reporter and the conditions under which he does his work. Standards are none too exacting. Reports of interviews with prominent personages are notoriously inaccurate. It would seem that newspapermen do not always try to repeat a person's exact words and for this reason many persons refuse to grant interviews, or allow them only upon condition that copy be submitted for approval before publication. On the other hand the carelessness of reporters frequently allows a speaker to repudiate unfortunate utterances!

The historian who uses newspapers as sources (and properly used they are of great value) must take pains to check all statements with care. It must be remembered, too, that newspapers include matter of many different kinds, and the critic's attitude must vary according to the nature of the item. Advertisements often have their uses as they throw light on customs or conditions no longer existing. Obviously editorials require a special type of criticism. Weekly and monthly news journals, moreover, are more trustworthy than the dailies, since the articles in them are prepared more carefully and deliberately. In sum, statements in newspapers are subject to the tests applicable to statements of other kinds, with rather more than the usual amount of suspicion that they may have been made by negligent persons.[50]

Great masses of source material of a kind with which the historian

[50] *Cf.* James Ford Rhodes, "Newspapers as Historical Sources," in his *Historical Essays* (New York: The Macmillan Company, 1909), pp. 81–97. Rhodes says that he never relied on newspaper statements unless they could be corroborated. See also Spahr and Swenson, *Methods and Status of Scientific Research* (New York: Harper & Brothers, 1930), 120–121. Hereafter cited as Spahr and Swenson. *Cf.* note 2, *ante.*

has to deal are found in diaries, memoirs, recollections, and autobiographies. The trustworthiness of these differs greatly. The writers are not equally truthful, competent, and unprejudiced, and if they were, the appraisal of their statements would still differ. A contemporary record, such as is made in a diary, is more likely to be accurate than a memoir written long after the events recounted. For this reason the critic is more inclined to believe John Quincy Adams's assertion in 1844 that Andrew Jackson approved, a quarter of a century earlier, the relinquishment of the claim of the United States to Texas, than to accept Jackson's denial, for the former made an entry to this effect in his notable diary, at the time, while in 1844 Jackson spoke from memory only.

Old people's recollections are notoriously fallible. Some years ago a graduate student in The Ohio State University personally interviewed an aged politician concerning his attitude toward Mr. Bryan during the campaign of 1896, and was informed by the gentleman that he had been unable to follow Mr. Bryan's leadership. Later the student found contemporary accounts of speeches by this Ohio politician advocating Mr. Bryan's election.

During the gold rush of 1849 a young Philadelphian went to California, where he remained for five or six years. Thirty-five years later he wrote from memory an account of his adventures. In this he says: "While the events recorded are yet bright in my mind and strictly true and correct, it is possible that some of them may be placed out of time and out of exact location." [51] The critic is compelled to doubt the accuracy of all details in a book of this type, although a group of such works taken collectively may give a trustworthy composite picture of an impressionistic kind.

While a contemporary record such as a diary escapes the danger to which memoirs are exposed through lapses of memory, it cannot be any more accurate and dependable than its author. The personal equation enters here, as in all statements. An incompetent eyewitness will make an imperfect report, whether it be in a court of law or in a private diary. An undisciplined mind may accept hearsay for fact, accusation for proof. A prejudiced mind will be reflected in comments on men and events. John Quincy Adams, while an accu-

[51] Anna Paschall Hannum, ed., *A Quaker Forty-Niner: The Adventures of Charles Edward Pancoast on the American Frontier* (Philadelphia: University of Pennsylvania Press, 1930), 392.

rate recorder of events, was prone to make interpretations of the actions of others based on the assumption that their motives were unworthy.

The rule that in order to get at the truth statements must be traced to their basis in reliable observation means, in one application, that the critic must inquire whether a statement under scrutiny is based on the observation of the maker or some one else. It has already been recognized that while the conclusions of a careful investigator belong in the second category, they may be so sound as to be considered authoritative. However, if the critic is not satisfied that this is the case, or if he is working upon an original and unsolved problem, he must not be content with second- and third-hand assertions or opinions, if it is possible to go behind them to the firsthand accounts. Hence the emphasis that is placed upon the sources.

ii. GOSSIP, RUMOR, AND SLANDER

Nothing is more common than for persons to repeat, often with embellishments, what others have told them, without any attempt to ascertain the truth. So rumor spreads and slander grows. Henry Ward Beecher once wrote a letter to a congressman in which he said that Postmaster Lincoln of Brooklyn had told him that Senator Pomeroy of Kansas had told him that he had called at the White House and found "the president [Johnson], his son, and son-in-law, all drunk and unfit for business, and that the President kept a mistress at the White House." The congressman sent Beecher's letter to Secretary Hugh McCulloch, who showed it to Secretary Gideon Welles of the Navy Department. When as a result Johnson's friends demanded an explanation from Pomeroy, he disavowed making any of the charges except that he had seen Robert Johnson "in liquor," and had thought that the son-in-law was in the same condition.[52]

A historian who encountered Beecher's letter and relying on his truthfulness as a clergyman used it as evidence bearing on Johnson's character without tracing the charges to their source would be led to a false conclusion. True criticism is intolerant of such slovenly procedure. Yet histories of the United States abound in stories which have originated in malice, faulty memory, or myth, and have been disseminated by partisans or gossips, accepted by uncritical his-

[52] Howard K. Beale, *The Critical Year* (New York: Harcourt, Brace and Company, [c1930]), 78–79.

torians, and copied and perpetuated by their successors. To restate the point, a person who merely passes along what he has heard is an incompetent witness whom the critic should thrust aside in his quest for the responsible author of the assertion. In a court of law such testimony would be thrown out without ceremony.

Prominent persons are especially likely to be the victims of such misrepresentations and their true character may be obscured by them. Hero worshipers make poor biographers as do also those who delight in "debunking" or are careless in their search for facts. Abraham Lincoln and his wife were the victims of William H. Herndon, Lincoln's biographer and one-time law partner. Several writers have dealt with these apocryphal tales about the Lincolns but many of them continue to circulate.[53]

iii. MYTHS, LEGENDS, AND TRADITIONS

When unfounded tales become current they are "myths" or "legends," regardless of how they may have originated. In some cases the authors are known, as in the case of the Herndon stories, and critics may be able to refute them. In other instances the stories have been passed along orally from generation to generation until their origin is forgotten and the original form lost. They spring up whenever trustworthy records are not obtainable.

Myths such as Herndon propagated are akin to gossip and are frequently exposed by critical scholarship. The historian can usually make nothing of those of the second class for want of evidence, documentary or archeological, to corroborate or disprove them. Some actual event may have been their source, but they grow with repetition and in time lose all determinable resemblance to the facts from which they sprang. The historian views these facts through a refracting medium the effect of which he has no means of discovering. Therefore, to statements in legends he cannot apply the usual tests. Imagine attempting to apply historical criticism to the labors of Hercules in the hope of finding some grain of truth embedded in the myth!

What archeology may sometimes contribute to the knowledge of

[53] Among the writers who have sought to set the record straight are: Montgomery S. Lewis, *Legends that Libel Lincoln* (New York: Rinehart & Company, c1946); David Donald, *Lincoln's Herndon* (New York: Alfred A. Knopf, 1946); and Ruth Painter Randall, *Mary Lincoln: Biography of a Marriage* (Boston: Little, Brown & Company, 1953). Regarding repetitions of the old stories see *Time*, January 30, 1950.

facts hidden in legends is illustrated by the experience of the German, Heinrich Schliemann, who became convinced by reading the *Iliad* that in antiquity there had actually been a war between the Greeks and the Trojans. In 1870 he made excavations at a spot in Asia Minor which he believed to be the site of Troy and found evidence which proved early contacts between its inhabitants and the Greeks. That was about all and it was not very satisfactory. Nothing was found to verify any *incident* in the Homeric tale or to confirm the existence of any of the personages of the drama. The wooden horse, Agamemnon, Priam, Helen, Paris, Ulysses, Hector, Achilles, *et al.* remain as they were before, creations of the poet's imagination. The *authorship* of the epic, the Homeric problem, is another matter, on which scholars are still working.

The status of traditions is hardly better. The present century has brought extensive archeological investigations in Egypt, the Holy Land, and adjacent countries which indicate that the Biblical account of the enslavement of the Children of Israel in Egypt and their exodus to the promised land of Canaan is traditional or legendary and without support of documentary or archeological evidence. The Old Testament accounts preserving these traditions were written centuries after the events they report, and no Egyptian records have been found relating to this early period of Hebrew history. The archeological discoveries in Palestine so far relate to a time when the Hebrews were already in that land, although subject to Egypt.[54]

Norse sagas are traditions written down several centuries after the events they purport to record. They are the basis of the theory that Norsemen visited North America long before Columbus made his memorable voyage. No cautious historian would deny that there may have been such visits, but most scholars are not yet convinced by the evidence adduced by devotees of the theory that Norsemen really reached America.[55] Nevertheless several scholarly organizations have joined forces to make a thorough investigation of a rune stone found in Minnesota containing a fragmentary account of what purports to be a visit by the Norse to that region.[56]

[54] Finnegan, *op. cit.*, 129 *et seq.*

[55] See, *e.g.*, Oscar J. Falnes's review of H. R. Holand, *America, 1355–1364*, in *MVHR* for September, 1947, pp. 288–289; and compare Kenneth Bjork's review of Frederick J. Pohl, *The Lost Discovery, ibid.*, March, 1953, pp. 747–749.

[56] *MVHR*, September, 1948, pp. 364–365, and September, 1949, pp. 365–367.

When the Constitutional Convention of 1787 adjourned it left its records in the custody of its presiding officer (George Washington), who deposited them in the State Department in 1796 subject to the orders of Congress. That body took no action concerning them for many years, and meantime had no source of information about the Convention's proceedings except the uncertain recollections of delegates who had later been elected to Congress. The dearth of information fostered the spread of misinformation, and in the course of a quarter century a number of myths sprang up which prompt publication of the records would no doubt have prevented. One of these related that Franklin's proposal to open each session of the Convention with prayer brought delight to Washington's "dignified face." Hamilton, however, was said to have opposed the motion on the ground that he saw no need of calling in "foreign aid"; upon which Washington gazed at him "with a mixture of surprise and indignation" on his face. Thereupon—so runs the story—the Convention instantly adopted the proposal, Hamilton alone indicating disapproval. (Franklin's motion was in fact made but was rejected.)[57]

Even a careful historian will sometimes think that he has sufficient evidence to support a statement when there are pertinent facts which he has not discovered. Such overlooked evidence may tend to a directly opposed conclusion. The following quotations point the moral:

> Many of the most wealthy and influential houses [families] in colonial Virginia were founded by men that could boast of no social prominence in England. . . . Adam Thoroughgood, although he came to Virginia as a servant or apprentice, became wealthy and powerful.[58]

Professor Wertenbaker could have marshalled an imposing number of cases to support his statement, but evidently overlooked the fact that an immigrant entering seventeenth-century Virginia as a

[57] Homer C. Hockett, *Constitutional History of the United States* (2 vols. New York: The Macmillan Company, 1939), II, ch. 4. (Hereafter cited as *Constitutional History.*) This chapter, based on Farrand's *Records*, relates several myths which arose in this period. The prevalence of misinformation was one of the reasons why Congress resolved in 1818 that the records should be published.

For other myths which scholars have sought to run to earth see *MVHR* for September, 1948, pp. 263–271; June, 1951, pp. 81–90; and September, 1952, pp. 347–348.

[58] Thomas J. Wertenbaker, *Patrician and Plebeian in Virginia* (Charlottesville, Va.: published by the author, 1910), p. 17.

servant was not necessarily from that class in the old country. He was unfortunate in citing the case of Thoroughgood, for

> the different records . . . show the continued emigration to Virginia of numerous persons who were connected by ties of blood or marriage with persons of high position in England. . . . Adam Thoroughgood . . . was a brother of Sir John Thoroughgood . . . who was attached to the Court.[59]

iv. TESTS OF TRUTHFULNESS

The statement of a person who for any of the reasons which have been considered is an incompetent person must be regarded as doubtful. It does not follow, on the other hand, that all statements of potentially competent witnesses are true. The question of whether a competent person is also truthful is quite a distinct one. He may know the facts and yet fail to tell them. This may be because he falsifies deliberately and intentionally; but the problem is not one of mere veracity. Influences of many kinds may lead to the distortion or coloring of a statement so that it misses the truth in one way or other without a deliberate falsification.

It is always wise to inquire whether the maker of a statement had a personal interest of any kind to be promoted by having his statement believed. One can hardly expect anything but a denial from a person accused of wrongdoing, nor anything but fair promises from a candidate for office. Most people have learned to hear the representations of salesmen with skepticism. A subordinate is expected to speak well of his superiors, at least in public; but if a discharged employee denounces the policies or conduct of his former "boss" he is to be suspected of pique or self-justification. Whether employed or dismissed one's statements involving his own interests or reputation are questionable. The critic needs to inquire into the present and past relationships between persons who make statements about others and those about whom they are made. One who accepts assertions by interested persons without further ado is childishly credulous or the victim of his own desire to believe regardless of evidence.

To what race, nation, party, sect, social set, profession, or other group did the maker of a statement belong. It is important to answer

[59] Philip Alexander Bruce, *Social Life in Virginia in the Seventeenth Century* (Richmond, Va.: printed for the author by Whittet and Shepperson, 1907), 51–52.

such questions because a prejudice—or at least a bias which may unconsciously influence even one who seeks to be unprejudiced—favorable to the group to which he belongs is to be apprehended, tending to warp his assertions from the exact truth. The critic must be constantly on the lookout for signs of these influences, for no one is ever entirely free from them. While prejudice and bias are commonly considered synonymous terms they should be distinguished. A bias is a natural leaning toward one's own interests or group or hypothesis, and influences even those who desire to weigh all evidence fully and honestly. A prejudiced person, on the other hand, *prejudges* issues regardless of the evidence or before it is presented. Special pleading may be the duty of the advocate (lawyer), but impartiality is as essential a quality for the historian as for the judge. One has only to read a few reviews in the historical journals to be convinced that many writers in the field of history violate this rule, either indulging in special pleading or in the selection of facts to support a pet hypothesis.[60]

The historian must expect to find all controversial matters treated with more or less bias. For example, he must approach the work of Catholic and Protestant writers on the Protestant Revolution prepared in both cases to encounter bias in spite of the efforts of the authors to be fair and impartial. He could not expect agreement between two historians of labor struggles if one had a capitalist background and the other belonged to a group of wage earners. Bias is sometimes found where one would least expect it. Even some of the books of the Bible betray it. The two books of Kings were compiled by unnamed persons from records now lost but to which many references are made ("Now the rest of the acts of Rehoboam . . . are they not written in the book of the chronicles of the kings of Judah," etc., etc.) show a Jewish bias against the neighboring Hebrew state of Israel. The purpose of these editors was to show that the misfortunes of both kingdoms were due to God's displeasure because they had forsaken him and adopted idolatrous ways; but they lay chief blame on "Jeroboam, the son of Nebat," reminding readers repeatedly that it was he who introduced idolatry into the kingdom of Israel and by this bad example led Judah, their land, also into apostasy.

George Bancroft's account of the Battle of Lexington shows a

[60] For an example see William C. Binkley's review of Elgin Williams's *The Animating Pursuits of Speculation*, in *MVHR* for December, 1949, pp. 517–519.

national bias which does violence to the facts. Depositions signed by many Americans who took part in the battle, including Captain Parker who was in command, show that Parker gave the order to disperse upon the approach of the British before the British officer, Pitcairn, commanded it. Bancroft had copies of these depositions, yet his story of the combat is a paean of praise for men who "stood motionless in the ranks, witnesses against aggression; too few to resist, too brave to fly." According to Bancroft (but not the sources) Pitcairn, seeing that the Americans did not heed his command to disperse, "discharged a pistol, and with a loud voice cried, 'Fire!'" Then, "in the disparity of numbers, Parker ordered his men to disperse. Then, and not till then, did a few of them, on their own impulse, return the British fire." As a matter of fact it is impossible to determine which side fired the first shot.[61] Bancroft's account is shaped by his ultrapatriotic bias. In extenuation of his misrepresentation of the facts it may be added that a faulty system of notetaking threw too great a burden on his memory.[62]

Since it is to be expected that interest, bias, or prejudice will result in more or less distortion of the truth, statements which might be expected to show such distortion but do not are apparently placed on a somewhat higher level of credibility. Especially is this true when the slant is *unfavorable* to the personal or group interest of the author. The Bible commends the man who "sweareth to his own hurt and changeth not" (Psalms xv: 4). Nevertheless the critic must be on guard against covert motives. A longing for notoriety has caused many a crime, and the same motive or others arising from perverted mentality has led many a person to confess a crime which he did not commit. A clever liar, moreover, may seek to throw the critic off guard by a false show of fairness, in order to gain acceptance of statements apparently fair to opponents but really detrimental to them.[63] Or an incoming official may speak in complimentary terms of his retiring predecessor of the opposite party, only because he wishes to be thought magnanimous. It is therefore worth while to repeat that each statement must be tested not only separately, but also in the light of all pertinent evidence.

[61] George Bancroft, *History of the United States of America, from the Discovery of the Continent* (author's last revision, 6 vols. New York: D. Appleton and Company, 1891–1892), IV, 155.

[62] *Post,* p. 139.

[63] Recall Mark Antony's funeral oration, *Julius Caesar,* Act III, scene 2.

It is wise for a writer to volunteer information about his relations with his subject in order to disarm suspicion of bias. In his history of the Adams family (the family of John Adams) James Truslow Adams promptly disavows kinship with his subjects, since kinship would create a presumption of friendly bias. Such a presumption is always in order where people make statements concerning their kindred, although critical examination may prove the presumption to be unwarranted. Nor is the bias always friendly; it may be quite the reverse. A descendant of John Wesley wrote a biography of him which shows an unsympathetic bias. The critic must make allowance for all bias, whether favorable or the contrary. A biographer who uses intemperate or extravagant language either in praise or blame of his chief character, or that person's friends or foes, detracts from a shrewd reader's confidence in the reliability of his work.[64]

A strong protestation of impartiality or affection should arouse suspicion. Hamlet had players put on an act to catch his father's murderers. When the woman in the scene goes to extremes in expressing her love for her husband, the queen, Hamlet's mother, betrays her guilt when she exclaims "The lady doth protest too much."[65] A favorable comment is often the prelude to an unfavorable remark; the two should be considered as inseparable. On the other hand an expression of admiration for members of an opposed or contrasted group if not followed by any comment of a different tone is evidenced of absence of the customary bias. If an account of Catholic missions among the Western Indians, written by a Protestant, is uniformly sympathetic and appreciative, the impression of impartiality is strengthened by a statement making clear the writer's own religious affiliations. Any conclusions based on such statements, however, should be tentative, and should stand or fall only after examination of all related statements.

A third type of inquiry asks whether the position of the maker of a statement was such as to require or permit conventional expressions rather than his real sentiments. The pious phrases of the President of the United States in the annual proclamation of a Day of Thanksgiving are worth nothing as evidence of his personal views on

[64] As an example see the review by Charles H. Metzger of John Richard Alden's *General Charles Lee, Traitor or Patriot,* in *MVHR* for December, 1951, pp. 501–503.

[65] Act III, scene 2.

religion; nor does the signature "Yours truly" warrant a young woman in bringing a breach of promise suit against her male correspondent. In days gone by men wrote letters to their deadliest enemies and signed themselves "Your obedient servant." The meaninglessness of formulae is plain enough in such cases as the last two, but some persons might not readily perceive that the same is equally true in the first. The danger of misconstruction increases in direct ratio with the critic's unfamiliarity with the class of documents in which the formulae are found, because of the greater difficulty in recognizing them. Problems of this kind are numerous in the history of ancient and medieval times, and fall within the field of the auxiliary science of diplomatics.

Somewhat similar are expressions uttered under such circumstances that they were likely to be colored by the desire to please hearers or readers. A courtier's words in addressing the king are not the only instances of studied flattery. It is often thought better to be complacent and agreeable than to utter unpleasant truths. Courtesy sometimes demands silence or words which do not reveal the speaker's whole thought. The efforts of young orators, debaters, and writers, however crude, are more often praised than subjected to constructive criticism because the critic fears the effect will be chilling. A recommendation addressed To Whom It May Concern, and handed to the person recommended, is likely to be less candid and consequently to carry less weight than if addressed confidentially to a prospective employer. Sheer laziness and desire to avoid irritating discussion often induces people to acquiesce in opinions which they do not share. Thousands of persons sign petitions to be rid of the bearers, whether the petitions express their desires or not. The unjust judge decided to avenge the widow "lest by her continual coming she weary me" (Luke xviii: 1–5).

Internal evidence often suggests pertinent criticism. If a writer betrays vanity, by the habitual ascription to himself of a conspicuous share in important actions or events, intimacy with prominent personages, or otherwise, his statements are suspected of exaggeration. Such bragging ways supply the chief reasons for questioning John Smith's story of his rescue by Pocahontas; a boastful tone pervades all of his writings. In his first account of his capture by the Indians there is not a word suggestive of intervention by the native princess. It was not until her marriage with John Rolfe, followed by her spectacular reception in England, had made her a celebrity (and, say the critics, not until her death had made denial of the account impossible), that Smith published the story of the rescue.

If internal evidence betrays a strong interest in literary form or effects on the part of a writer there is reason to fear that he may have distorted facts. Although a writer should cultivate a pleasing style, historical accuracy is almost certain to suffer if his motive becomes *chiefly* literary.[66] The love of rhetorical flourishes, picturesque details, dramatic narrative, or a fondness for portraying intense emotion or conduct of exceptional nobility, may prevail over the desire to tell the precise truth. An example of the last kind is the Parson Weems story of George Washington and the cherry tree. Akin is the correction of Washington's mistakes by Jared Sparks in his edition of Washington's writings. Bancroft wrote in almost as exaggerated a strain as Weems when he described the actions and feelings of the people of Lexington upon hearing of the approach of the British troops on the morning of April 19, 1775:

> . . . How women, with heaving breasts, bravely seconded their husbands! how the countrymen, forced suddenly to arm, without guides or counsellors, took instant counsel of their courage! The mighty chorus of voices rose from the scattered farmhouses, and as it were, from the very ashes of the dead. Come forth, champions of liberty, now free your country; protect your sons and daughters, your wives and homesteads; rescue the houses of the God of your fathers, the franchises handed down from your ancestors! [67]

These heroics were the product of Bancroft's imagination. The contemporary statements of participants in that day's doings show no consciousness of the momentous character of the events. Bancroft distorts the truth in two ways: by indulging in rhetoric of this kind, and, as already pointed out, by allowing national prejudice to blind him to the facts as told by the sources.

Some writers embellish their narratives with picturesque but unhistorical details for the sake of vividness. One might describe a home-coming of Thomas Jefferson thus: "The red disc of the sun was just sinking from view behind the western hills, and purple twilight was already gathering in the vales as Jefferson drew near to Monticello." This literary sentence might have value if true to facts,

[66] Homer C. Hockett, "The Literary Motive in the Writing of History," in *MVHR*, March, 1926, pp. 469–482.
[67] *Op. cit.*, IV, 154.

but if drawn from the writer's imagination must be classed with other untruths. Data of the kind needed to support such expressions are rare in historical documents and must not be supplied by a writer who has no basis for them. When that is the case the truth might just as well be that the arrival was at midnight in a pouring rain! Distortion of this kind is so common that the critic must suspect the accuracy of statements in such colorful language. Besides they cast doubt on the writer's accuracy in treating matters of real importance. It is well at this point to recall the self-restraint of Thucydides.

Authors whose field is the twilight zone between fiction and history—"fictionalized history," which is more akin to the novel than history—adopt the picturesque style to make their books interesting, or write biographies with as many intimate touches as the novelist employs in depicting the thoughts and emotions of his heroes. Such writing has currently a great vogue; but it should be remembered that while history will not be read if it is not interesting, it *should* not be read—or written—if it is not true. Such wandering from the strait and narrow path deserves, and often receives, reproof by the reviewer. An appropriate review of a bit of errant history comments that "the writer does not allow historical accuracy . . . to prevent him from telling any good story, thereby achieving the end of entertainment." [68] Another scholarly historian writes a brief but excellent essay on the contrast between the aims and output of real historians and these purveyors of counterfeit goods.[69] This review is recommended as collateral reading for the student. Unfortunately the general reader and the novitiate in the historical field do not always have the benefit of expert judgment of the writings they encounter; to both is offered the warning that it is so difficult to discriminate between the imaginary and the real in fictionalized history that the safe course is to treat all of it as fiction and turn elsewhere for trustworthy information.

The film industry habitually disregards facts when dealing with historical themes, paying even less attention than fictionalizing historians to the boundaries between truth and fancy. If used at all for

[68] James H. Shideler, reviewing Edwin Corle's *The Royal Highway*, in *MVHR* for March, 1950, pp. 684–685.

[69] Arthur Eugene Bestor, Jr., reviewing Edward Nicholas's *The Hours and the Ages, ibid.*, June, 1950, pp. 116–117.

educational purposes movies should be accompanied by competent comment.

Another species of distortion ignores the actual sequence of events, which to be sure may be drab enough, and seeks to make a dramatic appeal by presenting happenings which took place at different times as if they occurred in artistic sequence, or experiences of different individuals as if they happened to a single person. During the progress of the debate over the admission of Missouri as a state, Thomas Jefferson declared that the controversy startled him "like a fire bell in the night." Unfortunately for the literary historian the utterance was not evoked by the beginning of the controversy nor yet at its climax. The effect would be more dramatic if the historian quoted the words out of their exact historical setting—but the account would be less true as history, which requires the sentiments of people to be attributed to them at the *time when they were held or expressed,* not when they *should* have been. The crucial moment often passes before the actors in the human drama are aware that it has arrived. Hindsight should not be confused with insight.

Speakers and writers frequently distort the truth by exaggerating the intensity of their own emotions or those of others for the purpose of exciting the responses they desire from audiences or readers. The eloquence of the orator, whether in the field of law, politics, or religion, is not the best medium for presenting facts. It is too often akin to the device of the attorney who simulates convictions which he does not hold and emotions which he does not feel in order to influence a jury and obtain a verdict for his client. If the allegation were proved that Daniel Webster was equally willing to plead for the other side in the Dartmouth College Case, his impassioned defense of his alma mater might still be admired as oratory but the estimate of his character would probably suffer. The lawyer's plea is sometimes like the trick of the thief who raises the hue and cry to divert attention from himself, or that of the demagogue who forsakes argument and slanders his opponent to cover his own crookedness. Nor is ridicule argument, except to answer a fool according to his folly. Even so, the question may be, Who is the fool?

Demagogues, who seem to be ever plentiful in American politics, stop at nothing in their efforts to discredit opponents. The evening before the polls opened in the presidential election of 1920 a handbill was distributed on doorsteps alleging that the Republican candidate had some Negro blood. This attempted appeal to race prejudice was vicious in two ways: in its false implication that it was a disgrace to have the least trace of Negro blood in one's veins; and in its leaving no time for the victim to deny the allegation.

V. DISCREDITED STATEMENTS

While negative criticism seeks every reason for doubting the truthfulness of statements many survive the most rigorous tests. Even then, as will be explained later, their truthfulness is not established unless corroborating evidence is forthcoming. Moreover there are some kinds of statements which are rejected even without being subjected to the usual tests. The historian must reject them when the tests he usually makes are not applicable. Such treatment is due statements reporting happenings which do not conform to the laws of nature as established by scientific methods. It requires no justification where myths, fairy tales, stories of magic, etc., are involved. Their summary rejection is implied in the rule that no statement can be accepted unless it can be shown to rest on trustworthy observation. If any one asserts them he must be regarded as ignorant, superstitious, the victim of hallucination, or some other form of mental aberration.

Some would contend that miracles present an exceptional case. This is due to their intimate connection with religious belief. If by a miracle is meant a supernatural occurrence, not in conformity with the laws of nature as expounded by the scientist, the historian is wise if he refrains from attempting to determine whether or not an alleged miracle actually occurred, for its truth or falsity depends on evidence which does not fall within his province. He follows the scientist's lead. He is bound to recognize that belief in miracles has greatly affected human life and conduct. Beliefs and their influence on mankind are historical facts which the historian must reckon with in this limited way, and that is as far as he can legitimately go.

Finally, every statement which is not in accord with the body of (supposedly) known historical facts must be considered as improbable, although the open-minded historian recognizes that the whole body of supposed facts must be held subject to revision if and when new evidence is forthcoming. Supposed facts and trusted conclusions are constantly being modified in the light of new discoveries.

3. The Recovery of the Past

a. *The Possibility of Recovery*

By this time the student may be tempted to conclude that it is useless to try to distinguish the true from the false sufficiently to make the historian's efforts worth while. The predominant note in critical method may seem to be doubt and negation. A few generations ago German historians set themselves to portray the past as it actually was (*wie es eigentlich gewesen*), but distortion of the facts has been and continues to be so common that prominent persons have denounced written history as little more than "fiction agreed upon." The late Henry Ford I is reported to have said that "history is bunk," and some of the prominent American historians of the generation now passing from the stage seem to have agreed. In a letter to the author of this Manual the late Carl Becker wrote "you cannot recover the past." In similar vein Charles A. Beard, regarded in his later years as the "dean of American historians," entitled his address as president of the American Historical Association "Written History as an Act of Faith." [70]

The present writer ventures to say that the majority of American historians hold less extreme views than the two just quoted. In the opening pages of this book he considers the conditions which limit the historian and attempts to show that they are not unlike those met by researchers in other fields. He maintains that despite gaps which can never be filled, enough knowledge of the past can be recovered to make the effort highly profitable. It is not difficult to recover a good deal of the past as it relates to Carl Becker. There can be no doubt that there was a Carl Becker, that he spent his youth in Kansas, that he studied under Frederick Jackson Turner at the University of Wisconsin, that he spent his last years as a professor of history at Cornell University, that he was a prolific writer, that a bibliography of his chief works could be prepared, etc., etc., etc. There can be no doubt that the English colonies in America fought a successful war for independence during the years 1775 to 1781, that George Washington served as commander-in-chief of the American forces, and that he became the first President of the Republic under the Constitution drafted in 1787. There can be no doubt that a war broke out in 1861 between the North and the South which ended in 1865 in the defeat of the Confederacy.

[70] *AHR*, XXXIX (1934), 219 *et seq.*

These instances chosen at random could be multiplied a thousand fold to prove that facts about the past have been in part preserved in recoverable form. In every case mentioned in the preceding paragraph the few facts given could be amplified by adding many others which are just as indubitable. That myths and errors have found their way into much written history must be admitted; but the purpose and justification of these pages lie in the effort to show that proper criticism may both establish facts and purge history of erroneous statements. Sound criticism has brought it about that many histories are now in print in which the truth is so preponderant that error is confined to details of relatively slight import; but while they may contain little that is not true, it goes without saying that none of them contain *all* the facts even now available which relate to their subject matter. History as written is necessarily made up of selected facts.

b. *Determinable Facts*

The historian may derive a certain amount of satisfaction from correcting an error, exposing a myth, or exploding a faulty hypothesis. Such achievements have their value in clearing the ground for more accurate work, which is the writer's proper objective. The historian's main purpose is to gather a body of ascertained facts which, properly presented, will clarify our understanding of the past and its significance for the present.

i. CONTRIBUTIONS OF (1) EXTERNAL AND (2) INTERNAL CRITICISM

In this connection it is appropriate to recall what has been learned about the contributions criticism makes in determining the facts about documents and the truth of the statements in them. Hence, now turning from negatives, we may consider further the ways by which facts may be ascertained or statements certified as true beyond reasonable doubt.

ii. ANONYMOUS STATEMENTS

When we dealt with the Book of Ruth, an anonymous document, our purpose was to determine the time of its writing. By comparing its liberal tone (internal evidence) with the tone of Ezra (external evidence) the approximate date was discovered. Without the knowledge of its correct time-setting in Jewish history its significance might be missed by readers. Anonymity was in this case of no great importance, the significance of the study being the conclusion that the writer represented a liberal group. There is no need of subjecting the *statements* in the document to a rigorous test of truthfulness. Critical study of the word-for-word report of the conversation between Ruth and Naomi would yield no valuable result. In short, this book (document) is to be taken as a whole and judged by its purpose—to persuade the Jews that they should abandon their narrow nationalistic prejudices. Ruth is not the only book in the Bible which needs to be dated and interpreted by finding the author's purpose. Job, Daniel, and Jonah are other good examples.

The relation between a document's purpose and the type of criticism applicable to it may be clarified by a further illustration. Probably no one would read a play of Shakespeare as a history textbook. To be sure many of the plays deal with historical events and personages; but the author's purpose was to produce dramas, not history, and it would be folly to discount his works because they do not meet tests applicable to historical writings. While the problem of authorship—whether Shakespeare or Bacon wrote certain plays—is of interest and properly belongs in the field of criticism, the *product* speaks for itself as the work of a genius. The same principle holds for historical novels; their merits should be judged by their purpose and not as sources of historical information.

Bearing in mind the relation between the purpose of a document and the appropriate kind of criticism to use on it, we may ask what tests may be applied to anonymous documents and statements. If external criticism fails to supply data concerning authorship, internal criticism is directed to the statement instead of the author. It must be remembered that by authorship more is meant than the name of the writer of a document. If he has written on politics, his country, state, and party if ascertainable may be as important as his name in indicating his probable bias. If he has written on religion knowledge of his creed or denomination will serve in the same way. "The Monk of St. Gall," whose name is unknown, is sufficiently identified by this appellation for some of the purposes of criticism.

Some of the tests already discussed may be applied to anonymous statements. The critic may ask questions which will test the probability of falsity or truthfulness, such as: Is the statement prejudicial to the end the maker evidently seeks to gain? If he voluntarily makes an admission which tends to thwart his purpose it evinces an effort to be truthful.

Would the falsity of a statement be certainly detected? It is supposed that John Smith would not have published the story of his rescue by Pocahontas while she was living and certain to hear of it, unless it was true; she would have denied a false account. The same reasoning would apply in the case of an anonymous statement which the maker evidently desired people to believe, as if false it would be expected to call forth an authoritative denial. Nevertheless it must be remembered that it is difficult for truth to overtake falsehood even though it is supported by evidence.

Is the statement of an indifferent nature? Many assertions are of such a casual or neutral sort that there is no conceivable motive for misrepresentation. If such statements are incorrect it is because of unintentional error. The probability of error may be weighed by asking such questions as: Is the statement such that, if true, it must have been a matter of common observation and knowledge for a long time, or over a wide area? If so, the probability of error is reduced to the minimum. The same is true if the statement is such that a superficial observation would suffice for a correct report. Finally, there are statements which could never have been thought of if untrue, such as that the precepts of the Sermon on the Mount were actually proclaimed by a great teacher.

iii. INCIDENTAL ALLUSIONS

Casual allusions in the literature of any people often reveal facts concerning their ways of life. Scripture references to chickens prove that, like sheep, they were among the common possessions of the ancient Hebrews. The collections of stories used by medieval preachers to illustrate their sermons are important sources of knowledge of life in the Middle Ages. Even the collection of fairy stories known as the *Arabian Nights* incidentally throws much light on the culture of the Mohammedans of Arabia during the reign of the Caliph Haroun-al-Raschid (766?–809).

Certain cautions must be heeded in interpreting such allusions. They reflect the time from which the document dates, but not necessarily that which it purports to describe. Moreover one must not confound the moral or aesthetic concepts of the writer with those of the age portrayed. Penelope's fidelity to Ulysses cannot be taken as typical of wives in ancient Greece. Nor can descriptions of objects be regarded as proof that they existed, although the author must have been acquainted with their component elements. If golden streets are mentioned the reference proves, not that they were actually to be found anywhere, but only that the writer was familiar with both gold and streets and had a lively imagination.

iv. STATEMENTS CONCERNING CUSTOMS

Contemporary statements concerning customs, doctrines, and great events of any period show the existence of such customs and institutions, if they endured for a long time or over a vast area and therefore must have attracted general attention and become matters of common knowledge. However, when such statements include incidental details these are subject to doubt unless they are of the kinds discussed in the preceding paragraphs. There is also an inherent danger in translations from one language into another. In some cases our English Bible uses the names of plants familiar to us for very different ones found in Palestine in Biblical times. The Spanish conquerors of Mexico had no means of describing native life except by using Spanish terms which could not convey a correct understanding of it.

In this connection it should be explained that ancient history wears an illusory appearance of greater certainty than modern. This is because the truth concerning modern events must be found by sifting great masses of evidence while the preserved materials relating to remote times are meager. The truth is that the facts of ancient history are much more difficult to ascertain because of the dearth of independent accounts. For example, it is customary to accept the account of the early Germans by Tacitus because it is almost the only one extant. His statements are accepted as facts, contrary to the rules of criticism, since they cannot be corroborated. It is a case of "take it or leave it." With that alternative before them historians commonly "take it," but their own writings should at least hint at the difference between statements resting on a single authority and facts established by two or more independent witnesses. One should not state positively that it was the custom of the early Germans to do so-and-so, but should use some saving clause such as "according to Tacitus it was the custom," etc. On foundations almost as uncertain some historians have built elaborate theories about the origin of English institutions. Others have followed the etiological narratives of Livy in dealing with the beginnings of Roman history with scarcely a suggestion that they are unhistorical. A good example of Livy's etiology is his explanation of the name of the City of Rome on the ground that it must have been founded by a man named Romulus.

V. STATEMENTS REGARDING DETAILS

The most difficult statements to deal with critically are those which, like Tacitus's descriptions of early German life, concern details. *The statement of one person should never be regarded as establishing the truth of details.* There would be little risk in accepting even a newspaper account, if contemporary, reporting that the Democratic National Nominating Convention of 1928 met at such and such a time and place, but if the account went on to say that Mr. So-and-so met Mr. Thus-and-so in a back room and reached certain agreements about the nomination, corroborating evidence would have to be demanded. If such evidence could not be found the story should be classed, tentatively, as on a par with the charges which Beecher disseminated against President Johnson.

However, it often happens in recent history that more than one statement is available with reference to a particular event. Each statement is then subjected to the tests of internal criticism and if not rejected is compared with the other statements by asking such questions as: Are they (1) independent observations (2) made by different observers (3) belonging to different parties, sects, or groups (4) working under different conditions? Essential agreement in the statements of such independent witnesses will establish the truth beyond reasonable doubt.

These considerations make it clear why an investigator must collect the statements on a given matter by members of opposing groups. Thus in studying a political campaign it is necessary to examine representative newspapers of all the parties presenting candidates.

It is to be noted that independent reports of observations are bound to differ in nonessentials, such as phraseology. Such minor variations are evidence of independence rather than error, and add to the conclusiveness of concurrent accounts. *Absolute likeness would prove dependence,* and reduce the several accounts to one. Where statements seem to agree, therefore, it is necessary to determine whether one has been borrowed from another, or whether they are really independent. Because Madison borrowed some of the statements which he found in the *Journal* his papers as published seem at some points to confirm the *Journal,* whereas the borrowed statements rest solely upon its authority. Such tests applied to the gospels of Matthew and Luke aid in distinguishing between the independent statements in each and those which both borrowed from Mark.

On the other hand, where statements seem contradictory it is necessary to determine whether the contradiction is real or only apparent; they may bear on different aspects of a matter. The six blind men who went to "see" the elephant did not contradict one another despite the differences in their reports. Nor did they corroborate one another; their comments dealt with different features of the object examined.

Sometimes independent accounts agree at certain points and are contradictory at others. Both John Adams and Thomas Jefferson were members of a committee appointed by Congress in 1776 to draw up the Declaration of Independence. About half a century later each gave an account of the operation. Adams asserted that the committee met and appointed a subcommittee consisting of Jefferson and himself to make the draft, that he persuaded Jefferson to do it, and that the latter's draft as reported to the main committee was accepted substantially as drawn. Jefferson denied that there had been a subcommittee, but said that he consulted Franklin as well as Adams and that they made several changes in his draft as the original copy still showed. Written notes he had made on the spot at the time, he alleged, supported his statement about the changes.

Here is both confirmation and contradiction; some facts are established and others left undecided. That Jefferson drew the draft is clear, and also the fact that he consulted Adams. Whether there was a subcommittee is uncertain; Adams may, as Jefferson said, have "misremembered" informal conferences as meetings of a subcommittee, while Jefferson may have forgotten a subcommittee because he "consulted" Franklin as well as Adams. His written memorandum is not conclusive of the point, for it merely says "the Committee for drawing the Declaration of Independence desired me to do it. It was accordingly done." Adams's statement about changes is contradicted by Jefferson, and his assertion is supported by the appearance of the document but not by his memorandum.[71]

No conclusion can be reached when statements of equal intrinsic

[71] *Cf.* discussion of this question in Henry Johnson, *Teaching of History in Elementary and Secondary Schools* (New York: The Macmillan Company, 1926), 432–434.

credibility are really contradictory. An example of such contradiction is found in the statements of eyewitnesses concerning the firing of the first shot at Lexington. Nor can a conclusion be reached if statements deal with different aspects of a matter, for this is equivalent to dealing with different subjects.

vi. CIRCUMSTANTIAL EVIDENCE

Statements which are not directly confirmed by independent assertions may command tentative acceptance if they fit in harmoniously with other facts which are indubitable. At the time of the controversy over the admission of Missouri to statehood John C. Calhoun is known to have been an extreme nationalist in his views of the powers of Congress, while by the end of the 1830's he had become the chief protagonist of the strict construction of its powers. This alteration of opinion concerning a fundamental principle would justify a student of the history of slavery in surmising that Calhoun had probably changed his views on the slavery issue also. In this case circumstantial evidence would, without other warrant, permit the student to state this probability. But he could not thereby escape the duty of trying to discover whether his surmise was supported by facts, for a minimum of skill in research would reveal them.[72]

It is believed that Andrew Jackson opposed the administration of John Quincy Adams because he thought that Adams had won the presidency in the House election of 1825 by means of a political deal with Henry Clay. Jackson himself never made a statement to this effect, nor was it made for him by any authorized spokesman. Yet circumstantial evidence of the fact is strong. Jackson greeted Adams cordially on the day of the latter's inauguration and showed no resentment over his own defeat. It had already been charged that Adams had promised Clay the post of Secretary of State in return for his aid in winning the House election. Jackson knew of this charge but his conduct at the inauguration indicates that he did not at that time believe it. When a little later Adams nominated Clay, Jackson asserted that he had been robbed of the presidency by a "corrupt bargain," and referred to Clay as "the Judas of the West." The inference is almost inescapable that the appointment of Clay convinced him of the truth of the pre-election charge, and caused his hostility to an administration which he might otherwise have judged on its merits.

[72] See Exercise No. 6, *post*, page 75.

4. Exercises in Criticism

It would be logical for a manual on method to begin with the ways of finding material, for the historian has nothing to apply critical principles to until he has gathered it. However, critical method may become through practice so much a part of him that in effect its application accompanies his research. As has been said already, the author of the present book deems it desirable for the beginner to become acquainted with critical principles before he begins his research, for then he may approach it with the proper mental orientation.

It would be almost impossible to formulate a complete statement of critical method. The merit of rules lies in their expression of that good sense and judgment without which it is a waste of time to engage in historical pursuits. Rules are, as has been said, based on experience and common sense, and may save beginners the necessity of learning by their own experience, which is "the hard way," attended by mistakes. Even with the help of rules, the student must himself cultivate a sound critical attitude and the ability to adapt his procedure to the requirements of his particular undertaking.

a. *A Plan of Review*

This advice may seem difficult to follow. If the presentation of the matter in the foregoing pages seems intricate and confusing, it is suggested that the student, instead of trying to memorize rules and use them as yardsticks to be applied mechanically, attempt, by way of review, to draw up a succinct analysis to reduce the "code" to its bare essentials, supplemented where necessary by examination of pages of the text and the footnotes. Using the Table of Contents as a framework, such a summary might take the following form (blanks to be filled by student). The analysis may be extended at the student's discretion:

External criticism examines ; internal criticism examines . The purpose of the former is ; that of the latter is .

External evidence differs from external criticism in ; internal evidence differs from internal criticism in .

The purpose of textual criticism is . It falls under the head of criticism.

Positive criticism does not aim to . Illustrate.

The criticism which tests the truth of statements is called . It asks such questions as .

The chief rule governing the acceptability of a statement of detail is .

b. *Sample Questions for Students to Ask and Answer*

How may the tone of a document aid in dating it?

What general rule requires the rejection of certain types of statement? What types?

Is it worth while to attempt to recover facts about the past?

Under what conditions may the historian use circumstantial evidence?

What is the value of a myth for the historian's use?

c. *Exercises*

The author regards the discussion of critical method as the most valuable part of this Manual, not only because it deals with something essential to success in writing history, but because it involves a discipline of mind and character which every one needs. Its value extends far beyond the requirements of the would-be historian. In these modern times a course in this subject might well replace the study of traditional logic.

However, the present writer is concerned primarily with the needs of students, teachers, and writers of American history. It is desirable for all of these to supplement the sort of review recommended above with a few problems requiring in a simple way the utilization of critical principles as a kind of bridge carrying them over to the problems of research. From the first to the last example, these problems grow successively somewhat more difficult; and since they require some research, a subject which has not yet been taken up systematically, needed suggestions are given in connection with each of them.

Some of these exercises are based on the discussions of method in this Manual, while others are based on statements in various textbooks from which students are likely to have gained their first considerable body of historical information. Instructors should be able to add other suitable questions and exercises as needed. Such is the prestige of the printed word with the average young person when he takes his first college course in history that his textbook may be remembered as an unimpeachable authority. Even the advice of a scholarly instructor was probably suspect if it differed from a statement in "the book." While this attitude is usually superseded by the time young people reach the graduate school, the best way to overcome it is by experience in the use of critical procedure. Then if not sooner they will discover that textbooks are peculiarly liable to err owing to the conditions under which they are produced.

It would be unreasonable to expect writers of that class of books to make no statements not based on their own critical study of the sources. They may be competent scholars, but the scope of textbooks is so inclusive that the writers are of necessity largely dependent on the statements of others, some of whom may not be as accurate as they should be. Through their errors false statements creep into print and are disseminated and survive until some critical investigator happens to detect them and publish the correction. Since the nature of the textbook writer's task makes it impossible for him to follow all the rules governing the author of a special study, it is the latter's task and duty to expose textbook errors if they happen to fall within the scope of his researches.

The correction of many such errors is quite within the competence of a capable student as an exercise in the application of critical method. Even if some one else has already made a correction, the student may, for the sake of practice, be allowed to discover the facts for himself, just as if the error had never been detected. However, he may not be able to discover that it is an error unless he is directed to examine critically some specified passage or statement. That much guidance the following exercises attempt to give.

EXERCISE No. 1. Professor Edward Channing, discussing the various sources from which Columbus could have got the idea that he could reach Asia by sailing westward, takes up each possibility in turn and in each case decides that there is no conclusive evidence that *it* was the source of his idea. What conclusion was the appropriate one for him to state? The student may use the index of the *Harvard Guide* (see pages 121–122) to ascertain which of Channing's writings should be examined to find his statements about this matter.

EXERCISE No. 2. Professor Arthur M. Schlesinger, Jr., writes of John C. Calhoun: "As he rode north from Pendleton in the Indian summer of 1837, his lips compressed, his face drawn with concentration, his manner absent and taciturn, he weighed his future course with infinite exactness."[73] Schlesinger's book was a Pulitzer

[73] *The Age of Jackson* (Boston: Little, Brown and Company, 1945), 242.

Prize winner. Is there any ground for questioning the accuracy of this description?

Exercise No. 3. A certain textbook says that James Otis, advocating universal suffrage in the 1760's, wrote that applewomen and orange girls had as good a right to share in making the compact of government "as the philosopher, courtier, and . . . politician." The words about applewomen and orange girls were not enclosed in quotation marks. A friend wrote to the author saying that New Englanders in Otis's time did not eat oranges. In reply the author cited Carl Bridenbaugh's *Cities in the Wilderness*,[74] which says that oranges, raisins, and figs were among the imports of Boston merchants before 1760. Let the student criticize both comment and defense.

Exercise No. 4. On the death of President Washington, Gouverneur Morris delivered a funeral oration in which he described Washington's appearance and quoted his words on a tense occasion in the Constitutional Convention of 1787, twelve years earlier:

> Americans!—let the opinion then delivered by the greatest and best of men, be ever present to your remembrance. He was collected within himself. His countenance had more than usual solemnity.—His eye was fixed, and seemed to look into futurity. "It is (said he) too probable that no plan we propose will be adopted. Perhaps another dreadful conflict is to be sustained. If to please the people, we offer what we ourselves disapprove, how can we afterwards defend our work? Let us raise a standard to which the wise and honest can repair. The event is in the hand of God." [75]

Morris was present in the Convention at the time but tells us that he took no notes of the proceedings. This alleged statement by Washington is still frequently quoted by writers and speakers. Let the student appraise its credibility.

Exercise No. 5. The *Readers' Digest* for November, 1953 (pages 157–180), contains a condensation of a book intitled *The Man Who Wouldn't Talk*. The student should read this article and decide what tests were needed to establish the book's authenticity. Afterwards he should consult the issue of the *Digest* for January, 1954 (pages 106–110), in which the editors confess that the book was a clever hoax which completely deceived them, and check their tests with his own.

[74] New York: c1938, p. 41.

[75] Farrand, *Records*, III, 381.

EXERCISE No. 6. Suppose an instructor tells a student that many textbooks say the passage of the Missouri Compromise of 1820 was effected by votes of Southern members of Congress and suggests that he check the truth of the statement. As we are assuming that this assignment is made before the student has received instruction in research the instructor might have to direct him to the vote as recorded in the proceedings of Congress. He should then be able to learn that the Compromise was passed by a majority in which the Northern members outnumbered the Southerners who voted with them. This fact, learned by personal examination of the evidence, has a much greater educational value for the student than accepting a secondhand statement from the most eminent authority. Going through the process yields not only information but training in essential historical "know how." [76]

EXERCISE No. 7. John C. Calhoun was a member of President Monroe's cabinet when Congress passed the Missouri Compromise bill. Before signing it the President requested the opinions of the cabinet members as to its constitutionality. The only record of their answers that has been found is an entry in the diary of John Quincy Adams, another member of the cabinet, who wrote that Calhoun agreed that the measure was constitutional. A student might be asked to find and evaluate the Adams memorandum guided by such questions as: What rule of evidence applies to this memorandum? He should not need to be told that Calhoun's later career might yield evidence on this point. Where should he look for it? It should occur to him that some biographer may have discussed the matter and that biographies of Calhoun would probably be found in the library. Or the instructor might suggest that he use the index of the *Harvard Guide* to find the names of his biographers and editors of his writings. Following such clues he should find that Calhoun admitted that he had favored the Compromise but later came to regard that opinion as a grave mistake.

Following this procedure would again contribute much more to the student's training than telling him exactly where he would find

[76] For textbooks giving the correct information see Homer C. Hockett, *Political and Social Growth of the American People* (New York: The Macmillan Company, 3d edn., 1940 and later reprints), 501; also Homer C. Hockett and Arthur M. Schlesinger, *Land of the Free* (New York: The Macmillan Company, 1944), 199. *Cf.* John D. Hicks, *A Short History of American Democracy* (Boston: Houghton Mifflin Company, [c1943]), 204; and other textbooks chosen at random.

the answer to his question. He would also profit if he compared the lives of Calhoun to see whether any of the biographers had solved the little problem.

EXERCISE No. 8. Bassett's widely used textbook, narrating events connected with the choice of President by the House of Representatives in 1825, says that Van Buren of the New York delegation

> hoped the state's vote would remain divided on the first ballot. Thus there would be no choice on that ballot, which would give him the opportunity at a later time to cast the New York vote for Adams and secure for himself the honor of president-maker.[77]

To a promising student at this stage of his training it should be obvious that Bassett's authority for this statement is some one whom he does not name. He would see that it would be wrong for him to accept it as a fact even if he quoted it with some such qualified phrase as "according to Bassett," for Bassett is not an "authority" but merely passes along some other person's statement. There is a possibility that Bassett's authority misrepresented Van Buren's intentions. If either Bassett or his unidentified authority is in error, the student would by his statement merely perpetuate the error by passing it along, and for such negligence cautious language would not atone. He must if possible test the truth of the allegation by tracing it to the person who first made it; he faces the task of finding Bassett's source and checking the original statement with any that Van Buren himself may have made.

This search might be difficult even for an experienced scholar. It is often true that evidence either to establish or refute a statement is not to be found and that the quest leads only to a suspended judgment. In the present case one should see that probably the first step should be to discover what Van Buren said, if anything. The college library catalogue would no doubt contain a number of entries under Van Buren's name and in one or more of the books listed something might be found bearing on the question. If the catalogue listed Van Buren's *Autobiography* the seeker would be in luck, for he should recognize that it is the book where he is most likely to find any comment Van Buren may have made. Part of the good luck would be the fact that the catalogue listed the *Autobiography*, for it is yet to be learned that it forms a part of a composite work, and

[77] John Spencer Bassett, *A Short History of the United States* (New York: The Macmillan Company, 1913), 380.

many catalogues do not make separate cards for the parts of such publications. Here again the *Harvard Guide* would give first aid by providing information as to the publication in which this item appears.

Once in possession of the *Autobiography*, however, the investigator has plain sailing for a while, for in it he would readily find the following:

> I obtained a meeting of the friends of Crawford in the New York delegation and proposed to them . . . that we should abstain to the end from taking part in favor of either of the three [other two] gentlemen returned to the House—Jackson, Adams, or Clay. [Van Buren, evidently writing from memory, is in error at this point, as Clay's name was not before the House; the three were Jackson, Adams, and Crawford.] I assured them that there was no danger that an election would not be made by others and that if the friends of Mr. Crawford stood aloof from the intrigues which such a contest would produce unavoidably they would form a nucleus around which the old Republicans of the Union might rally if the new Administration did not act upon their principles as we apprehended would be the case. They resolved with perfect unanimity to pursue that course, and I do not believe that a single individual of our number ever thought of departing from it; certainly not one did so depart. Judge Hammond was therefore misinformed in regard to their intention to vote in any event [that is, if the first ballot did not result in a choice] for Mr. Adams.[78]

Following a clue which turns out to be a good one often leads to another. A part of our student's good luck is that Van Buren's statement discloses the name of the author of the statement quoted by Bassett, *viz.*, one "Judge Hammond." He can now turn to the library catalogue or consult the *Harvard Guide* again with the expectation of finding the book written by Hammond and the following passage which it contains:

> I have it from the best authority that Mr. Van Buren and his most immediate friends of the Crawford party meant, at the next balloting to have given Adams the election. They wished to have had it in their power to have said to Mr. Adams, "your friends and Mr. Clay's cannot make you president—We give you the office." [79]

[78] John C. Fitzpatrick, ed., *The Autobiography of Martin Van Buren* (AHA *Report* for 1918, II), 149–150.

[79] Jabez B. Hammond, *The History of Political Parties in the State of New York* . . . (4th edn., Buffalo: Phinney & Co., 1850), 190.

Comparison of this statement with Bassett's leaves little doubt that Hammond's *History* was Bassett's source, even though it may have come to the latter through some intermediate writing. However that may be, Bassett did not discover that almost seventy-five years before the publication of his textbook Hammond had retracted the assertion about Van Buren. The correction appears in a note in the Appendix of the same edition of his *History*:

> I have ascertained that the statement in the text is materially incorrect. I have lately been informed from unquestionable authority, that shortly before the election of the President, a meeting was held by the members of the New York delegation, friendly to the election of Mr. Crawford, at which, upon a full view of the subject, they decided with great unanimity, to adhere to Mr. Crawford to the end, and leave the election to be made by others. I have this statement from a gentleman of high standing who was then a member of Congress, and was present at the caucus. It is, however, due to myself to add that I had the best reasons and high authority for the allegations contained in the text. I was at Washington at the time of the election, and was in favor of the election of Mr. Adams. From various conversations which were held in my presence with the Crawford members from this state, *some days before the election,* I was led to believe that on the second ballot they would vote for Mr. Adams. But I did not assert the fact on such grounds. In the year 1841, I was told by a leading and impartial friend of Mr. Adams, then a member of the House of Representatives, that *he knew the fact*, that the Crawford members from this state would after the first ballot have voted for Mr. Adams. . . . Some time before the election several of Mr. Crawford's friends had assured him that such would be their course, and he had never been informed of the caucus I have mentioned where the persons with whom he conversed changed their determination. My friend did not intend to deceive me, but was himself deceived. . . .[80]

Having found this evidence our investigator is ready to appraise it critically and draw his conclusions. As for Bassett's secondhand statement, the only value it has is as an example of the persistence of error when once put into circulation. The evident contradiction between Van Buren's statement and Hammond's first one disappears with the latter's correction. Hammond appears in the role of an honest but not very critical historian whose reliance on unnamed

[80] *Op. cit.*, Note C, 540.

authorities is not reassuring. While his corrected version agrees with Van Buren's testimony he still fails to identify his "high authority" and "best authority" for his original allegation, nor does he name the "impartial friend of Adams" on whose word he relied so completely. Thus he deprives the critic of the means of checking further. Moreover, it is conceivable that his "unquestionable authority" for the retraction was Van Buren himself, in which case there is only one authority for the alleged caucus agreement, and that authority is a man (Van Buren) who had a personal interest in having his explanation believed and whose memory shows signs of failure.

That Van Buren was Hammond's authority seems unlikely, however, since the *Autobiography* neither hints at an effort to bring about a correction nor reveals any knowledge that one had been or would be made. Moreover some doubt remains about the correctness of the "correction." But conceding Hammond's limitations, the evidence is fairly conclusive that there was *at one time* a disposition on the part of Crawford's friends to switch their ballots to Adams after the first ballot. According to Hammond, conversations in his presence in 1825 showed this intention, and a friend of Adams assured him in 1841 that he knew of this intention at the time. The assumption that there was such a plan fits in with Van Buren's account of the calling of a caucus, by supplying a motive for it, and adds to the probability that Van Buren wished to bring about a change of mind. Van Buren's testimony thus confirms rather than contradicts Hammond's original statement that the Crawford men intended to vote for Adams on the second ballot. Nor does Van Buren's statement that they changed their minds contradict the statements made to Hammond on which he based his original assertion, for it relates to another phase of the matter. Events throw no light on what the Crawford men would have done on a second ballot, as the first resulted in Adams's election.

A beginner would find it a good exercise to make a careful analysis of the evidence in a problem such as this, along the following lines:

1. What are Bassett's statements?
   ANSWER:
   a. Crawford men in New York delegation intended to abandon him after first ballot and vote for Adams.
   b. Van Buren, as leader, made this plan hoping to secure for himself the honor of President-maker.

2. What value attaches to Bassett's statements?
   ANSWER: No more than attaches to those of his source.
3. Who is his authority?
   ANSWER: Not named. Probably Hammond.
4. What are Hammond's statements?
   ANSWER:
   a. Some Crawford men, including Van Buren, intended to vote for Adams on second ballot.
   b. "They" wished to have the honor of deciding the election.
5. Does Hammond make these statements as his own observations?
   ANSWER: Partly.
6. What is their basis?
   ANSWER:
   a. Various conversations of Crawford men from New York, in his presence, some days before election, revealed intention to vote for Adams on second ballot.
   b. In 1841 a friend of Adams told him he knew of this intention, as Crawford men had assured him of it some time before the election.
7. Do these statements warrant the allegations in the text of Hammond?
   ANSWER:
   a. They support the first statement.
   b. They do not warrant the statement as to motive. It is a mere surmise and must be dismissed.
8. Are there any statements which seem to contradict Hammond's first allegation?
   ANSWER:
   a. An unknown authority mentioned by Hammond in Note C.
   b. Van Buren's autobiography.
9. What do they say?
   ANSWER: A caucus was held at which the Crawford men resolved to adhere to him to the end.
10. Is there any indication in Hammond's statements that the Crawford men intended to vote for Adams on the second ballot in spite of the caucus?
    ANSWER: No.
11. Does Van Buren deny that Crawford men had at one time planned to switch to Adams?
    ANSWER: No.
12. Is there then any real contradiction in the several statements?
    ANSWER: No. They concern different matters.

13. To what do the statements reduce?

    ANSWER:

    a. Hammond: Some Crawford men indicated an intention of supporting Adams on the second ballot, but
    b. At a caucus they decided to adhere to Crawford to the end.
    c. Van Buren: I called a caucus and proposed that the Crawford men should stick to him to the end. This was agreed to.

14. What of the probable truth of these statements?

    ANSWER:

    a. Hammond is a semiexpert investigator. His first statement rests upon observations of more than one witness to whom he listened, and is probably true.
    b. Van Buren's statement may be questioned on several grounds:

       1) It was made long after the event, and betrays lapses of memory.

       2) He was personally interested as his reputation was more or less at stake.

       3) It is supported only by the testimony of an unnamed person, mentioned by Hammond, who may have been Van Buren himself.
    c. On the other hand:

       1) If the unnamed authority was Van Buren, his autobiography might be expected to give some hint of the fact.

       2) If it was rumored that the Crawford men were planning to switch to Adams, Van Buren would have had a reason for calling a caucus *if he opposed* the plan. His statement fits in with Hammond's first.
    d. Van Buren's statement is not certainly but yet quite probably true.

After such an analysis, a historian, say a textbook writer, who wished merely to give his conclusions without troubling his readers by reviewing the evidence, would write somewhat as follows:

> According to the available evidence, Crawford's friends in the New York delegation manifested a disposition to switch their votes to Adams after the first ballot. Van Buren, however, declared many years later that he had opposed this course, and that in a caucus of the Crawford men in the delegation it had been decided to support Crawford to the end. As Adams was elected on the first ballot and Van Buren's account lacks adequate corroboration, it remains somewhat uncertain what course the New York men would have followed in the event of further

balloting. Certainly there is no sufficient warrant for the assertion sometimes made that Van Buren was scheming to pose as President-maker, by throwing the decisive weight into the scales in favor of Adams on the second ballot.[81]

[81] Any one wishing to pursue exercises similar to those suggested above will find twenty topics presented in problem form by as many specialists in the volume by Richard W. Leopold and Arthur S. Link, eds., entitled *Problems in American History* (New York: Prentice-Hall, Inc., 1952).

PART II

The Master's Essay

PART II

The Master's Essay

1. The Prospective Teacher as a Writer of History

It is necessary to repeat that the first step of the trained historian is to gather the material needed for writing the history of whatever he has chosen to write about, and that the next is to subject the material to critical examination. As a matter of fact, however, he gathers his material with the principles of criticism in mind. To enable the beginner to do the same it is necessary to introduce him to critical method before he begins the search for material. The purpose of the first part of this book is to give him this introduction. The exercises with which it concludes involve the use of some of these principles and also some research, and in a simple way combine these two essential steps of the historian's work. Especially the last exercise is a fair sample of what must be done in preparation for writing a master's thesis, the chief difference being its more limited scope.

The author assumes for the time being that the user of this Manual will be a college graduate who has majored in history and is beginning to work for the second degree. The probability is that as an undergraduate his training in historical method has been slight. It may have been only that given to all members of his history classes, whether they were majoring in the subject or not, in connection with the preparation of assigned topical reports. One reason for this scant attention to method is that no room can be found in the crowded undergraduate curriculum for a course devoted to it. The present tendency to expand the curriculum at the expense of the humanities is a factor in creating this situation; it often results in making the basic history course a part of a general survey of the social sciences or world civilization. Such a hodgepodge thins history down to the vanishing point and cannot be expected to possess the characteristic values of historical studies. Nor can it contribute much to the preparation of competent teachers of history. On the contrary, it may add impetus to the disposition of public-school officials to entrust history to a teacher whose only qualification is the ability to keep a day or two ahead of the assignments he gives pupils in the textbook.

More encouraging is the growing recognition that it is necessary to give prospective history teachers special training. As yet the demand stems chiefly from university teachers of the subject, seconded by some of the high schools and their staffs. These leaders urge the general acceptance of a specified minimum of preparation for teaching history in the public schools. Some schools require the teacher to have a master's degree in the subject, and a few stipulate the doctorate. Under present conditions it would seem reasonable to encourage promising would-be teachers to seek at least the master's degree. The best hope of improving the quality of instruction in the public schools seems just now to center about that effort. One of the hopes of the author of this Manual is to promote this movement as far as may be by guiding the candidate for the M.A. in his first venture in writing history. He seeks also to inspire prospective teachers with a sense of the high values they deal with, so that they may strive to give their pupils something more than drill in memorizing facts.

2. Choosing a Subject

The suggestions now in order are for the student who must choose a subject for the essay which is part of the requirement for the second degree, and who must learn how to find the materials needed for writing it. It is obvious that he must have some acquaintance with the general field in which his subject falls. He may be most likely to find such a subject within the scope of one of the courses he has pursued. Even the basic text may suggest one or more such subjects. At any rate he should choose a topic which has aroused his interest in the course of actual study, and it should be chosen by him, not for him. It will then be more likely to hold his interest, challenge his best efforts, and appeal to his sense of personal responsibility for results. The desideratum is a maximum of independent initiative and a minimum of direction. It is nevertheless wise, and usually a requirement, that each student have a faculty adviser who will help him avoid a theme for which he lacks proper preparation, or the scope of which is not properly defined, or for which there is not sufficient available material. Every topic requires its own kind of preliminary training; if it is in economic history the writer must be acquainted with the principles of economics; if in diplomatic history he should know the elements of international law and probably French, German, Spanish, or some other foreign language or languages.

Inexperienced persons have a tendency to undertake studies which have too broad a scope. It must be remembered that the purpose of this first undertaking is less to gain information than it is to become familiar with the historian's tools. The project must be so restricted as to permit adequate treatment in the time available. The investigation of Van Buren's part in the House election of 1825 should warn the candidate that a surprising amount of time and effort may be required for the research needed to solve one single problem.

Several related problems could grow out of the one concerning Van Buren, and might well arise from that study. By pursuing Van Buren's activities further, or by including the related doings of other men, an essay broad enough for the M.A. might easily result. Thus a project begun on a modest scale may grow, and a modest beginning is advisable. However, it is more likely that a proposed study may be stated at first in terms which will require limitation as the scope of the theme is more clearly perceived. One might plan to study "The Attitude of Republican Leaders toward the Fourteenth Amendment," but the abundance of the material to be examined, or the time required to cover it properly, or other conditions not foreseen at the outset, might make it necessary to be content with a fragment of the contemplated study, such as, say, "The Attitude of Republican Leaders toward the Fourteenth Amendment during the Debate on Its Passage," or "The Fourteenth Amendment as an Issue in the Congressional Campaign of 1866." At this point the student might turn to the topics suggested later on in present Part II on pages 128 and 129.

The tendency of the scope of a project to expand as the investigation proceeds, while possibly necessitating a contraction of the original purpose, may mean in the long run that an essay for the master's degree can be added to and become a doctoral dissertation. Whatever the final form of the understanding, a study must have a unity of its own.

The essay should be an original study. This does not mean that it must treat of a subject never before touched, but that it should be handled in an original way. The exercise on Van Buren shows that one who has initiative and insight can often go over old ground and find new evidence which will correct errors or improve the interpretation in older treatments. "The student should cultivate the faculty of detecting facts overlooked by others, or new relationships in old facts. The mark of a gifted investigator is that he finds [facts and interpretations] where others have never thought of looking, or have looked too superficially."[1]

The term "thesis" commonly used to designate the composition required of the candidate for the master's degree is not well chosen, as the basic meaning of the word is a proposition to be maintained or defended. "Essay," in the sense of an analytical or interpretative study, is a more appropriate term, for the writer seldom has at the outset a proposition to maintain. His task is exploratory, and, unlike a theorem in geometry which is stated in advance, cannot lead to a Q.E.D. (*quod erat demonstrandum*). He has nothing to defend until he reaches some conclusion; that conclusion is what he must be prepared to defend. The investigation may be founded on a hypothesis, but a hypothesis is not something to be defended. The historian should be as much interested in finding that it is wrong as that it is right, for always his proper purpose is to discover the truth. He wanders from what is for him the strait and narrow path if he becomes so enamored with his hypothesis that he selects his evidence to prove it and neglects evidence pointing to a different conclusion.

Any topic suitable for the essay should necessitate some use of the critical method. An investigation nearly always requires a combination of internal and external criticism, and of course the principles to be applied will vary according to the problems encountered. Even in the case of a first effort there is no reason for wasting time on a subject of no intrinsic importance. While practice in correct procedure is the main purpose of the beginner, he should cultivate the attitude of one who expects his study to be read or even published. Several examples have been mentioned on preceding pages

[1] Allan Nevins, *Masters' Essays in History*, 6.

of essays written by candidates for the master's degree which are real contributions to history.[2] Such studies are often accepted in whole or in part for publication in historical magazines. Sometimes even a senior undergraduate writes a baccalaureate "thesis" which is published because of its unusual merit.[3]

Just as Bassett's textbook suggested the problem in Exercise No. 8, so a textbook used by a student might arouse his interest in a problem suitable for the master's essay. Suppose that he wished to go beyond the textbook in studying President Arthur's relation to the movement for reform of the Civil Service. The subject involves a problem in criticism, since the candidate will know that prior to becoming President, Arthur was regarded as a spoilsman, and that his conduct in office was contrary to what this reputation led the public to expect. The question then is, does the evidence indicate that his sense of responsibility in office caused a change of heart, or is his conduct to be attributed to some other cause?

3. The Search for Material

To write an acceptable essay the candidate must have access to a library containing ample collections which he has learned how to use. The collections must include a variety of materials, such as government records and documents; newspapers; the chief general histories; works of leading statesmen; biographies; monographs; and periodicals. The library must also be provided with the various bibliographies, guides, indexes, etc., to all of these. The investigator must be able not only to use the library catalogue, but also to select the proper aids to help him prepare a list of the books, articles, documents, and other works he is likely to need. This list is the tentative bibliography, tentative because as research goes on items will be added or discarded.

A meritorious production must rest largely on sources, but writings which are secondary in one sense may be sources in another. Hammond's *History* was a secondary work, yet an important source for the study of Van Buren. Theodore Roosevelt's *Winning of the*

[2] See studies of the text of the Randolph Resolutions and the authorship of Washington's Farewell Address, *supra*, pp. 35, note 32; 24, note 12.

[3] A master's essay by Eugene H. Roseboom on "Ohio in the Presidential Election of 1824" is printed in the *Ohio State Archaeological and Historical Quarterly*, XXVI, 153–224. See comment on a baccalaureate "thesis" on *The Early Settlement of Georgia*, in *MVHR* for December, 1949, pp. 502–503.

West would be a secondary history of that subject but a source for any one studying Roosevelt as a writer of history.

a. *The Tentative Bibliography*

i. EQUIPMENT

The student should arrange his bibliographical data systematically as he collects it. He should have a supply of paper slips on each of which one item (and only one) may be entered. The size of these slips is a matter of individual preference; the plan first tried is often changed in the light of experience. Many persons use 3 x 5 cards, which is the size used in the card catalogue of the college library. Others prefer larger slips or cards. Stationers can supply cards in several standard sizes and cabinets for filing them varying from inexpensive pasteboard trays to large metal cases. Many workers do not use cards at all, but make their notes of both bibliographical and subject matter on slips of paper of uniform size. Slips half the size of a sheet of typewriter letter paper (8½ x 11) are quite satisfactory in the long run, and the uniform size permits all notes to be filed in one cabinet. Small cards do not have much space for subject-matter notes, and large ones are wasteful since notes frequently require only a few words. The use of two cabinets of different size, one for bibliography cards and one for subject-matter notes, is likely to prove unsatisfactory.

ii. FIRST ITEMS

Thus equipped the student must decide where to look for the first items of the bibliography. For the subject "President Arthur and Civil Service Reform" he might first consult the library card catalogue, or having taken his subject from a textbook, he might start with titles it cites. In it he would no doubt find references to biographies of the men who were involved in the reform movement both as advocates and opponents, and citations of pertinent writings of other kinds, as well as the general background history of the topic.[4] A card for the tentative bibliography should be made for each item deemed important. The following forms are correct for this purpose

[4] See, for example, Arthur M. Schlesinger, *Political and Social Growth of the American People, 1865–1940* (New York: The Macmillan Company, 1941), Index under Civil-service reform, and appendix, "List of Books Cited."

and also for the final bibliography, except that in the latter it is desirable to use authors' full names instead of initials:

Oberholtzer, E. P.,
A History of the United States since the Civil War. 5 vols. New York: 1917–1937.

Howe, G. F.,
Chester A. Arthur (American Political Leaders). New York: 1934.

Stewart, F. M.,
The National Civil Service Reform League. Austin, Texas: 1929.

Fish, C. R.,
The Civil Service and the Patronage (Harvard Historical Studies, XI). New York: 1905.

Sageser, A. B.,
The First Two Decades of the Pendleton Act (University of Nebraska *Studies,* XXXIV–XXXV). Lincoln, Nebr.: 1935.

Underscoring indicates that the words should be *italicized* when printed. If this and other matters of form are practiced from the beginning later tasks will be much easier.

iii. THE LIBRARY CARD CATALOGUE

If the student lists first the titles found in the textbook he may next consult the library catalogue to learn whether the library contains these books. He may find that it does or does not have all of them or that it gives other titles. Already he would of course have become more or less familiar with the catalogue, yet may not have learned some things that will help him in using it.

Efficient use of a library requires a knowledge of the system of classification and cataloguing employed. There are several systems and the investigator must acquaint himself with the one used in the institution in which he works. Nowadays the dictionary catalogue is used so much oftener than any other that it is the only one described here.[5]

In this type of catalogue all main entries are arranged in one alphabet, much as words are in a dictionary. Every book is represented by several cards: one is filed under the surname of the

[5] For fuller discussion consult Margaret Hutchins, *et al., Guide to the Use of Libraries.*

author of the book, another under the first word (not an article) of the title, and a varying number under appropriate subject headings. One subject card may indicate the nature of the whole book, another a topic given prominence in a part of it, and others bibliographies, biographies, or critiques which it contains. Still other cards may be filed under the names of editors, translators, compilers, joint authors, and the series title, if there is one. Under subject entries cross-reference cards are used, in addition, to call attention to other subject entries under which related works may be found (as, under Civil Service one might find a cross reference reading: See also Spoils System). Cross references are also used to refer from an author's pen name to his real name.

While all main entries appear in one alphabet, some of them have subdivisions within which the items are arranged in a subordinate alphabet, because such groups of cards have a unity of their own. Thus under the letter U will be found a main heading: United States as *author*. Here are listed in alphabetical order (1) all publications issued by the Department of Agriculture; (2) those published by the department or bureau next in alphabetical order, *e.g.*, the Bureau of Animal Husbandry (the determining word here being *Animal*); (3) those of the Bureau of Biological Survey, etc.

Then follows another main entry—United States as *subject*—with similar subdivisions, such as Army, Census, Commerce, Education, History, etc. Under History again, there are many subdivisions, according to period, topic, or geographical section. This process of subalphabetization is capable of indefinite extension. Many of the cards in these subdivisions duplicate, of course, those in the primary alphabet.

There are certain other departures from a strictly one-alphabet arrangement in the dictionary catalogue. For example, all names beginning with New as a *word* precede all beginning with New as a *syllable*. Thus New Albany is followed by New Jersey and New York before Newark appears; New Zealand precedes Newald. A series of identical names of persons, as John Smith, are filed in the order of the birth dates of the persons. If the same word is the name of a person, place, and thing, the respective cards are filed in this order, i.e., the name of the person before that of the place, etc.[6]

[6] Many libraries use in their catalogues cards printed by the Library of Congress primarily for its own use but made available to other libraries by purchase. Only one form of card is printed—the author card. The purchasing

Some libraries deviate from the arrangement of cards just described. If this is the case in the library where the student works it will not be difficult for him to ascertain just what plan is in use.

IV. USE OF SUBJECT ENTRIES

Let us now return to the student. After ascertaining which of the titles in his bibliography are in the library, he should examine the catalogue cards under names and subject headings. Pursuing the topic relating to "President Arthur and Civil Service Reform," his textbook knowledge would suggest that he look up entries under such names as George H. Pendleton, George William Curtis, Dorman B. Eaton, Roscoe Conkling, and Presidents Grant and Hayes as well as Arthur; and such subject entries as Civil Service. Under this last he would probably find again the book by Fish, on *The Civil Service and the Patronage*. For each new item a slip should be made out in the form already described, and if new data pertaining to any item are found they should be noted. Every bit of available information bearing on the value of an item for the investigation, and all data needed if the book finds a place in the final bibliography, should be included. (For further directions about the data see pages 129–134.) Information about authors (external criticism) should supply facts bearing on their competence. Thus the fact that Carl Russell Fish was a professor of American history in the University of Wisconsin is *prima facie* evidence that his book is a scholarly production. However, at this stage few facts about authors will be found and the special search for them should be postponed. Directions for this quest will be given later.[7]

V. BIBLIOGRAPHICAL DATA FROM BOOKS

Another very good way to locate bibliographical items is to examine the bibliographies and footnotes in books as they are added

---

library obtains the required number and adds all needed headings in the space above the author's name.

The Library of Congress maintains an author card catalogue, of which a printed edition has been made: *A Catalogue of Books Represented by Library of Congress Printed Cards Issued to July 31, 1942* (167 vols. Ann Arbor: 1942–1946). This is supplemented by an additional 42 vols. printed in 1948, and an annual volume since that date. Since 1950 these catalogues have contained subject entries.—*Harvard Guide*, 110. (See Index under *Library of Congress Subject Catalogue.*)

[7] For pages giving information about authors see Index under Masters' essays. (See *post, Library of Congress Subject Catalogue*, pages 126, 257.)

to the tentative bibliography. Besides book titles this examination should bring to light articles in periodicals, newspaper matter, citations of government documents, and various other sources of information. As advised above, slips for these items should include all information afforded by the works examined, that bears on their value for the investigation, and, for those likely to be retained in the final bibliography, all pertinent bibliographical data. It may be helpful to include a memorandum telling where the item was found. Thus from the bibliography on pages 252–256 of Fish's *Civil Service* would be obtained the following reference to be entered on a slip in this form:

> Bernard, George,
> Civil Service Reform versus the Spoils System. New York:
> J. B. Alden, 1885. [Fish, C. S. & P., bib.]

After a few titles have been collected it is advisable to go to the shelves in the book stacks and handle the books one by one. This may require a stack permit which may be obtained from the proper library official. If a volume is not found in the place indicated by the call number, the attendants will aid in locating it. Examination will show that some of the books bear on the subject under investigation while others have no important relation to it and may be discarded. While examining entries under Civil Service the student may have found the following:

> Civil Service Reform Association,
> Bibliography of Civil Service Reform and Related Subjects.
> Published for the Women's Auxiliary to the Civil Service Reform Association. New York: 1900.

Such a work would of course be carefully examined for references not otherwise obtained, or subject matter of importance. The investigator might be well repaid for his pains, or, as in the above instance (assuming the person interested in Arthur's term), might find few helpful references or facts. After a little experience it should take him only a few minutes to make this sort of appraisal of a book. The importance of any item retained should be indicated by a comment on its slip. The form for Fish's book (for page see Index under his name) is an example of such comments, enclosed in brackets.

While looking over books in the stacks it is well to glance at adjacent shelves as it is possible that other useful books on kindred subjects may be found there. If a reference is found to a book which is not in the library a note of it should be made. If it appears to be of considerable value for the investigation, the library may purchase it on request or on the recommendation of the Department of History. If it is out of print and not obtainable by purchase it may be possible to borrow it for a brief time through the system of interlibrary loans. Or possibly a photostat or microfilm copy can be obtained. The library officials or the History Department should be consulted in such matters.

Books not actually used in writing the essay should ordinarily not be included in the final bibliography unless they appear to be of special importance. In that case they may be listed with a comment explaining both their apparent value and the reasons for not using them.

Footnotes found on those pages of books where the investigator's special subject is discussed, such as those on pages 217–222 of Fish's book if he is studying the Civil Service under Arthur, are of great value early in his work while he is getting his bearings. Such notes often cite the exact location in the sources where the bills, acts, reports, or speeches are printed which form the heart of the subject. It is wise to take these citations just as they are found, disregarding for the time the form in which they should be entered in the final bibliography, although data for it should be noted if at hand.[8]

No publications of the Federal Government are cited more often than those which contain the reports of debates in Congress. Numerous references for the student to note will be found in such forms as the following, to which he should add headings suggested by the context, and citations of the source where the item was found:

Congressional Record, 47 Cong., 2 sess., 283, 463–464.
Congressional Record, 47 Cong., 1 sess., 5704, 6016; 2 sess., 204–208, 241, 284, 318; Congressional Globe, 41 Cong., 3 sess., 1936.

A glance at the context on the pages where these citations occur will suggest the appropriate headings and comments:

Pendleton Act

Senate Debate, 1882. Cong. Rec., 47 Cong., 2 sess., 283, 463–464. [Fish, C. S. & P., 218.]

[8] The proper forms for citations in footnotes and bibliography are considered on pp. 150 f.

Pendleton Act

Senate Debate, 1882. Cong. Rec., 47 Cong., 1 sess., 5704, 6016; 2 sess., 204–208, 241, 284, 316, 318. *Cf.* Cong. Globe, 41 Cong., 3 sess., 1936. [Fish, 219.]

Note that in citations of debates in Congress Arabic numerals denote columns instead of pages. Hints of pertinent matter in documents of various kinds which might otherwise be overlooked may be caught from footnotes:

Discussion of Pendleton Act

55 Cong., 2 sess., Sen. Docs. I, No. 24. [Fish, 220.]

Text of Pendleton Act

Stat. at Large, XXII, 403–407. [Fish, 221.]

Arthur's Reform Message of Dec. 5, 1881
Richardson, Messages, VIII, 11, 60.

Like Fish's book, others will yield similar items in random order, making the usefulness of separate slips apparent, since related slips can be brought together in filing:

Campaign Assessments

Cong. Rec., 47 Cong., 2 sess., 141–143.
[Speech of Sen. Hale in defense of practice of levying cam. ass. on officeholders. Cited by Sparks, Natl. Devel., 197.]

Garfield's Message Concerning Appointments and Removals
Richardson, Messages and Papers, VIII, 147. [Sparks, 188.]

The citations of presidential messages in a work associated with the name of Richardson suggest that certain classes of source material of government origin have been collected, edited, and published under government auspices. Among these are the messages of Presidents, the laws, the decisions of courts, opinions of attorneys general, treaties with foreign nations, and other documents relating to foreign affairs. After encountering a few references to such publications the investigator will perceive the necessity of obtaining the full bibliographical data for them. In many cases this can be done readily by referring to the bibliographies in the works in which the footnote citations are found; and, in addition to the specific citations which have been noted, a slip should be prepared for the collection referred to. For example:

> Richardson, James Daniel, comp.,
> A Compilation of the Messages and Papers of the Presidents, 1789–1897. 10 vols. Washington: Government Printing Office, 1896–1900.

Similarly numerous references will probably be gathered to the *Statutes at Large of the United States*, such as:

> Act Forbidding Campaign Contributions by Federal Employes
> Stat. at Large, XIX, 169 (1876). [Sparks, 188.]

Sooner or later a slip for the *Statutes at Large* will be made out in the form shown *post.* (For page see Index under Statutes.)

As citations of Supreme Court decisions are picked up they may be noted thus:

> De Lima v. Bidwell, 182 U.S. 1.
>
> [Status of Porto Rico after cession to U.S. Applicability of tariff to imports from the island. Cited by Latané, Am. as a World Power, 145.]

The forms for citing decisions of the Supreme Court have become conventionalized. Instead of placing the volume designation after the title in the usual way (as, *History of the United States*, VI, 142), Arabic numerals denoting the volume precede the title. Thus 182 U.S. 1 is equivalent to *Reports of the Supreme Court of the United States,* CLXXXII, 1. The form has the obvious advantage of brevity yet is perfectly understandable. Previous to 1875 the name of the reporter was used in place of the initials U.S.; thus 8 Cranch 49 is equivalent to Cranch, reporter, *Decisions of the Supreme Court,* VIII, 49. (See also *post.* For page see Index under Courts.)

In taking references from newspapers the name of the paper as it is printed on the first page—the heading—should be given in italics, the date of the issue in which the item is printed, and if possible the page. If the name of the paper does not indicate the home of the publication it (state or city) should be interpolated in parentheses. This is not necessary in the case of weekly and monthly magazines of wide circulation, such as *Harper's Magazine, Nation, Reader's Digest,* etc. The nature of each item should be noted, an editorial being distinguished from a news item, or communication from a private correspondent, etc. In this class of citations it is particularly important to note the work from which the reference is taken if not from the paper itself, as credit must be given to that work as well as the paper. Examples:

The New York Times, Dec. 18, 1895.
[Editorial on Pres. Cleveland's message on Venezuelan boundary dispute.]

Baltimore Sun, July 6–11, 1904.
[Report of Dem. Natl. Nom. Conv. Cited by J. H. Latané, America as a World Power, 232.]

Public Opinion, XIX, 541, 547, 552, 586, 649.
[Extracts from press comment on the Venezuelan boundary dispute, summer and fall, 1895. Cited, D. R. Dewey, Natl. Problems, 307.]

Springfield Republican (Mass.), Feb. 3, 1890.
[Ed. comment on conduct of Reed as Speaker. Cited, Dewey, Natl. Probs., 154.]

The Christian Science Monitor (Boston), July 8, 1929. [Comments]

The foregoing examples are designed to indicate the data the student will gather and the comments he may make on the slips for his own use. They do not represent the form for citations in footnotes and the final bibliography. These will be considered later.[9]

b. *Bibliographies, Catalogues, Guides, and Indexes*

It would be difficult if not impossible to place under the above head aids confined to the needs of candidates for the master's degree. All those presented here are just as useful to the student working for the doctorate, or to the professional historian. The first-year graduate will employ some of them in his research, and no one can draw a hard and fast line and say to him "thus far you shall go and no farther." It is a matter of selecting the guides applicable to the particular subject under investigation by the particular student.

No one should suppose that he is expected to try to memorize the contents of this section. It is intended for references. It must be repeated that the choice of subject by the candidate for a master's

[9] See *post*, pp. 150 f.

degree should be made with the guidance of an adviser and with due regard to the resources of the library in which he is working. Most candidates for that degree should choose a subject on which all of the work can be done in one institution.

i. BIBLIOGRAPHIES OF BIBLIOGRAPHIES

In 1903 E. C. Richardson and Anson E. Morse undertook to compile a comprehensive bibliography of works on American history published during the previous year. This was the beginning of the series entitled *Writings on American History,* which has been described as "the world's outstanding bibliography of contemporary writings in a national field." The volume for 1902 was brought out in 1904 by the Library Book Store, Princeton, N. J. A second was prepared by Andrew C. McLaughlin and others and published by the Carnegie Institution in Washington in 1905. For want of editors and sponsors no volumes were compiled for 1904 and 1905, but the enterprise was resumed in 1906 under the editorial direction of Grace Gardner Griffin, who carried on the work until relieved by James R. Masterson in 1949—an unmatched record.

After the first two volumes appeared several years elapsed before the project found a permanent publisher. The annual volumes for 1906, 1907, and 1908 were published by the Macmillan Company; those for 1909, 1910, and 1911 by the Government Printing Office. Next the Yale University Press brought out the volumes for the years 1912–1917. Finally, in 1918, the *Writings* were made a part of the American Historical Association's *Annual Report.* This was a fortunate and logical arrangement, for in 1889, soon after the Association's formation, it had been incorporated as a subsidiary of the Smithsonian Institution, entitled to share the funds appropriated by Congress for its publishing program.

These vicissitudes did not prevent the publication of a volume of the *Writings* for every year from 1906 through 1940. None were prepared from 1941–1947. When Masterson became editor issues for 1948 and 1949 were published in 1952 and 1954 (AHA *Reports* for 1950 and 1951) respectively. Through the years the work of compilation had grown heavier as the bulk of current publications increased, and the time between the year covered and publication increased accordingly. The growing load of the Government Printing Office added another reason for delay. Still more serious was the rising cost of printing. The problem of financing, troublesome from the first, now became critical. Editor Masterson came to his task hoping to be able to cover the missed years 1941–1947, but found when the volume for 1950 was ready for printing that funds did not permit it. The Association Council has been investigating the possibility of using some cheaper method of producing the required number of copies.

These increasing difficulties made it necessary to curtail the coverage of the volumes for 1948 and 1949, and, after 1945, to abandon printing anything in the yearly *Reports* except the proceedings. In the beginning (1906) the editors aimed to include all significant writings on the United States and British America published either in these countries or Europe, whether in the form of books, pamphlets, or articles in periodicals. The prefaces for the issues of 1948 and 1949 explain the changes that have been made in this program.

Every volume of the *Writings* has devoted a section to bibliographies; these save the investigator much labor. Each volume is also elaborately indexed. But from year to year users have found the necessity of examining the increasing number of indexes more and more time-consuming and irksome. Out of this need came the plan in the middle thirties to prepare a cumulative index designed to cover all volumes through 1938. David M. Matteson undertook this task which it seemed might be completed by 1950. This hope was dashed by his death in 1949, but the project is still under way and of the projected two volumes more than half of the work has been finished. Funds to finish it were made available by Mr. Matteson's generosity, for he not only served virtually without compensation but left a legacy of some $47,500 to complete the project. Although some further delay will occur, workers in American history may look forward to a time in the not distant future when they will have this index to aid them in getting at the contents of the *Writings*. Even as matters now stand, with some years not covered and no general index, the series is the best single aid in preparing a bibliography of topics in the field.[10]

Easier to consult is the *Harvard Guide to American History*, already mentioned for its utility as "first aid" in finding Van Buren's *Autobiography*, Calhoun's *Works*, etc. It is the product of six associated professors of Harvard University, several of whom are Pulitzer

[10] See p. 253 f.

Prize winners.[11] Its antecedents go back to a *Guide to the Study of American History* compiled by two Harvard professors, Edward Channing and Albert Bushnell Hart, and published in 1896. In 1912 a revised edition was issued in which the original collaborators were joined by Frederick Jackson Turner.

The present book is in a sense a revision of this second edition of forty years ago. From the most important older works and the output of the forty years the editors have made a "rigorous selection" of "items most useful for present-day needs." Parts I and II, comprising 244 pages, discuss the nature of history, the techniques of research and writing, the materials of history, and aids to research, including list of sources and helpful publications of many kinds. The remainder of the text, pages 249 to 543, divides American history into chronological sections for each of which, following a brief summary, elaborate references are given for the topics it treats. The very full index fills pages 547 to 689. The index omits titles except of reference works, usually gives only initials of authors' and editors' given names, does not identify publishers, but gives place and date of publication. Appraisals are rare, and topical citations are scanty. Under Civil Service, for example, an investigator gets no hint of the existence of Fish's book. If the student used the author's name, the index would direct him to but one entry, and that in a list of references on the period of Republican Supremacy, 1801–1815. There he would find: C. R. Fish, *Civil Service and Patronage* (1904), ch. ii. For additional data, such as this Manual mentions in discussing the Civil Service, he would have to look elsewhere. The frequent references in this Manual to the *Guide* bears witness to the author's belief that it amply fulfills the editors' hope that "as a reference tool it may simplify" the problems of the student.

The library catalogue, the *Writings*, and the *Harvard Guide* will aid in finding bibliographies of bibliographies. Among them would be the compilation by Coulter and Gerstenfeld,[12] which "brings together . . . bibliographies of history, and those general bibliographical manuals which are essential to research . . . arranged by period, by country, and by episode . . . all briefly annotated and

[11] Oscar Handlin, Arthur Meier Schlesinger, Sr., Samuel Eliot Morison, Frederick Merk, Arthur Meier Schlesinger, Jr., and Paul Herman Buck, comps. Cambridge, Mass.: The Belknap Press of Harvard University Press, 1954.

[12] Edith M. Coulter and Melanie Gerstenfeld, *Guide to Historical Bibliographies*. Berkeley: University of California Press, 1935.

described. . . . Detailed subject index. . . ." A standard work and more recent is one by H. P. Beers, editor, *Bibliographies in American History.*[13] It lists bibliographies by periods and has additional sections giving subject bibliographies especially for the social sciences. State bibliographies are another feature. A periodical of the same general character, arranged topically, is the *Bibliographic Index, 1937–1946.* Monthly issues were cumulated in annual volumes, the latest of which was published in 1946.[14]

One other bibliography for American history should be mentioned in this connection, although like the Coulter book it is not limited to the one field. This is *A Guide to Historical Literature*, prepared by an editorial committee of the American Historical Association headed by G. M. Dutcher. It lists and appraises the chief historical writings of all times and all countries, includes selected bibliographies, and often cites reviews.[15]

The *Harvard Guide* brings together on pages 105–109 lists of bibliographies on numerous subjects. Such of these as are particularly suited to the purposes of this Manual may be found there under appropriate heads.

Among older works which are still serviceable is Larned's *Literature of American History.* It lists 4145 of the books most likely to be found in libraries at the close of the nineteenth century, and for each gives a brief statement of merits or demerits by a competent critic. Supplements for 1900–1904 give similar estimates of a few contemporary publications. A bibliography of this series follows:

Joseph Nelson Larned, ed., *The Literature of American History. A Bibliographical Guide.* Boston: Houghton Mifflin Company, 1902.

—— Supplement for 1900 and 1901, ed. by P. P. Wells (American Library Association *Annotated Lists*). Boston: American Library Association Publishing Board, 1902.

—— Supplements for 1902 and 1903, ed. by P. P. Wells (*Annotated Titles of Books on English and American History*). Boston: American Library Association Publishing Board, 1903–1904.

—— Supplement for 1904. Boston: American Library Association Publishing Board, 1905, and *A. L. A. Booklist*, Feb., 1906.

[13] 2d edn., New York: 1942.

[14] Dorothy Charles and Bea Joseph, eds. New York: The H. W. Wilson Company, 1945–.

[15] New York: The Macmillan Company, 1931. 2d edn., 1949.

ii. BIBLIOGRAPHIES IN COMPREHENSIVE HISTORIES

It should be borne in mind that some of the general histories contain bibliographical matter of value. The chief materials for almost every phase of American history prior to 1789 are discussed in the "Critical Essays on the Sources of Information" which follow each chapter of Justin Winsor's *Narrative and Critical History of America*.[16] Suppose the topic under investigation to be the Stamp Act controversy. On pages 72 and following in the sixth volume of Winsor (as is readily ascertained by use of the index) are given references to sources of all kinds on that subject so far as they had been assembled by the historical scholarship of Winsor's day. Of course, since the publication of his work there have been discoveries of additional sources, and critical studies have been written. These must be sought by using other guides such as are mentioned in this Manual. Similarly *The American Nation: A History*;[17] *A History of American Life*;[18] and other general histories, have chapters or sections containing bibliographical matter. In the first mentioned the final chapter of each volume is a "Critical Essay on Authorities"; the same is true of the other series.

By using these and similar aids the student of the Stamp Act controversy may discover that a bibliography of the act and associated legislation is printed in a *Bulletin of the New York Public Library*, and from this bulletin he would learn that pamphlets on the subject are in the library of the New York Historical Society.

Both the Winsor and the Hart series are out of print but still to be found on the shelves of many libraries. The appraisals in the Hart series do not include any publications issued since 1918. Plans are on foot for a new many-volume series to supersede *The American Nation*.[19] There are many other comprehensive histories; a list will be found in the *Harvard Guide*, pages 209–210.

iii. BIOGRAPHIES

Supplementing the guides to materials are those giving information about authors and editors. The most useful and reliable com-

[16] 8 vols. Boston: Houghton Mifflin Company, 1884–1889.

[17] Albert Bushnell Hart, ed., 28 vols. New York: Harper and Brothers, 1904–1918.

[18] Arthur M. Schlesinger and Dixon Ryan Fox, eds., 13 vols. New York: The Macmillan Company, 1927–1948.

[19] See *MVHR* for December, 1946, p. 514.

pilation of such biographical sketches is the *Dictionary of American Biography.*[20] Its articles are limited to deceased notables.

Information about living authors may be found in many cases in *Who's Who in America,* published biennially since 1899. Beginning with 1939 a *Monthly Supplement* has bridged the years between issues. Two volumes entitled *Who Was Who,* published in 1942 and 1950, assemble articles on deceased notables from all issues of *Who's Who.* The same company publishes several other biographical guides: *Who Knows—and What; Who's Who in the East; Who's Who in Commerce and Industry; Who's Who on the Pacific Coast;* and *Who's Who in Latin America.*[21]

The Jacques Cattell *Dictionary of American Scholars* has 12,000 or more sketches of recognized scholars in all fields and includes many names not found elsewhere.[22] The Dargan *Guide to American Biography* divides entries according to periods down to 1815 and from that date on arranges them according to subject.[23]

There is much biographical matter in current magazines and books. *Current Biography,* a monthly, guides one to this class of material. Its issues are cumulated annually and a volume published in 1950 indexes all entries for the years 1940–1950.[24] Similar is the *Biography Index*; volume one cumulates entries from January, 1946, to July, 1949.[25] *Webster's Biographical Dictionary* contains 40,000 sketches of prominent personages of all times.[26] A fraction of its space is devoted to Americans.

Since we are concerned primarily with information about authors

[20] Allen Johnson and Douglas Malone, eds., 22 vols. New York: Charles Scribner's Sons, 1928–1944. A plan to supplement the *D. A. B.* for the colonial period was formed a few years ago, the editing to be done by Louis K. Koonts and Kenneth P. Bailey, of the University of California at Los Angeles. (See *MVHR* for March, 1945, p. 651.) This project has apparently fallen by the way.

[21] All of these members of the *Who's Who* family are published by A. N. Marquis & Co (now Marquis-Who's Who, Inc.), Chicago, except the last-named, of which Stanford University is co-publisher.

[22] 2d edn., Lancaster, Pa.: The Science Press, 1951.

[23] Marion Dargan, *Guide to American Biography, Part I, 1607–1815; Part II, 1815–1933.* Albuquerque, N. Mex.: University of New Mexico Press, 1949–1952.

[24] Maxine Block *et al.,* eds., New York: The H. W. Wilson Company, 1940–.

[25] Bea Joseph and Charlotte W. Squires, eds., New York: The H. W. Wilson Company, 1946–1949.

[26] Editorial Board of G. & C. Merriam Company, *Webster's Biographical Dictionary: A Dictionary of Names of Noteworthy Persons with Pronunciation and Concise Biographies.* Springfield, Mass.: 1943.

and editors of historical writings as a means of judging of their competence, it is somewhat disappointing to find that so much of it must be sought in guides of a general character such as those mentioned. Dictionaries of authors include writers of all descriptions. There are, of course, full-length lives of many historians, but there are also a few books which are devoted especially to shorter studies of them. One of the earliest of these was Jameson's, which deals chiefly with the leading historians of the nineteenth century.[27] A quarter of a century later Bassett followed with a volume of excellent essays about men some of whom Jameson had also discussed.[28]

Bibliography, biography, and historiography are closely associated. This is evident in a volume by O'Neill, which not only discusses the biographies of Americans, including historians, but sketches the biographers and appraises their work.[29] About the same time the *Jernegan Essays* presented studies of twenty-one of the leading American historians each written by a student who had received his training under Professor Marcus W. Jernegan, of the University of Chicago.[30] A similar book, with essays on men whose work had been in the wider field of social science, had been published a decade earlier.[31] Discussions of American historians and their works form the subject matter of Kraus's book.[32]

Historical *characters* rather than *writers* of history are the subjects of most biographies. Like general histories, biographies of the first class often contain material bearing on historical subjects and thus come within the range of the historian's interest and research. The reader may recall the use made of Hammond's *History of New York.*

[27] John Franklin Jameson, *The History of Historical Writing in America.* Boston: Houghton Mifflin Company, 1891.

[28] John Spencer Bassett, *The Middle Group of American Historians.* New York: The Macmillan Company, 1917. Useful comment on some of the historians in this same group will be found in George Peabody Gooch's *History and Historians in the Nineteenth Century* (New York: Longmans, Green and Company, 1913), *passim.*

[29] Edward H. O'Neill, *Biography by Americans, 1800–1936; A Subject Bibliography.* Philadelphia: University of Pennsylvania Press, 1939.

[30] William T. Hutchinson, ed., *The Marcus W. Jernegan Essays in American Historiography.* Chicago: University of Chicago Press, 1937.

[31] Howard Washington Odum, ed., *American Masters of Social Science.* New York: 1927.

[32] Michael Kraus, *A History of American History.* New York: Farrar & Rinehart, Inc. (now Rinehart & Company, Inc.), 1937. A new edition entitled *Writing American History* has been published by the University of Oklahoma Press (Norman: 1953), but this Manual follows the original edition, which hereafter will be cited as Kraus.

Few students would be likely to seek a biography of Hammond unless he himself was the subject of study. His characteristics as a historian were obvious enough to make an extended study of him superfluous for our purpose, since for it only what he said about Van Buren was of consequence for us.

When biographies become important in one's research one will find a list of the chief ones in the *Harvard Guide*, pages 177–206.

iv. INDEXES

a) *Periodicals*

Much of the best work of writers appears in periodicals both of the general and professional classes, and it is important to know how to ascertain expeditiously whether anything of significance for one's study is to be found in them. Considering the number and variety of these journals and the random order in which their offerings are made, it might seem that every article of their contents was doomed to early oblivion. Even the indexes which they provide at regular intervals help but little, for no one can run through the annual indexes of *The Century Magazine*, *Harper's Magazine*, and scores of others in the faint hope of finding something related to one's subject. The situation would indeed be hopeless were it not for the comprehensive indexes.

The pioneer attempt to index American periodicals was begun in the 1880's by William Frederick Poole. The first volume of *Poole's Index to Periodical Literature* was brought out in 1882, but appeared in revised form in 1891.[33] The work was a subject index of the contents of the most important American and English periodicals from 1802 to 1881.

Five supplements under the original title were prepared by Poole and others with the cooperation of the American Library Association, each covering four or five years and bringing the *Index* down to the close of 1906. In its entirety the series covers a period of 105 years and lists a total of nearly 600,000 articles by subject in more than 12,000 volumes of nearly 500 periodicals. An abridged edition, known as the "Baby Poole," was printed in 1901, covering articles in

[33] 2 vols. Boston: Houghton Mifflin Company, 1882 and 1891. It is interesting to note, in connection with the hypothetical study of "President Arthur and Civil Service Reform," that the 1882 Poole lists about 100 articles discussing some phase of the civil service problem. *Cf.* Fish, *op. cit.*, 217.

a selected list of 37 periodicals which were still being published in 1899. One supplement to the abridgment was brought out in 1905, for the years 1900–1904. All supplements and abridgments came from the press of the Houghton Mifflin Company.

The basis of the later supplements to *Poole's Index* was the *Annual Literary Index*, put out by the *Publishers' Weekly* of New York from 1893 through 1905. These volumes included an author index which Poole did not have, hence they are still of some utility. Of chief present-day value, however, are the lists of bibliographies and the indexes of dates of principal events. The latter is usable as a guide to issues of newspapers in which accounts of important events were printed.

In 1905 the character of the *Annual Literary Index* was changed somewhat by the *Publishers' Weekly* and its name altered to *Annual Library Index*. In this form it ran through six volumes with author, title, and subject indexes to periodicals, lists of bibliographies, and the index of dates. It was in turn superseded by the *American Library Annual* (same publishers) with the same features minus the index to periodicals; it ran through five years (to 1917). Meantime the *Readers' Guide to Periodical Literature* had been inaugurated in 1900. At first it indexed only fifteen periodicals. It absorbed the *Cumulative Index* in 1903 (a monthly which the Cleveland Public Library had sponsored to index some fifty periodicals by authors, titles, and subjects of articles, which is still of some use because it covered some magazines which *Poole* did not index),[34] in 1911 took over the periodical index feature abandoned by the *American Library Annual*, and finally the supplements to *Poole* after their discontinuance. These steps gave it the foremost position in the field, and led to the initiation of a *Supplement* in 1916 to care for the additional work assumed.

In its primary form the *Readers' Guide* is a monthly publication. The March, June, September, and December issues cumulate all previous entries of the year in one dictionary catalogue, making the December number a useful semipermanent index until superseded in its turn by the cumulations published at longer intervals. The first of these was for the years 1900–1904.[35] The total number of articles

[34] *The Cumulative Index to a Selected List of Periodicals.* 8 vols. Cleveland: The Cumulative Index Company, 1897–1903.

[35] New York: The H. W. Wilson Company, 1900–.

indexed in the permanent volumes long ago passed the million mark, and the periodicals now covered include not only the most important of the general publications but many of the prominent professional journals, including such social science magazines as *The American Historical Review* and the *American Political Science Review*.

As a new departure, the *Supplement* necessitated the indexing of certain periodicals from 1907. Beginning in 1921 its name was changed to the *International Index to Periodicals* because, besides covering more scholarly journals than before, it indexed some 75 foreign periodicals as well as more than one hundred domestic publications. Five issues appear yearly, the January number cumulating the entries of the preceding year.

Supplementing all of the foregoing is the *Magazine Subject-Index*. It covers about 79 American and British periodicals, especially those of historical interest, which neither *Poole*, *The Annual Library Index*, nor the *Readers' Guide* included. More than half of these journals were indexed from their first issues; some went back as far as 1876. A peculiar value of this index for the historian is that it includes state historical society periodicals.[36] The *Annual Magazine Subject-Index* [37] is a continuation which maintains this emphasis on history and, like the *Writings on American History*, continues the Griffin *Bibliography* described in the next paragraph.

For many years there was no comprehensive index for the numerous periodicals put out by national, sectional, state, and local historical societies. The articles in only the more important of these are included in the general indexes, and no guide for them as a class existed previous to the publication of A. P. C. Griffin's *Bibliography of American Historical Societies*. This work fills the second volume of the American Historical Association *Report* for 1905. It lists national societies in one alphabet, while local societies are grouped in alphabetical order under their respective states. Under the name of each society is given the complete table of contents of every number of its periodical publications. The whole is well indexed by authors and subjects. It serves a good purpose for students who need to go back fifty years or more for materials of this kind.

Cumulative indexes have become so numerous that there is need

[36] Boston: Boston Book Company, 1908.
[37] Boston: F. W. Faxon Company, 1909–.

of a guide to them, and at least one has been prepared.[38] Many investigators have occasion to use Canadian periodicals. For these there is a subject and author index which was published quarterly from 1928 to 1948 at Windsor and Toronto under the title *Canadian Periodical Index*. It was superseded in 1948 by *Canadian Index*, published in Ottawa.

Much material of value for the historian is published in the cognate fields of economics, sociology, political science, literature, biography, travel, law, etc. Some of the indexes which have been described cover many of the periodicals containing such matter. For some classes special aids are available. This is true of law, a field of considerable importance for students of history. There is a helpful guide by Hicks.[39] For statutes of both the United States and the several states there is a bibliography.[40] The most comprehensive coverage of legal periodicals is *An Index*, chiefly by subjects, not only of American law journals, but those of Canada, England, and the British colonies.[41] The first volume covers colonial and early American journals from 1791 to 1886; the next begins with 1887. Since 1908 the volumes have been based on the annual cumulations of the *Index to Legal Periodicals*, a quarterly (since 1926 cumulated triennially).[42]

Many universities with law schools publish legal periodicals; some of these have cumulative indexes. For information about them see *Harvard Guide*, page 112. On the same page there is information about the *American Digest* and the *Current Digest*, both of which summarize cases in the courts.[43]

It is sometimes important to know where files of periodicals may be found, since no one library can be expected to contain all of those mentioned in guides and catalogues. For this purpose some cata-

[38] D. C. Haskell, *Checklist of Cumulative Indexes to Periodicals in the New York Public Library*. New York: 1942.

[39] F. C. Hicks: *Materials and Methods of Legal Research*, 3d edn., Rochester: 1942.

[40] Lawrence Keitt, ed., *Annotated Bibliography of Bibliographies of Statutory Materials in the United States*. Cambridge: 1934.

[41] L. A. Jones and F. E. Chipman, eds., *An Index to Legal Periodical Literature*. 5 vols. Boston: Boston Book Company, 1888–1933.

[42] Published in connection with the *Law Library Journal*. New York: The H. W. Wilson Company, 1909–.

[43] Consult pages 111–112 of the *Harvard Guide* for titles of periodical indexes in many fields, and pages 170–173 for list of general magazines.

logues have been prepared covering the collections of groups of libraries. A good example is the *Union List of Serials in Libraries of the United States and Canada.*[44]

b) *Newspapers*

In the past research involving newspapers was a tedious task. Some writers of comprehensive histories who had access to large collections of them paged through the files chronologically, transcribing or paraphrasing their accounts of events. Professor John Bach McMaster was one of those who followed this practice, and it accounts for the peculiar organization of his history.[45] Recent aids have relieved research of much of the drudgery the older historians could not escape. For the years previous to 1820 an indispensable guide to newspapers is the bibliography compiled by Clarence S. Brigham.[46] One of its important features is the information it gives about the location of files and the availability of reproductions in photostat or microfilm. Winifred Gregory's *American Newspapers* (New York, 1937) supplements Brigham by covering newspapers in the United States and Canada for the years 1821–1936. Other lists of nation-wide scope are the *American Newspaper Annual* and the specialized *Check List of Negro Newspapers in the United States, 1827–1946.* For these see *Harvard Guide*, page 175.

Many of the larger libraries as well as states and cities issue check-lists, guides, or catalogues from time to time giving information about their newspaper files and other important classes of material. Many newspapers have been indexed and some have been microfilmed. A trial bibliography of the former has been compiled from

[44] Winifred Gregory Gerould, comp., 2d edn., New York: The H. W. Wilson Comany, 1943; supplements 1945, 1951. For bibliography of union lists see index of Constance M. Winchell, ed., *Guide to Reference Books,* 7th edn. Chicago: American Library Association, 1951. (Revision of book with same title by Isadore G. Mudge *et al.*, eds., Chicago: American Library Association, 1936.)

All extant periodicals in the United States published between 1741 and 1825 inclusive have been microfilmed, thus making them available by purchase in this form to libraries throughout the country. —*Harvard Guide,* 171.

[45] *A History of the People of the United States.* 8 vols. and a supplementary volume. New York: 1883–1913 and 1927.

[46] *History and Bibliography of American Newspapers, 1690–1820.* 2 vols. Worcester, Mass.: American Antiquarian Society, 1947. A reprint from the Society's *Proceedings*, n.s. XXIII and succeeding volumes. A few omissions are supplied by Carl Bridenbaugh in a review in *AHR* for January, 1948, pp. 346–347.

replies to an inquiry addressed to some 800 depositories listed in Gregory's *American Newspapers.*[47] *The Virginia Gazette* is one of the most valuable newspapers for the historian of the colonial period, largely because it republished items gathered from many contemporary papers. A microfilm edition recently brought out covers almost 200 more issues than an older photostat prepared by the Massachusetts Historical Society; the total number of issues of the *Gazette* now microfilmed is 1719. The accompanying index is "the first of its kind for a colonial newspaper." [48] The *New York Tribune* from 1841 to 1907, and the *New York Times*, 1851–1858, 1860, 1863–1905, have also been filmed. Indexing and microfilming are spreading rapidly among the newspapers of wide circulation, and more and more libraries of colleges and universities are acquiring copies for research purposes.

One of the early experiments in indexing newspapers was that of the California State Library in making a card index of more than 8,000 newspapers some of which date back to 1846. Recently the *Chicago Daily Tribune* began to index its files from 1847 on, and the City of Chicago is indexing its collection from 1833. The Ohio State Archaeological and Historical Society is sponsoring a selective index of seven of the oldest or most important papers of the state. Microfilms will be placed in the libraries of the seven cities where they were published. These are only straws which show how the wind is blowing.

The development of interinstitutional cooperative services is more and more relieving the investigator of the need of traveling from place to place in search of his material. (See *Harvard Guide*, 60.)

c) *Historical Journals*

Of course no publications are more important to the historian than those devoted to history. Many are published by local, state, or regional organizations and a few are supported by national organiza-

[47] Herbert O. Brayer, "Preliminary Guide to Indexed Newspapers in the United States, 1850–1900." *MVHR* for Sept., 1946, pp. 237–258. *Harvard Guide* mentions a number of the more important indexed newspapers, and lists by periods the papers of "general utility" for the historian, on pages 175–177.

[48] Lester J. Cappon and Stella F. Duff, comps., *The Virginia Gazette, 1736–1780*. 2 vols. Williamsburg: The Institute of Early American History and Culture, 1950. See *MVHR* for June, 1951.

tions. More or less complete files of these are in the larger public libraries and the major university libraries. Most institutions giving graduate instruction in the social sciences will have the journals of national scope and at least some of those published in their own areas. *The American Historical Review*, the American Historical Association *Annual Reports, The Mississippi Valley Historical Review* and its volumes of *Proceedings*, all serving a nation-wide constituency, are indispensable publications for institutions giving advanced degrees in American history to possess. Many other journals representing kindred fields of social science—political science, economics, sociology, law, etc.,—are almost as necessary for the student of American history as the historical journals.[49]

Although several of the indexes already described, especially the *Annual Magazine Subject Index*, the *Readers' Guide*, and the *Writings on American History*, include entries for important articles or studies in these publications, the student should bear in mind the following especially important indexes:

The American Historical Association *Annual Report* for 1914 contains a general index of *The American Historical Review* up to that date, while the *Report* for 1944 includes a classified subject bibliography with explanatory comments on the articles, notes, suggestions, and documents published in the *Review* during its first fifty years. For *The Mississippi Valley Historical Review* there are now three indexes published at ten-year intervals: the first covered volumes I–XV; the second, volumes XVI–XXV; the latest, volumes XXVI–XXXV (1939–1949). Each of these indexes is a "comprehensive, analytical combination of author, title, reviewer, and subject headings." In addition to the indexes there is a *Topical Guide* for the *Review* and the *Proceedings*. It was published several years ago and is therefore not up to date.

V. APPRAISING BOOKS

Any one engaged in preparing a tentative bibliography for a master's essay is presumed to have made a casual examination of the books he has listed and to have rejected some of them as useless for his purpose. Those which have been retained after this initial ex-

[49] For lists of societies, colleges, etc., publishing journals or series of studies in the social sciences, together with the titles of their publications, see *Harvard Guide*, 163–170.

amination must sooner or later be subjected to a more critical test. At this point the beginner should be diffident about the soundness of his judgment and should seek the opinions of expert judges. There are various ways of finding their estimates. For books published before the end of the nineteenth century Larned's *Literature of American History* is helpful, as has been pointed out. Comment that is usually reliable is to be found for later publications in the reviews published by the historical magazines, such as *The American Historical Review* and *The Mississippi Valley Historical Review.* Guidance in finding reviews in historical periodicals will be given by the various indexes already described. For the years since its publication began the *Book Review Digest* is especially useful. It is a monthly with semiannual and annual cumulations, and condenses book reviews from more than fifty English and American periodicals including the literary supplements of leading newspapers. A sentence or two, or a plus or minus sign for favorable and unfavorable judgments, indicates the trend of opinion, while specific references guide the student to the issues of the periodicals where the reviews were published.[50] Of similar nature is the *United States Quarterly Book Review*,[51] which focuses the opinions of many reviewers on each work dealt with.

c. *United States Government Publications*

i. GUIDES TO USE

The publications of the Federal Government form one of the most important classes of materials used by American history students. They are so varied in character that it is difficult to carry in mind much information about them except what is impressed on the memory by constant use. Beyond a few directions, therefore, the best plan is to present a list of the more helpful guides. Some of these should be in the library where the investigator works.

A work of general utility is the *Guide to Reference Books*, by Mudge *et al.*, and its several supplements. It is the predecessor of Winchell's edition under the same title (see *ante*, 110, footnote 44). One of the features of this series is the section on Government

[50] New York: The H. W. Wilson Company, 1905–. Cumulative indexes are in vols. for 1926, 1931, 1941, and 1946.
[51] Washington: The Library of Congress, 1945–.

Publications. There are several other books to which the student should have access if he is making use of this class of material.[52] The second of the two mentioned in the footnote is described thus: "Basic collections and studies of federal laws, congressional debates and proceedings, United States documents and court reports, presidential papers, departmental and state government publications are all catalogued and briefly described. . . ."[53] A third guide is the Everhard *Handbook*, and a fourth by Childs, although devoted chiefly to publications by the states, may be mentioned here.[54] Both Brown and Childs guide one also to statistical materials.

ii. PROCEEDINGS OF CONGRESS

In addition to these guides some of the publications of the Federal Government commonly used by graduates should be described here. The records of the Confederation congresses preceding the adoption of the Constitution have been published during the present century under the able editorship of Worthington C. Ford and Gaillard Hunt.[55] The debates in Congress since 1789 have been printed under various titles, as follows:

Debates and Proceedings in the Congress of the United States, 1789–1824. 42 vols. Washington: 1834–1856. (Commonly known as the *Annals of Congress.*)

Register of Debates in Congress, 1825–1837. 29 vols. Washington: 1825–1837.

Congressional Globe, Containing the Debates and Proceedings, 1833–1873. 109 vols. Washington: 1834–1873.

Congressional Record, Containing the Proceedings and Debates, 1873–. Washington: Government Printing Office, 1873–.

All of these but the *Record* were published as private enterprises sanctioned by the Government; but since publication by the Government began many improvements have been made. Beginning

[52] Edith F. Clarke, *Guide to the Use of United States Government Documents*. Boston: Boston Book Company, 1918; Everett S. Brown, *Manual of Government Publications*. New York: Appleton-Century-Crofts, Inc., 1950.

[53] *MVHR*, Sept., 1950, p. 376.

[54] Elfrida Everhard, *Handbook of United States Public Documents*. Minneapolis: H. W. Wilson Company, 1910.

James Bennett Childs, *An Account of Government Document Bibliography in the United States and Elsewhere*. 3d edn., Washington: Government Printing Office, 1942.

[55] *Journals of the Continental Congresses, 1774–1789*. 34 vols. Washington: 1904–1937.

with the *Register* the record of a session of Congress is called a "Volume," although often divided into several units for printing. These units are called "Parts." Each volume is indexed, but the subject entries are inadequate.

It is important to note that the earliest date of publication of any of these records is 1825. Moreover even as printed the record is incomplete. The Senate held secret sessions during the early years, and the printed record of its proceedings is most meager. The deficiency is filled to some extent by the diaries of certain members. For the first two years one kept by a Pennsylvania member of the Senate is available, while for the early years of the nineteenth century that of William Plumer fills a similar gap. Both of these diaries were published in comparatively recent times.[56] Before 1825 the dearth of information about the doings of Congress was comparable to that concerning the proceedings of the Constitutional Convention of 1787. Yet citizens were not quite without means of knowing what was going on, for most sessions were open to the public and some newspapers followed the debates and published important speeches in whole or in part, as well as notes of the proceedings. One of the foremost of the papers was *Niles' Weekly Register*, which flourished from 1811 to 1849. Many local papers reprinted the parts of its contents which had general interest, and in turn it disseminated their significant or interesting local items.[57]

Many valuable documents might have been lost if it had not been for the enterprise of this journal. An example of its service was the publication of Rufus King's speech on the Missouri Compromise. The speech was delivered in February, 1819, from notes which King did not write out in full until late in that year. *Niles' Register* published it on December 4. *The Congressional Register* reports speeches from 1825, and the printing of the *Annals* was not begun until a decade later. The *Annals* covered the years beginning with 1789, but were compiled from such records as the editors could lay

[56] Edgar S. Maclay, ed., *Journal of William Maclay, United States Senator from Pennsylvania, 1789–1791*. New York: 1890.

Everett Somerville Brown, ed., *William Plumer's Memorandum of Proceedings in the United States Senate, 1803–1807*. New York: The Macmillan Company, 1923.

[57] *Niles' Weekly Register*, known in its later years as *Niles' National Register*, was published in Baltimore, by Hezekiah Niles. The history of this notable journal has been written by Norval Neil Luxon in a book entitled *Niles' Weekly Register*. Baton Rouge: Louisiana State University, 1947.

hands on, and their publication did not reach the era of the Missouri controversy until about 1840. Meantime *Niles' Register* preserved King's speech for use by the editor of King's writings published three-quarters of a century later.[58]

The publishers of the *Annals of Congress* failed to find other contemporary documents which fortunately came to light later. A significant part of the history of the Missouri Compromise turned on President Monroe's decision. By the time, a generation after the Compromise, when the issue arose again concerning the power of Congress to prohibit slavery in a new state or even in a territory, it had been learned that Monroe had faced these issues and had hesitated until letters from his Virginia friends apparently decided his action. A tyro who was content with what the *Annals* yielded would miss these documents which were belatedly published in the *Congressional Globe*.[59] The question is, how could he be expected to find them.

These illustrations show how difficult the historian's task is when he deals with problems related to the legislation of the early years. The deficiencies of the *Annals* in respect to the records of both houses of Congress make it necessary, even in tracing legislation, to follow not only the *Annals* but the *Journals* of both houses, for in them are preserved the record of motions, votes, and other steps in procedure. Both houses have published these records of regular business annually since 1789, but publication of the *Journal of the Executive Proceedings of the Senate . . . 1789–1905*, in ninety volumes, although dating from 1789, was not begun until 1828. The executive sessions relate to nominations submitted by the President for confirmation and treaties submitted for ratification.

iii. STATUTES AND DOCUMENTS

Since publication of the *Congressional Record* was begun the *Journals* have lost much of their earlier significance, as the index of the *Record* includes a history of bills and resolutions on which there was action during the session. The index gives every stage of the progress of each bill and the number of any reports or documents relating to it. In the early days acts as passed were printed in appen-

[58] Charles R. King, ed., *Life and Correspondence of Rufus King*. 6 vols. New York: 1894–1900.

[59] 30 Cong., 2 sess., App., 63–67.

dices in the volumes of the *Annals*, etc., but unfortunately for the historian, bills as originally presented or reported from committee are seldom incorporated either into the *Journals* or the debates. Great bundles of the printed sheets on which they came before the houses were for years piled away in almost inaccessible places in Washington. The proceedings preserve the record of amendments, and the essence of the original proposals is usually recoverable by examination of the debates and the acts as passed.

In later years the acts of each session have been published as passed in the temporary forms called Slip Laws and Pamphlet or Session Laws. All the laws passed by a Congress (covering the biennium) are collected into one volume, under the title *Statutes at Large*. The volume for the years 1789–1873 were collected and published in seventeen volumes (Boston: Little and Brown—later Little, Brown and Company—1845–1873), but since 1874 they are again being issued in annual volumes by the State Department. This series contains the laws and resolutions, proclamations, treaties, and other international agreements for each Congress.

As time passes and other legislation is enacted some statutes become obsolete or are modified, so that new publications become necessary containing the general and permanent statutes in force.[60] These revisions are indispensable, of course, for the legal practitioner, but for the historian the original statutes, even if amended or repealed, may be of equal or even greater importance, making the *Statutes at Large* invaluable. The *Revised Statutes* are described as follows:

> *Revised Statutes of the United States . . . Embracing the Statutes . . . General and Permanent in Their Nature, in Force on December 1, 1873.* 2d edn. Washington: 1878.
>
> *Supplement to the Revised Statutes of the United States, Embracing the Statutes, General and Permanent in Their Nature, Passed after the Revised Statutes.* 2d edn. 2 vols. Washington: 1900–1901.
>
> *United States Code 1946 Edition Containing the General and Permanent Laws of the United States in Force on January 2, 1947.* 5 vols. Four Supplements, 1947–1951.

[60] See Clarke, *op. cit.*, 130 *et seq.*, for fuller directions for tracing legislation; and Spahr and Swenson, *Methods and Status of Scientific Research*, 183, for discussion of the various forms in which revisions of statutes are published.

iv. INDEXES AND GUIDES

Indexes have been made for the Federal statutes, two of them under the supervision of the Library of Congress and another now about a century old. (See *Harvard Guide*, 115, 121.)

Save for their voluminous character there is little difficulty in following congressional debates if the dates of their beginnings are known approximately. An examination of a volume of the *Annals, Globe,* or *Record,* will make evident how they are to be used. Helpful, however, are the comprehensive *Tables* prepared by Church and Smith.[61]

The House and Senate *Journals* are also easily used. But to find data in the documents on a given topic is a very different matter. One of the earliest efforts to provide guidance to documents dates from 1832, when a collection was begun entitled *American State Papers: Documents Legislative and Executive.*[62] This series, running from the First Congress through the Twenty-fifth, contains groups of indexed volumes on *Foreign Relations, Military Affairs, Public Lands, Finance,* etc., and *Senate, House, and Executive Documents.* A continuation beyond the terminal date carries the coverage in some cases to 1876 and 1895.[63]

Much documentary material was printed in appendices in the *Annals, Debates,* etc. Much was also collected by committees of the two houses because of its bearing on proposed legislation, and is now to be found in their reports. Nearly every important administrative official makes an annual report and many of these are printed. An element of confusion results from the transfer from time to time of these officials from one department to another. For example, from 1832 to 1849 the report of the Commissioner of Indian Affairs was a part of the report of the Secretary of War; but after 1849 the Commissioner was under the Interior Department and his report became a part of the annual statement of its head. Numerous other shifts of similar nature have been made.

Other events occur which make it difficult to follow the records.

[61] Alonzo Webster Church and Henry H. Smith, *Tables Showing the Contents of the Several Volumes Comprising the Annals of Congress, Congressional Debates, Congressional Globe, Congressional Record, Statutes at Large, United States Supreme Court Reports . . . Arranged by Years and Congresses.* Washington: Government Printing Office, [1892].

[62] 38 vols. Washington: 1832–1861.

[63] For further details consult *Harvard Guide*, 122.

In all these reports there is material of great historical value. An intricate system of reports has been evolved, well calculated, it would seem (although, of course, not by design) to bury data beyond recovery.

The annual issues of the *Journals of the Continental Congress* (see *ante*, page 114, note 55) are indexed and contain bibliographical notes, but without some kind of comprehensive index the investigator would be bewildered beyond hope. The first attempt at such an index was made by Benjamin Perley Poore, acting for the Government, which published the product of his labors in 1885.[64] Entries are in chronological order and in each case include an abstract of the document and information as to where it is to be found. The whole is indexed by authors, titles, and dates, but the subject entries are inadequate.

Supplementing Poore for the years 1774–1789 is a private undertaking edited by Paul Leicester Ford.[65] Also supplementing Poore for the documents of the early constitutional period is the compilation by A. W. Greely.[66] Other deficiencies of Poore's *Catalogue* are partially remedied and Greely's compilation continued by the *Tables of and Annotated Index to the Congressional Series of United States Public Documents.* Part II (the *Annotated Index*) is a "minute alphabetical subject index" of the congressional series of documents from the Fifteenth Congress to the Fifty-second (1817–1893). Its list is a selection of the more important documents, about half of the total number.[67] Still another compilation covers the departmental series of documents as well as the congressional. Although its list of the former documents is incomplete,[68] it serves as a bridge over the gap between Poore's *Catalogue* and the *Catalogue* prepared by the

[64] *Descriptive Catalogue of the Government Publications of the United States, September 5, 1774–March 4, 1881.* This and other publications, some of which are mentioned later on, have a place in the Congressional Documents. The citation for Poore's *Catalogue* in this series is: 48 Cong., 2 sess., *Sen. Misc. Doc. 67.*

[65] *Some Materials for a Bibliography of the Official Publications of the Continental Congress.* Boston: 1890.

[66] *Public Documents of the First Fourteen Congresses, 1789–1817.* 56 Cong., 1 sess., *Sen. Doc. 428.* A supplement is published in the AHA *Report* for 1903, I, 343.

[67] Superintendent of Documents. Washington: Government Printing Office, 1902.

[68] John G. Ames, ed., *Comprehensive Index to the Publications of the United States Government, 1881–1893.* 2 vols. 58 Cong., 2 sess., *H. Doc. 754.* Also printed separately. Washington: 1905.

Superintendent of Documents for publications issued after March 4, 1893.[69] Thus this work continues the *Comprehensive Index* and the *Tables of . . . Public Documents.* This "Doc. Cat.," as it is sometimes called, appeared in primary form as the *Monthly Catalogue of United States Public Documents* (after 1939 known as the *United States Government Publications Monthly Catalogue*), with a list of all current Government publications. The *Monthly Catalogue* issues for each year (July to June) were cumulated to form an indexed volume, but these annual volumes were superseded when the complete and permanent biennial volumes came out. The biennial volumes, one for each Congress except the Fifty-fourth which has two, have elaborate author and subject indexes. However, the biennial series was discontinued in 1940, but the *Monthly Catalogue* is still issued and an annual index is supplied at the close of the calendar year. Since 1936 the latter has listed important documents duplicated by various processes as well as all current printed documents.

Since 1928 the Superintendent of Documents has published a semimonthly list of *Selected United States Publications*, with entries by title. These Government publications are supplemented by others printed privately, such as Hirshberg and Melinat, eds., *Subject Guide to United States Government Publications.*[70]

Of special importance is the Hartwell *Checklist*, which is "an approximately complete checklist of all public documents issued by the United States Government during the first century and a quarter of its history." It begins with the documents in the *American State Papers* and ends with those of 1909. The second volume is an index. This list supersedes the *Tables* of the *Annotated Index*, overlaps and supplements Ames, and in part parallels the *Catalogue* of the Superintendent of Documents beginning with publications of 1893. But while the Hartwell work is a checklist, that of the Superintendent of Documents is a catalogue.[71]

[69] *Catalogue of the Public Documents of Congress and of All the Departments of the Government of the United States . . . 1893–1940.*

[70] Chicago: 1947. For description of this guide and others of more or less use to the student investigator see *Harvard Guide*, 114 (publications about hearings before Government committees); 119 (J. K. Wilcox, "New Guides . . . "); and 120 (Merritt, *United States Government as a Publisher*).

[71] M. A. Hartwell, ed., *Checklist of United States Public Documents, 1789–1909. Congressional: to the Close of the Sixtieth Congress: Departmental: to*

V. COURT REPORTS

On page 97 the method of citing Supreme Court cases was explained. In the days when they were cited by the name of the reporter the titles used were not uniform, although the most common one was *Reports of Cases Argued and Adjudged in the Supreme Court of the United States*. There were only slight variations from this wording. The reporter's name preceded the title, and following it came the years covered by the volumes he reported, the number of volumes, and the place and dates of publication. In abbreviated form the list of the reporters and the years covered by their several reports are: A. J. Dallas, 1790–1800; William Cranch, 1801–1815; Henry Wheaton, 1816–1827; Richard Peters, 1828–1843; B. C. Howard, 1843–1861; Jeremiah S. Black, 1861–1862; J. W. Wallace, 1863–1874. Since 1875 the title has come first, thus: *United States Reports: Supreme Court, 1875–* , the reporter's name following.

This last is the full bibliographical form but citations are commonly given as shown on page 97 of this Manual. The total number of volumes filled by the reports of Cranch and his successors from 1790 to 1876 was ninety. The first of the *United States Reports* is numbered 91, being thus continuous with the numbering of the earlier series. A case cited in the first volume of the reports after 1874 would therefore be 91 U.S., followed by the page where the case is printed, or where the words quoted are to be found, or the place to which the reader's attention is directed.

There are many well-indexed books on constitutional history or constitutional law, or reprinting leading cases in whole or in part, which cite cases in the way described. There are also bibliographies and guides to the reports of both Federal and state courts.[72] A student will often find it wise to read the full text of a case or decision and make his own analysis. If a summary will suffice, the *United*

---

he End of the Calendar Year 1909. 3d edn. Washington: Government Printing Office, 1911.

This checklist does not include the maps in the Congressional Series, but a descriptive list of these, now printed for the years 1817–1843, will when completed be a record of maps in the series to 1861. Helpful on occasions is Everhard's *Handbook*.

[72] C. C. Soule, *Lawyer's Reference Manual of Law Books and Citations*. Boston: 1883; brought to 1942 by F. C. Hicks, *Materials and Methods of Legal Research*, 3d edn. Rochester: F. A. Eldean, *How to Find the Law*. St. Paul: C. B. Putnam, 1949. For all of these see *Harvard Guide*, 116, 119.

States Supreme Court Digest may be used for cases in the highest Federal tribunal.[73] Cases in the lower Federal courts are reported in a series of volumes beginning with decisions of 1789 and continuing to date.[74] Supplementary papers on some of these cases are on file in the offices of the clerks of these courts or in the Library of Congress.[75]

Students engaged in legal or constitutional studies are likely to have use for the opinions of the attorneys-general.[76] Such a collection is available.

vi. DOCUMENTS AND PLAIN TITLES

From time to time documents of special classes have been collected and published. They are often assigned to places in the documentary series. Some illustrations of this practice have been mentioned in footnotes on pages of this Manual. Other compilations of this kind are: C. J. Kappler, *Indian Affairs, Laws, and Treaties,* published in 1902 (57 Cong., 1 sess., *Sen. Doc. 452*); Thomas Donaldson, *The Public Domain* (47 Cong., 2 sess., *H. Misc. Doc. 45, Pt. 4*); James D. Richardson, *Messages and Papers of the Presidents* (53 Cong., 2 sess., *H. Misc. Doc. 40*); and William M. Malloy, *Treaties, Conventions, International Acts, Protocols and Agreements between the United States of America and Other Powers, 1776–1937* (61 Cong., 2 sess., *Sen. Doc. 357*). (This is properly the designation of volumes I and II of Malloy, which were issued in 1910. A supplement was published in 1913 which is designated thus: 62 Cong., 2 sess., *Sen. Doc. 1063*; while a third volume is *Sen. Doc. 348* of the Fourth session of the Sixty-seventh Congress. A fourth volume was published in 1938.)

It has already been said (page 99) that the American Historical Association was incorporated by Congress in 1889 as a subsidiary of the Smithsonian Institution. Its reports afford another illustration of the unexpected kinds of matter which Government documents may contain. Presented by the AHA to the Smithsonian, the reports are transmitted by the latter to Congress and are then printed as House

[73] 18 vols. St. Paul: 1944–1945. Continued in supplements.

[74] *Federal Cases; Federal Reports; Federal Supplement; Court of Claims Reports* are the titles of these publications.

[75] See *Harvard Guide*, 123.

[76] E. F. Hall, *et al.*, eds., *Official Opinions of the Attorneys-General of the United States Advising the Presidents and Heads of Departments in Relation to their Official Duties, 1791–1948.* 40 vols. (through 1948). Washington: 1852–.

Documents. To take one at random, the *Annual Report* for 1896 is placed in the document series as 54 Cong., 2 sess., *H. Doc. 353, Pts. 1 and 2.*

The search for such documents is simplified by the fact that most libraries catalogue them separately. Many are published with what are called Plain Titles as well as the designation of their place in the documents; that is, with the same kind of title page that is found in ordinary books. The AHA *Reports* have this dual form. The *Harvard Guide*, on pages 123–125, lists many documents which have plain titles but does not give the documentary description.

vii. DOCUMENTS ON FOREIGN RELATIONS

Many indexes and guides have been prepared for documents on special subjects. The field of foreign affairs has fared well in this respect. Besides the volumes compiled by Malloy there is a similar collection edited by Hunter Miller.[77] There are also many volumes of diplomatic correspondence with other nations assembled by various editors; other volumes on arbitrations and adjudications; treaties to promote peace; international law digests; etc.[78]

There are four works on foreign relations which constitute a sequence deserving of special mention: the volumes on *Foreign Relations* in the *American State Papers* (see *ante*, page 118); the Hasse *Index*;[79] the Department of State *Papers Relating to Foreign Relations*;[80] and the Bemis *Guide*. Beginning where the Hasse *Index* ends, the work of editing and publishing records had reached 1935 by the year 1952. Supplements had been issued in the meantime for numerous series. The full list will be found in the preceding citation of the *Harvard Guide*. The Bemis work (*Harvard Guide*, 107) is described in the footnote below.[81]

In a way the Hasse *Index* bridges the gap between the indexed volumes on *Foreign Relations* in the earlier series of *American State*

[77] *Treaties and Other International Acts of the United States of America, 1776–1863.* 8 vols. Washington: 1931–1948.

[78] See the list in the *Harvard Guide* under the heading Federal Records Relating to Foreign Affairs, 123–124.

[79] Adelaide R. Hasse, *Index to United States Documents Relating to Foreign Affairs, 1828–1861.* 3 vols. Washington: The Carnegie Institution, 1914–1921.

[80] *Papers Relating to the Foreign Relations of the United States, 1861–.* Washington: –1952.

[81] Samuel Flagg Bemis and Grace Gardner Griffin, eds., *Guide to the Diplomatic History of the United States, 1775–1921.* Washington: Government Printing Office, 1935.

Papers, and the *Papers* edited and published by the State Department. There is some overlapping, in fact, throughout the group, yet they are mutually supplementary.

Previous to 1950 the text of treaties formed a part of the volumes of *Statutes at Large*. Beginning with the treaties of that year the State Department has prepared a volume each year under the title *United States Treaties and Other International Agreements*. The first was published in 1953.

d. *General Catalogues of Books*

Several attempts have been made to compile comprehensive dictionaries or catalogues of books published in the United States, including colonial times, or about the United States but published elsewhere. Complete files of these catalogues are not likely to be found except in a few of the larger libraries of the country, and their accessibility is consequently restricted. They are more likely to be useful to an occasional candidate for the doctorate than to those who are seeking the master's degree. The descriptions which follow may be referred to as needed. However, some of the current publications which grew out of them are among the most useful tools of the historical student.

The pioneer in the field of comprehensive book catalogues was Orville Augustus Roorbach. During the years 1852–1861 he compiled a four-volume catalogue of American books published after 1820, under the title *Bibliotheca Americana*. Soon afterwards Joseph Sabin undertook the more ambitious project of making a dictionary of books, pamphlets, and periodicals about America including those published elsewhere. He adopted Roorbach's title with additions descriptive of his own compilation, and arranged the entries in the alphabetical order of the authors' names.[82] The first volume appeared in 1868 and the nineteenth in 1892. The *Dictionary* had then reached the name Simms. At that point the work was interrupted and not until the early 1920's was it resumed. Wilberforce Eames compiled two more volumes, the second of which was published in 1929, reaching the name William Smith. The last editor was R. W. G. Vail, who completed the undertaking, the words "present time," used

[82] Joseph Sabin *et al.*, eds., *Bibliotheca Americana. A Dictionary of Books Relating to America from its Discovery to the Present Time*. 29 vols. New York and Portland, Me.: 1868–1936.

in the title, having in the course of years acquired a meaning quite other than that which Sabin had in mind.

A feature of the Sabin *Dictionary* is its frequent mention of libraries which possess copies of the rare books it lists. A similar feature is found in the dictionary of Charles Evans. While the Sabin project was in a state of suspended animation Evans attempted a dictionary for the years preceding Roorbach's initial date which would carry full bibliographical data about each entry. Each volume is indexed by author, subject, and publisher. Most of the works Evans lists are now out of print and quite rare, making especially useful the information he gives about libraries in which copies may be found.[83]

After 1861 the Roorbach enterprise was supplemented by James Kelly who produced two volumes covering the publications of the decade following Roorbach's terminal date. Kelly abandoned Roorbach's Latin title and adopted an English equivalent—*American Catalogue*.[84] About that time the *Publishers' Weekly* made its initial bow (1872), and supplanted Kelly as the basis of a new project which appropriated the name he had used for his work. The first volume of this *American Catalogue of Books*, based on the *Weekly*, listed books in print (that is, offered for sale by the publishers) on July 1, 1876. From 1886 to 1910 there was a form which had temporary value, known as the *Annual American Catalogue*, which cumulated the entries in the *Publishers' Weekly*.

The *Publishers' Weekly* is the standard journal of the American book trade, and continues to provide a means of keeping up with current books, as each issue contains a list of the week's publications as well as announcements of forthcoming books. The *American Catalogue* has given way, however, to the *United States Catalogue*, published by the H. W. Wilson Company of New York, which has become the chief producer of library guides and indexes. The original home of the Wilson Company was Minneapolis, but later it removed to New York City. The *United States Catalogue* made its appearance in 1900 (in Minneapolis) with an issue listing books in

[83] *American Bibliography: a Chronological Dictionary of All Books, Pamphlets, and Periodical Publications Printed in the English Continental Colonies and the United States . . . 1639–1820*. 12 vols. Chicago: Blakely Press, 1903–1934.

[84] *American Catalogue of Books Published in the United States from January, 1861 to January, 1871*. 2 vols. New York: 1866–1871.

print in 1899. Later issues catalogued new publications during periods of three or five years, thus forming a continuous record to 1928. The subject entries are of value for compilers of bibliographies, and the data given are very complete and accurate. At intervals volumes have been devoted, like the first, to listing books in print at specified dates. The publication includes not only the output of commercial concerns, but works printed privately, regular importations, Canadian books not also published south of the border, university, society, and state publications, and those of the Smithsonian Institution, the National Museum, the Bureau of American Ethnology, and some other government departments and agencies, both Federal and state.

The *Cumulative Book Index* issued by the same publishers bears much the same relation to the *United States Catalogue* that the *Publishers' Weekly* formerly held to the *American Catalogue*. Published every month since 1898, the *Index* cumulated its entries semiannually and annually. The yearly cumulations bridged the years between the volumes of the *United States Catalogue* until 1928. Since then it has been an annual supplement to the *Catalogue*, indexing current books in the English language by author, title, and subject.

In 1948 the Library of Congress published an alphabetical subject catalogue of accessions represented by the printed cards it had prepared for distribution since 1945. This guide, the *Library of Congress Subject Catalogue*, is continued in quarterly issues of which the last for each year cumulates the entries for the four quarters. It is essentially a continuation of the *Catalogue of Books Represented by . . . Printed Cards* described *ante*, page 92, note 6.[85]

e. *Bringing Research to a Focus*

Enough has been said in the last thirty-one pages about the materials of research to bewilder any beginner who does not keep in mind the fact that his task is to *select* what he needs for his specific undertaking. He is fortunate if his training has included a proseminar or course in research in which he has had practice in choosing the appropriate aids for compiling bibliographies on various subjects, finding specified documents, or tracking down what a statesman has

[85] Other catalogues of value for advanced research are described in *Harvard Guide*, 110.

said or done about some particular matter. Such training should prevent waste of time when he has to pursue independently the preparation of a master's essay, a task which shifts his attention from general research to that for a specific subject.

The general review on the preceding pages covers most of the area within which candidates for the master's degree are likely to do their investigating. Indeed, it covers ground which candidates for the doctorate must also traverse. No student at either of these levels will need to use all of the aids which have been described, on any one study; nor will they furnish all guidance needed by every candidate, especially one working for the doctorate, to all the material he may need.

The concept of the scope of history has grown immensely during the past few decades. Until near the close of the nineteenth century a common view was expressed by the saying "History is past politics and politics present history." Before that, history was frequently confined to accounts of the deeds of rulers and the wars between their respective countries. A few eighteenth-century writers glimpsed the importance of the everyday life of the people, but for a long time that notion of history failed to command general attention. Nowadays the close relations between history and other social sciences are widely recognized and much heeded by writers. The effort to understand and account for the issues involved in international relations and diplomacy which so often led to armed conflict has largely replaced the former accounts of wars in which strategy and tactics were chief interests. History now embraces not only politics but economics, religion, industry, and education in their full extent. Indeed, no phase of human conduct or thought is any longer regarded as closed to the historian.

It is quite impossible to attempt in this Manual a comprehensive survey of the facilities and procedures for productive writing in the whole of this vast field. In a later division (Part III) further comments and suggestions will be offered for advanced researchers. Here reference is made again to the *Harvard Guide* as the best single work citing materials helpful to this class of students. Its extensive index unlocks its resources for them. For candidates seeking the M.A., the best advice, as has been said already, is to undertake subjects of modest scope for which the institutions where they are working have, or can readily procure, the needed materials. The considerable research required to trace Van Buren's part in the House election of 1825 should be sufficient warning that an apparently simple topic may prove to be surprisingly intricate.

A doctoral candidate might attempt a biography of a character not previously studied sufficiently, but for a master's study a more suitable subject would be the share of some prominent person in a significant event or events. A good beginning for such a project would be to list the biographies of which he was the subject. This can be done most readily by consulting the *Harvard Guide* index under the person's name. The card catalogue would then show which of the biographies are in the library. Comparing statements in them with one another, with those in general histories, and with the man's own writings would no doubt bring to light differences in the point of view, contradictions, or other discrepancies. These differences would be the matter to which critical tests should be applied in conformity with the procedures already discussed. Sometimes the examination of court decisions, a variety of government documents, or other classes of material would be involved. The chief value of such a study would lie in the making of it, although it might sometimes be a real contribution to historical knowledge.

As examples of this type of essay the following suggestions are offered. Many other topics will readily occur to a student's supervisor, or, better still, to the student himself.

Henry Clay's part in one or more of the following: The Missouri Compromise; The Presidential Election of 1824–1825; The Issue of the United States Bank in the Presidential Election of 1832.

Was John C. Calhoun the Author of the South Carolina Exposition of 1828?

What Were Calhoun's Views of the Powers of Congress over Slavery in the Territories?

President Monroe and the Missouri Compromise.

President Monroe on Internal Improvements.

A Comparison of the Views of Jefferson and Madison on Constitutional Construction.

Thomas H. Benton on Westward Expansion.

The Authorship of President Jackson's State Papers.

Alexander H. Stephen's Views on Slavery Issues.

A Critique of John A. Bingham's Explanation of the Fourteenth Amendment.

Chief Justice Waite and the Doctrine of Property Affected with a Public Interest.

Theodore Roosevelt's Concept of a "Twilight Zone" of Constitutional Power.

Theodore Roosevelt's Theories Concerning Big Business.

President Taft and the Ballinger Affair.

Woodrow Wilson and the Doctrine of the "New Freedom."

Another type of essay would examine conflicts of group or sectional interests and the effects on legislation. Examples:

The Geographical Distribution of the Congressional Vote on the Missouri Compromise and Its Significance.

The Contest over the Wilson-Gorman Tariff Act and Its Significance.

The Sectional and Economic Alignment on the Issue of the Free Coinage of Silver and Its Interpretation.

The Political, Economic, and Social Alignment on the *Laissez Faire* Philosophy.

4. Assembling Materials: Bibliographical Forms

As the number of bibliographical slips increases the plan for filing them will need to be expanded. One division may be devoted to Newspapers and another to Articles in Periodicals, Annuals and Publications of Learned Societies. Another will probably be required for Government Publications probably with subdivisions such as Federal, State, and Local or Municipal. Before filing slips in any of these classes appropriate headings should be written at the top of each. Within each class or subdivision an alphabetical order should be used, an article by Bassett in the periodical list going under B, one by Esary under E, etc. This plan will scatter references to articles by different writers in the same magazine and bring together those by the same writer in different periodicals. Newspaper items, on the contrary, should be collected under the name of the paper, all slips referring to the *New York Times*, for instance, or *The Chicago Tribune* being brought together regardless of authorship. Each slip should be given a topical heading and topics should be arranged alphabetically; under each topic, if the slips are numerous, a chronological order will usually be best. Cross references are useful to bring together items on the same topic from different papers.

The reason for the difference in the methods of handling newspaper and periodical matter will appear in the discussion of the form of the final bibliography. The topical segregation of periodical matter is taken care of in filing notes on subject matter. As the tentative bibliography grows this plan of arrangement should gradually give it final form, leaving at last little more to be done than to transcribe it.

In the suggestions concerning the tentative bibliography the student was urged to note for each item the data which would be needed if it should be retained for the final bibliography. The purpose of that advice will now be evident in its use in giving the bibliography its final form.

a. *Books*

Every book in the completed bibliography should be described or identified by the inclusion of the following data, as far as applicable to it: (1) Name of author, editor, or compiler, the family name coming first. This order is due to the fact that the bibliography is arranged in the alphabetical order of the family names. When a card is first made out, if the student has only the family name and initials of the given name as shown in some of the examples, the initials should be filled out. This can usually be done by inspecting the author card in the library catalogue, *e.g.*, Howe, [George] F. The bibliography should have the name as it appears on the title page of the book, but filling out initials in this way preserves the identity of the author if another of his works is used with his name in a different form. (2) Exact title as it appears on the title page (not cover) of the book. (3) The identification of the edition if it is not the first. (4) The number of volumes if there are more than one. (5) The place of publication (the home office if more than one is named on the title page). (6) Name of the publisher. (7) Date of publication.

If there is more than one volume and they have been published at different times, the dates of the appearance of the first and last should be indicated thus: 1882–1888. If publication is still in progress that fact should be indicated by leaving the second date blank: 1950–. If the date of publication does not appear on the title page the copyright date from the following page may be substituted thus: c1928. If that date is also lacking the abbreviation n.d. (for no date) should be used. If the date or dates of publication are supplied from external sources they should be enclosed in brackets without the c, thus: [1928–1930]. If no place of publication is given that fact is indicated by using n.p. (no place). If the place of publication is supplied, it should be enclosed in brackets to indicate that fact: [Albany].

The publisher's name is often omitted from a bibliographical entry although it is a good means of identifying the book. It also facilitates ordering it. Some authors and publishers place the publisher's name before the city where the book was published; some use the reverse order. This Manual gives the place of publication first, following the practice of the American Historical Association and the Mississippi Valley Historical Association, and many others; but the order found in the book itself may be followed.

Catalogue cards contain various other kinds of information, such as the number of pages in a book, the size of the page, and whether there are maps or illustrations. These need not be noted unless they are of significance for the study, which may be the case especially with maps. It will save time in asking for a volume again if the call number is placed on the slip. Any available information should be noted, as already advised.

With the additions suggested the slip for Fish's book would appear as follows:

AH5 Fish, Carl Russell,
H33 The Civil Service and the Patronage (Harvard His-
v. 11 torical Studies, XI). New York: Longmans, Green and
Company, 1905.

[Author was prof. of hist. in Univ. of Wis. Book covers 1789–1901. Ch. X on "Civil Service Reform, 1865–1901." Pp. 217–222 on Arthur's presidency. Bib. 252–266.]

If a volume is one of a series by different authors under a common editor or series title, the slip should indicate the *volume used* and its relation to the series, as follows:

Sparks, Edwin Erle,
National Development, 1877–1885 (vol. XXIII of The American Nation, Albert Bushnell Hart, ed.). New York: Harper and Brothers, 1907.

If a volume in a series under a general title contains several studies by different authors the following form should be used:

Chandler, William E.,
"Chester A. Arthur" (in The Presidents of the United States, 1789–1914, by John Fiske . . . and many others. James Grant Wilson, ed. 4 vols. New York: Charles Scribner's Sons, 1914), III, 195–237.

Carefully prepared bibliographies, such as the one in the Fish volume, usually give all needed data with the exception sometimes of the publisher's name. Footnotes, however, do not usually give full data because their purpose is not primarily bibliographical.[86] One finds, for instance, in a footnote on page 216 of Fish's book a reference to Lambert, *Progress of Civil Service Reform in the United States,* and it is necessary to turn to his bibliography for fuller information. There, under the division headed Pamphlets and Other Contemporary Discussion, are found the data for the following bibliographical note (here, however, the publisher's name is lacking and if supplied must be looked for elsewhere):

Lambert, Henry,
Progress of Civil Service Reform in the United States. Boston: 1885.
[Fish, C. S. & P., bib.]

b. *Articles in Periodicals*

The forms for books differ somewhat from those for other classes of items. Suppose that one finds a footnote reference to an article in a periodical. As in the case of a book the footnote citation may be in abbreviated form, necessitating the examination of the magazine itself to obtain the data for such a bibliographical note as the following:

Cary, Edward,
"The Administration and Civil Service Reform." International Review, VI, 227–233 (March, 1879).

Several alternative forms are possible. One would be:
Cary, Edward,
"The Administration and Civil Service Reform," in International Review for March, 1879 (VI, 227–233).

Actually it is redundant to cite both volume and date, but with either form the page numbers are important. When alternative forms

[86] Discussion of the difference between footnotes and bibliography will be found on pages 150 f.

are permissible it is desirable to adopt one and use it consistently. (For illustrations of varying practice see *ante*, pages 54, footnote 60; 59, footnote 66; 63, footnote 70; and 89, footnote 3.)

The underscoring for *italics* in citations of periodical articles is under the name of the periodical, while the title of the article is enclosed in quotation marks. The data concerning publisher and place of publication, required in the case of books, are replaced by the citation of the volume of the magazine, the page limits of the article, and the date of the issue in which it appears. Appropriate headings, comments on the author and the character and value of the article, as well as a note showing where the item was cited, should be included in these entries just as in the case of books. A similar form may be used in citing encyclopedia articles, but between the name of the encyclopedia and the volume containing the article, the number of the edition should be given: *Encyclopedia Britannica*, 14th edn., XI, etc.

c. *Publications of Learned Societies*

Articles in the reports, annuals, and volumes of studies published by universities, historical societies, and other organizations of the learned follow in the main the rules applicable to articles in periodicals and essays in composite books. They are enclosed in quotation marks when they do not fill entire volumes:

> Bassett, John Spencer,
> "The Regulators of North Carolina (1765–1771)." American Historical Association Report for 1894, 141–212.

If there is any danger of confusing figures for dates with those for pages the abbreviation p. or pp. may be inserted between the date and pages.

> Esary, Logan,
> "The Organization of the Jacksonian Party in Indiana." Mississippi Valley Historical Association Proceedings for 1913–1914, pp. 220–243.

In these items the names of the organizations are not italicized, but only the words which are regarded as the titles of the publications which appear periodically. In calling at the delivery desk for either of these articles one could probably not use the name of the author or the title of the article, but would have to ask for the *Report* or *Proceedings* of the organization for the year in question, just as in calling for a magazine in which a desired article was printed it would be necessary to give the date of the issue or the number of the volume.

However, if an entire volume is devoted to one study, the title of the study should be underscored like a book title:

Gephart, William F.,
Transportation and Industrial Development in the Middle West (Columbia University Studies in Economics, History, and Public Law, XXXIV). New York: Columbia University, 1912.

Houston, David Franklin,
A Critical Study of Nullification in South Carolina (Harvard Historical Studies, III). New York: Longmans, Green & Co., 1898.

In these illustrations the titles of the series in which the monographs appear are italicized, as well as the titles of the monographs. In the first illustration, however, the series title does not include the name of the university, while in the second it does. For the sake of consistency due care should be taken to note and follow such variations.

The parts of a composite volume are often catalogued. This is quite likely to be true in the case of university studies, several numbers of which are often bound together. When catalogued each such study is given its distinctive number in the volume of the series when it is cited.

Sufficient information has been given on pages 97 ff. concerning the proper forms for newspapers when listed in the bibliography.

5. Taking Notes

It is not to be supposed that the bibliography must be completed before the study of subject matter and the taking of notes are begun. On the contrary, the examination of material and notetaking will naturally and most economically accompany the collection of items for the bibliography; and new items will probably be found and used down to the very moment of completing the final revision of the essay. Indeed, as knowledge of the subject grows the perspective will improve and the quest for material needed to make the study complete will be more intelligently directed. The ability to discriminate between the relevant and the irrelevant in the tentative bibliography will also sharpen so that the final form may be prepared with good judgment.

a. *What to Take and How to Take It*

During the process of becoming familiar with the background history which serves as a setting for the theme, one chief purpose of reading is to make sure of the knowledge which is a part of the preliminary equipment for the special undertaking. Any notes which may be taken at this stage are mainly auxiliary to this purpose. The background facts may be obtained from secondary treatises, and as far as notes of dates, outlines of events, or other matter will aid the memory they should be taken. But it is assumed that the reader of an essay, as well as the writer, is acquainted with the general facts set forth in standard secondary treatises, and the writer will owe him no apology for treating such data as a common stock of knowledge.

To illustrate: while reading Sparks, *National Development*, one might, to aid the memory, make a memorandum of the date of President Arthur's accession; but in writing on "President Arthur and Civil Service Reform" it would be absurd to cite Sparks, or anyone else, as authority for this date.

It does not follow that a general history is never to be cited. It is quite possible that the writer of such a work expresses an opinion upon some phase of the subject under investigation. An opinion or judgment of such an author is not a background fact, but a specific item, which the monograph writer may wish to contrast or compare with the conclusions of other writers, not excepting himself. Such use is a part of the critical process. In case of such use, a citation of the place where the expression of opinion occurs will have to be given. In other words, facts relating to one's particular subject must be dealt with, both in taking notes and in writing the study, quite differently from background facts.

The distinction between these two classes of data should be kept constantly in mind, in order that proper notes may be made of those facts or statements for which the authority or source must be cited when the essay is written. This is not always easy, because there are facts which serve as links between the general and the special, and partake of the nature of both; and it is often difficult to decide how to treat them. The passage of the Pendleton Act is a well known fact of general history, and at the same time it is an outstanding fact in the history of civil service reform under Arthur. Should the dates of passage of the bill by House and Senate be regarded as general or specific facts? Only common sense can answer such questions. If a writer decides to cite authority in a matter of this kind, he should cite the best, *i.e.*, the record of the proceedings in Congress, rather than a general history.

The application of these reflections to the question of notetaking is that facts which pertain to the particular theme, as distinguished from those of general history, should be made note of and filed in the form in which they will be most useful when the investigator begins to write.

Starting with background reading, one proceeds to works relating more specifically to one's theme, selecting first those which appear most valuable for the purpose, and turning more and more to sources as one becomes aware of the phases of the theme which permit or demand original treatment.

What should be taken in notes depends very greatly upon the use to which it is anticipated the matter will be put. In practice the chief difficulty is to anticipate the use with accuracy; it may be but vaguely defined at the outset, and as it becomes clearer it may show that the earlier notes are not in satisfactory form. During the early stages of an investigation, it often happens that the notes taken are too voluminous. The fear of omitting something which may be needed later is quite likely to produce this result. This is perhaps better than the mistake of failing to note something which is afterwards found to be essential. Both errors are wasteful of time and should be avoided as far as possible.

A warning is not out of place against the danger of allowing one's attention to be distracted by interesting items not related to one's theme. The novice who engages in the examination of old newspapers is peculiarly susceptible to this temptation, and unless he steels himself against it, he is likely to discover that he has wasted much precious time. Another golden mean which must be assiduously sought is the course which runs between too great a dependence upon the memory, on the one hand, and the taking of unnecessarily full notes on the other.

Like the reporter's scent for news, the historian's instinct for data really pertinent to his study develops through use. The beginner will often discover that the notes which he took in the earlier stages of a study must be recast, supplemented, or boiled down. This labor will be minimized if the loose-leaf system, as explained below, is used, and a separate slip made for each item.

While the use expected to be made of the matter is the best guide in taking notes, the character of the document from which they are taken has something to do with their form. Presumably few if any are needed on background reading. A monograph on a topic closely related to that in hand may require an abstract, in which conclusions, points of view, and evidence especially stressed, are noted. In making such an abstract the investigator may appropriately employ any system of abbreviations or short cuts which will be intelligible to him, except where he makes actual quotations.

Only the most significant views or statements need be quoted as a rule, although it may be necessary sometimes to copy the whole of an important document. Whenever a passage is quoted it must be inclosed in quotation marks and the utmost pains must be taken to reproduce *exactly* the words, spelling, punctuation, capitalization, etc., of the original. If there are errors, the investigator must not correct them, but should indicate that he has followed the original by inserting in brackets, immediately following the error, the Latin word *sic*, thus: [sic]. Brackets should be used in every case where one interpolates words of one's own within quotations.

There is frequent need of interpolations, as an expression may occur in the quotation which refers to something which precedes the quoted words in the original, and would not be intelligible without explanatory comment. Suppose that one wishes to quote a passage concerning Washington's military leadership and his name does not appear in the part quoted. In such a case the name should be supplied in the following way: "This great captain [George Washington] was one of the ablest generals of the eighteenth century." *Do not make the mistake of using parentheses ( ) instead of brackets* [] *for this purpose.* Words in parentheses are likely to be mistaken for part of the quotation.

If it is desired to omit certain words within a quoted passage, an omission is indicated by three periods at the point where the words are left out. If the words would have ended a sentence, the omission is indicated by four periods, thus. . . .

These suggestions about quoted passages are equally applicable in notetaking and in using quotations in the essay. If not heeded when notes are taken, there will be doubt when the moment comes to use the quotation, and time will be wasted in referring to the source to check the accuracy of the copy.

Returning to the relation between the character of a document and the notes to be taken: an abstract of the whole may be needed, with an exact quotation of the central part. Speeches and court decisions may usually be handled in this way. Similarly, in the case of a bill or statute, one section may contain all that need be copied verbatim, the other sections being designated merely by captions indicating their nature. It is almost impossible, however, to paraphrase statements made in technical language, such as is used in laws, constitutions, and court decisions, without losing some of the essential meaning or doing violence to it. The further caution is needed that especial care must be taken, in all cases where passages are quoted, not to divorce them from their context in such a way that they will seem to mean what the document as a whole, or its author, does not mean. The abstract, condensation, or quotation must be so made that the meaning of the original is preserved with exactitude.

In making abstracts, condensations, or summaries, comments often occur to the student which he desires to jot down at the proper point in the notes. Care is needed to distinguish these comments from the notes on what has been read. Perhaps the best device for effecting this is to form the habit of inclosing one's own comment in brackets, just as if the notes consisted entirely of quoted matter.

A type of notetaking which presents especial difficulty to the novice is that in which numerous speeches are made on the same subject, as for example in a congressional debate on a matter of great public interest, such as the Compromise of 1850. The mere mass of matter is often almost terrifying, because of the time that would be required to sift it carefully. It is usually not very difficult to discover the few chief speakers on each side, and it is generally true that the other speakers add very little to the arguments of these leaders. This fact makes it feasible to examine a few speeches intensively, giving the rest only a cursory inspection to make sure that nothing of significance is overlooked. This method may be adapted to many kinds of investigation where the mass of material seems, at first glance, to be ominously large.

When one has a definite idea of the use which will be made of the notes on a book, monograph, article, or speech, they may be broken into convenient units for distribution in the appropriate topical divisions of the note file. This is made possible by the use of the system described in the following section.

b. *The Loose-Leaf System*

It is a fundamental rule of modern practice that each item or note must be entered on a separate slip of paper. The older historians were hampered by lack of this simple mechanical device. When George Bancroft began to take notes more than a century ago, preparatory to writing his *History of the United States*, he could think of no better plan for organizing them than to provide himself with a number of bound volumes of blank paper, one for each year, with a page for each day. As he read he entered his notes of events on the pages corresponding to the dates of their occurrence, thus giving a chronological arrangement to the whole mass of notes. The limitations of this method, and the burden it threw on his powers of memory, account for some of the faults of his *History*; yet for many decades writers continued to record notes in bound books, laboriously compiling indexes when the notetaking was completed as the only means by which all notes bearing on the same topics could be brought into view for dealing with the topics. When during the 1880's some of the leading libraries discarded the printed and bound catalogues which made impossible the insertion of accessions in their proper alphabetical position, and adopted instead the present type of card catalogue, which can easily be kept up to date, historical writers, as well as others, promptly adapted the new method to their needs, and thus the loose-leaf system came into use for notetaking.

Briefly stated, the merit of the method consists in the facility with which notes taken at random are brought into actual physical contact. The full benefits of the system will not be obtained unless one is skillful in breaking notes into the convenient units referred to in the preceding section. To say that only one item should be entered on a slip is easy, but it is not so easy to determine what one item is. The terms "unit" and "item" as used here have the same meaning, but the practical question remains, whether an abstract of a book, speech, or document is one item or many. It can only be answered that the same abstract may, for one purpose, be a single item, while for another purpose it may be two or more. A note taken while the prospective use is still uncertain will often include several items, as will be judged later, so that parts may have to be recopied and distributed in the appropriate places, or cross-reference slips will have to be made and put in each of these places, referring to the inclusive item.

c. *Headings and Citations*

When bibliography notes were being considered, allusion was made to the variety of choices in the matter of the sizes and kinds of cards or slips for use in notetaking. It was then suggested that there were advantages in using the same kind of paper for both bibliography and notes, since both could then be filed in the same cabinet. It cannot be expected that workers will agree in their preferences in such matters, and there is no need of agreement. Each person must determine his preference by his own experiments.

The present writer uses a filing cabinet with drawers wide and deep enough to receive an ordinary sheet of typewriter paper (8½ x 11 inches)—the same type of cabinet that is used in business offices for filing correspondence. This size affords room for the bodily insertion of manuscripts on full-sized sheets, pamphlets, and reprints or articles from journals. For notetaking, however, he uses half-size sheets (5½ x 8½). These are large enough to hold a good many words, and at the same time cheap enough to allow one to write only a line or two on a sheet without the pricks of conscience due to wastefulness.

Whatever size sheets are chosen, certain data are essential on every note. The notes proper, consisting of abstracts or quotations or both, may run over on to a second page or more. But in addition to the notes there must always be given: (1) an exact citation of the source whence they were taken; and (2) a heading showing the contents of the note and affording a clue to the filing of the slip.

If more than one sheet is required for the note, the heading should be repeated in brief form at the top of each and the page or sheet numbered. There is no hard and fast rule as to where the citation shall be placed on the slip, but trouble will result if it is omitted entirely. The habit should be formed promptly of recording it with meticulous care. For this reason it is a good practice to place it on the sheet before anything else is written. The heading can be added whenever a suitable wording is thought of. The form of citation may be as brief as is consistent with positive identification of the source of the information; and the citation should be repeated on the following sheets if more than one is required for the item. Otherwise, if a sheet becomes misplaced, difficulty may be experienced in replacing it properly.

It frequently happens that a running summary of several pages of a book can be placed on a series of pages of notes. It is well in that case to indicate the point in the notes at which the successive pages of the original begin by inclosing the page numbers in brackets at the point in the notes just preceding the abstract for that page. This makes it always possible to cite the exact page of the authority when making a citation during the process of writing.

These points may now be illustrated by the following form:

President Hayes and Civil Service
Sparks, Nat. Dev., 154–

Hayes championed reform from beginning of term. [155] Did not wait for Cong. to approp. money for C. S. Commission, but forbade govt. officials to levy camp. assess. [156] In this way aroused wrath of the politicians. [157] Reappointed James, reformer,

Pres. Hayes & C. S.–2.
Sparks.

as N. Y. postmaster. [158] Removed head of N. Y. customs office. [159] Led to contest with Stalwarts.

d. *Filing Notes: Relation to Outline*

Loose-leaf notes, if skillfully broken into units and given proper headings, are self-indexing and easily filed according to subject. The obsolete method of using a bound book scattered notes on the same matter, but the loose-leaf system brings them together. As knowledge of the subject under investigation grows, its divisions and subdivisions should rise above the mental horizon and form at the same time a tentative outline for writing the essay and a guide to the probable use to be made of each new fact added to the notes. This growing perception of the probable use to be made of the items suggests, as has been said, the proper units into which notes should be broken, and the net result of the whole process is that the scheme of notetaking and filing gradually approximates the outline which the writer will use as a guide in composing the essay. If, when he begins to write, his notes are arranged in the file in conformity with the outline of the essay, the mechanics of his procedure may be said to approximate perfection.

If the sheets used for notes are 5½ x 8½ inches, it will be difficult to use guide cards in the filing cabinet. A convenient substitute will be found in the manila folders in common use in business office letter files. One edge of a folder of this kind stands a little higher than the other when in place in the cabinet, thus giving space for words describing the contents where they will be visible. The bibliography slips, arranged in groups according to the subdivisions, with the items in each group in alphabetical order, may be placed in the first folder of the file, and other folders as needed may be used for the notes pertaining to each main division of the subject. An elaborate study may require separate folders for subdivisions, with some system of notation to distinguish the subordinate divisions from the main ones. It is not necessary to repeat the main headings on every folder. If they are numbered I, II, etc., the continuation is sufficiently indicated by repeating these numerals with the proper designation of the subdivisions:

I. The Master's Essay
    1. The Prospective Teacher. . . .
I.
    2. Choosing a Subject
I.
    3. Finding Material
        a. The Tentative Bibliography

It will now be apparent that while in the bibliography a number of articles by the same writer, published in the same or different magazines, would be brought together, the *notes* on each article would be distributed in the file according to the topic dealt with in each article. The plan places the data for each topic just where it will best serve the writer's purpose.

The scheme of filing may be developed indefinitely and adapted to the needs of the student who continues his activity as a writer or teacher of history. A course of lectures may be worked out and notes in any quantity may be filed exactly in the order in which the lectures are to be given. As notes are added the outline can be expanded so that both may always be exactly coordinated with the lectures.

6. Writing the Essay

a. *The Working Outline*

By the time an investigator has collected his material his outline should have begun to take shape in his mind. The evolution of the outline should keep pace with the gathering of data, and with the completion of this process the arrangement of the data should have been brought into conformity with the plan of presentation. Before beginning to write it is advisable to set down the outline in black and white. It will then serve as a guide for writing and in final form will become the table of contents of the finished study. Moreover, working out the outline will encourage a thoughtful review of the whole body of data, and this should yield the following results: (1) mastery of the data; (2) perception of the relation of parts to the theme as a whole; (3) certainty that sound conclusions have been reached on all problems; (4) clear definition of objectives. No writer should put pen to paper until he knows what he can do with his material, and the suggested review and outline are essential preliminaries to rapid and accurate writing. With such preparation the effort at expression in suitable words will help to clarify ideas still further.

As an analysis of the proposed contents of the text, the working outline should be divided into main and subordinate parts. Each main division should possess either a topical or chronological unity of its own, and the subordinate ones should form a logical outline of the topic covered in that portion of the study to which they belong. The plan of the outline must be determined by the nature of the materials revealed by this review, and in turn the materials should be given their final arrangement, in the order of the divisions of the outline. Further changes in the outline and in the arrangement of the data may result from the new insight which should come with the effort to present the theme, and hence the final table of contents may show some improvement over the working outline.

b. *The Preliminary Draft*

If these suggestions are followed, the step from outline to first draft should be an easy one. The outline may be regarded as a skeleton and the notes as the flesh. The preliminary draft should put flesh on the bones, and to do this a writing out of the essentials of the matter in the notes is required.

Even a first draft should be more than a series of quotations. The novice sometimes misconceives the task of composition as a mere putting together of quoted passages, as beads are strung. For the most part, careful paraphrases are preferable to long quotations. The use of the gist of the statements of others in the student's own words permits him to display his powers of interpretation, criticism, and presentation to better advantage, and is conducive to a more flexible and graceful style. His own words are needed especially to introduce quotations; to state the substance of long passages from sources or other writers, so that the words actually quoted may be limited to those containing the pith of the passage; to explain quoted passages; and to bridge over gracefully from one quotation, topic, or paragraph to another.

When quotations are used an effort should be made to vary introductory phrases. If one is preceded by the words "Said he": the next time a phrase may be interjected at the first natural break in the quoted words, thus: "I shall never believe," wrote Washington, "that . . .," etc. A quotation of six lines or more is often printed in smaller type and shorter lines than the text, and when so printed the quotation marks may be omitted.[87] On the typewriter a similar effect can be produced by using double spacing for the text and single spacing for the quoted passage. The contrast between text and quotation is emphasized by slightly shortening the quoted lines. The words used to introduce the quotation should be a part of the paragraph which precedes it.

To compose an essay largely of quotations would be equivalent to setting raw materials before the reader. If this only were done the writer would stand convicted of having neglected the critical work by which facts are obtained from statements and made the basis of interpretations and conclusions. Often, it is true, a scientific writer finds it desirable to exhibit some of the raw materials in order to show the critical use which has been made of them, and to show that the conclusions arrived at are valid. But he must not stop with a display of the raw materials without such use of them, leaving the critical work and conclusions to be made by the reader.

The writer should make a conscious and deliberate effort to free his own statements from all the influences—prejudice, ignorance,

[87] See *ante* pages 54 ff. and 72 for illustrations.

negligence, emotion, excitement, etc.—which he has learned to regard as tending to warp the statements which compose his raw material: *he must apply to his own statements the same critical tests which he has practiced in examining his sources.*

The primary purpose of the preliminary draft is to mobilize every essential of narration, exposition, argument, and conclusion fully, clearly, and accurately. Into the draft should be brought all of the facts which are to enter into the completed essay. It must be remembered that facts are of various kinds or orders. An event is a fact of one kind. If an opinion or belief has been held, whether it is true or false, *that it has been held* is a fact on a different level. Much history has been made by the fact that people held false beliefs. The presidential election of 1828 was probably decided by the erroneous conviction of many voters that Adams had gained office in 1825 by means of a bargain with Clay. Propaganda of any kind should be recognized for what it is, and must be distinguished from arguments based on evidence.

An institution is a fact; a relationship between facts is a fact. Sound generalizations or conclusions are facts. The writer who confines his production to a simple narrative of events, void of interpretations based on the perception of relationships, turns out a barren story, mere annals or chronicles. The analysis of Van Buren's part in the presidential election of 1824–1825 exemplifies in a small way how data should be handled for interpretative history.[88] Such history while more difficult to write and proportionately liable to error when attempted by a second-rater, is also much more worth while if the writer has real ability.

While making this first draft little heed need be paid to literary quality. It is easy for persons with strong literary feeling to waste time in polishing the first few paragraphs, but this temptation should be resisted. When the substance has been committed to writing a revision of the literary form will be possible with a minimum of effort. If the writer is a graduate student, his work should not be submitted for criticism until he has given it the final literary touches —unless he is prepared to be misjudged, or unless his supervisor wishes to examine the draft solely with reference to content. Especially should the adviser not be asked to read each chapter separately. The student should do his best to turn out a completed piece of work by independent effort.

[88] See *ante*, pp. 76–82.

It is essential to develop the draft with careful attention to the logical sequence of ideas and topics. It is helpful to remember also that in presenting matter to readers one should proceed from what they may be presumed to know to that which the essay is supposed to add to their knowledge. In other words, a writer of history must give his special theme its proper setting, not merely by a formal introduction at the beginning of the book, but at every stage where it is required for clearness and symmetry.

c. *Forms*

The rules governing the forms employed in writing history do not fall in that immutable class to which the laws of the Medes and Persians were alleged to belong. In fact, there is considerable variation in the practice of writers, as any one may discover by the most superficial observation. It would be convenient if writers of history could agree on a uniform code of rules. In the absence of such agreement every one is at liberty to pursue his own course, provided only that his practice is reasonable, consistent, and effective.

Nevertheless it is good judgment for beginners to follow the forms used by the members of the historical fraternity in the United States as shown by their publications, such as *The American Historical Review* and *The Mississippi Valley Historical Review*. These usages have won their way as the result of the experience of earlier writers. Novices are sometimes disturbed by discovering that the leading American historians of the nineteenth century did not use the present forms. There are still competent scholars who do not. The student's patience may be less severely taxed if he can see that there is a good reason for each requirement of the current code or any defensible alternative.[89]

i. FOOTNOTES: PURPOSES AND USES

As a part of the task of making the preliminary draft, the footnotes and bibliography should be put in proper form. If directions

[89] The student may find it informing to compare the practices recommended in this Manual with those shown by the footnotes in the essay on "Herbert L. Osgood," in *The Marcus W. Jernegan Essays in American Historiography*, edited by W. T. Hutchinson, and published by the University of Chicago.

Many publishers issue style books for the guidance of writers. Among the best are those put out by The Macmillan Company and the University of Chicago Press. However, publishers are usually willing to conform to the wishes of authors who have a reasonable system of their own.

already given have been followed carefully, it will now be comparatively easy to master the additional techniques.

Footnotes are used for several purposes: (1) to cite the authority for or source of statements in the text; (2) to relieve the text of matter which interferes with its flow and tends to distract the reader's attention or to lessen his interest, such as technical discussions and incidental comments;[90] (3) to cite other discussions or give additional information on topics in the text;[91] (4) for cross references;[92] (5) or for a combination of two or more of these purposes.

The first of these uses demands further explanation. It is due to the acceptance by contemporary historians of the view that a historical treatise is a scientific product. As the laboratory experiments performed by one scientist may be repeated by another as a check on the results reported, so the authorities on which the conclusions of a writer rest may be used by others to check his conclusions. The broad rule emerges that a writer should *cite his authority or source for every fact, opinion, or conclusion* (not his own) *stated in the text.*

This rule does not apply merely where the words of another are quoted. Of course the source of a quotation must be indicated; but a citation is just as necessary when words are paraphrased or only the substance given. It must be remembered that most of the data which a writer of history uses are not his at first hand, but are derived; his own opinions, conclusions, and interpretations are the only original contributions he can make.

This fundamental rule is subject to one exception: background facts, the common facts of general history which it may be assumed every intelligent reader knows, require no citations. Yet such facts should not be omitted, since to deprive the discussion of its setting mars the symmetry of the presentation. Besides many readers need to have common historical facts brought to mind in order to grasp the relations of the special study to the larger whole of general history, and to appreciate the contribution which the study makes.

While it is essential that the source of each derived statement be made clear, it is not always necessary to give a separate reference for each. Where several facts or alleged facts drawn from the same source are presented consecutively, it is permissible to cite the

[90] For illustrations see footnote on page 92 f.

[91] As is done on pages 8; 30, note 23; 31, note 26; 32, note 27; 48, note 50; 51, note 53.

[92] *Cf.* page 89, note 2.

source but once, at the conclusion of the paragraph, or series of paragraphs, if the continuity of the passage is clear to the eye.[93] If there is any room for the reader to doubt that all of the statements are from the same source, the citation should not be deferred beyond the end of the first paragraph, and additional citations should be given after each statement in the series. In such successive citations all after the first require only the word *ibid.*, with the page citation.[94] It is better to err on the side of too many citations than to give too few.

An alternative where a series of paragraphs condense a single authority is to indicate that fact in the initial note, which may read to this effect: "In this account of . . . the writer has followed So and so," with indication of the pages where the matter condensed is to be found in the work cited. Further references may then be dispensed with. A careful writer, however, will seldom be content to rely on a single account; hence occasions for notes in this blanket form should be infrequent.

It must also be remembered that the purpose of a citation is to indicate the source to which the writer is *indebted*, whether it be the primary source or a secondary account. If the writer gets data from an author who quotes a document or another writer, the authority is the work *consulted*, not the one to which it refers. The dangers of secondhand information have been discussed in the section on criticism. Scholarly work demands firsthand use of sources. But if a secondary writer quotes a source and the investigator relies on the secondary writer for his knowledge, he takes the risk of error and should be honest enough to admit it. It is a species of dishonesty to cite a source known only through a secondary work without indicating that fact in the citation.

It should be obvious that to cite a secondary statement based on a particular source in addition to citing the source does not add to the weight of evidence unless the secondary statement includes a judgment or interpretation. In such a case the relationship should be made clear. Nor does the citation of two or more secondary statements of an alleged fact derived from the same source add to the probability of its truthfulness or strengthen a statement in the text which repeats it. Such citations are not uncommon in the work of novices and show a lack of understanding of the principles of

[93] For examples see p. 46, note 45; 77, note 78.
[94] See p. 47, notes 46, 47, 48, 49.

criticism. Of course the *comments* of secondary writers may be important.[95]

If a magazine article has been used, the article, not the magazine, is the authority; the latter is mentioned only to show where the article may be found. If a book used belongs in a series, the authority is the particular volume, not the series; in fact, the authority is the particular statement. This rule is often disregarded. In a similar way a collection of source material cannot be an authority. For a specific statement a writer's authority is never a collection, but some particular document reprinted in it, such as a letter or speech by an indicated author. In a citation the document should be both identified and located by citation of volume and page of the collection.

ii. ILLUSTRATIONS OF USAGE

The text and footnotes on the preceding pages are intended to supply illustrations of usage. They should be examined in connection with the following explanations:

1. The index figures used in the text to call attention to footnotes should be elevated slightly above the type line, both when printed and when typewritten. The corresponding figures in the footnotes should be elevated in the same way and set slightly to the right of the margin of the page, with no space between the figures and the words which follow. As an alternative typed notes are sometimes given thus: (1), (2), etc.

2. Notes should be numbered consecutively throughout each chapter or main division, beginning with 1 in each, unless the total number in the study is less than 100, in which case the numbering may run consecutively through the entire work. Alternative uses are (1) to make the page the unit for numbering; (2) to place the notes at the end of each chapter instead of at the foot of the page; (3) to place them at the end of the book, grouped by chapters and numbered from 1 for each chapter. This last plan has the advantage of keeping the text page free, but invites neglect of the notes by the reader.

3. The figures for footnote numbers should never be placed at the beginning of a paragraph, title, sentence, or quoted passage. The normal position is at the close of the sentence which contains the statement requiring a citation. If the sentence requires more than one, the figures should be placed at the appropriate points within

[95] See p. 27, note 16.

the sentence, unless the reference cites two or more authorities for the same statement. In that case they should be placed in one footnote with a semicolon to separate them.

4. In footnotes the number of a volume should be given in capital roman numerals and page numbers in Arabic figures. Lower case roman numerals should be used in citing pages of the preliminary portions of books, if they are used, as is the case in this Manual.

5. The words *volume* and *page* and their abbreviations may be omitted if the foregoing directions are observed, except in cases where the figures might be misunderstood to stand for something else. A reference to a chapter number usually requires the use of the abbreviation chap. or ch., since the numerals following might otherwise be mistaken for volume or page references. Chapter numbers are usually given in capital roman numerals, but sometimes in Arabic.

6. If a treatise is without a bibliography, the bibliographical data should be given in the first footnote in which a reference is made to a work. To illustrate: certain notes on preceding pages have been drawn in the form which would be proper if the Manual contained no bibliography. One example is the reference to Bourne's *Teaching of History.*[96] The footnote with the bibliographical matter appears in this form:

> Henry E. Bourne, *The Teaching of History and Civics* (New York: Longmans, Green and Company, 1903), 35, footnote 1.

However, the form for this book in a bibliography would be:

> Bourne, Henry E., *The Teaching of History and Civics.* New York: Longmans, Green and Company, 1903;

and in that case the footnote would read:

> Henry E. Bourne, *The Teaching of History and Civics,* 35, footnote 1.

The family name comes first in the bibliographical form because entries in the bibliography are given in alphabetical order; no such reason applies to a footnote. Bibliographical matter is really grafted on a footnote, the note's purpose being to support a specific statement by a particular citation. On the other hand, the purpose of a bibliography is to describe a work in its entirety. It gives its description once for all, while the notes refer to each authority as often as

[96] *Supra,* page 27.

may be necessary—that is, every time its support is needed for a statement. The two functions do not naturally blend; hence an essay should always contain a formal bibliography, and matter of that kind should be kept out of the notes. If an article is to be published in a periodical, however, the bibliography must usually be dispensed with and data of that kind must be placed in the footnotes.

7. After a footnote has given the information about a work cited—name of author, title, and, if there is no formal bibliography, the necessary data of that kind—there are two ways to avoid repeating such detail in later citations. If the *next citation* is to the same work, *ibid.* (abbreviated form of the Latin *ibidem*, meaning *the same*) may be used. Standing alone it takes the place of author's name, title of book, and volume and page numbers; in fact it is the equivalent of ditto marks. If a different volume or page is intended, the numerals for these must follow *ibid.*

Since *ibid.* always refers to the work last cited, its use a page or more later would require turning back to identify it. To avoid both turning back and the necessity of repeating the former note in full, a shortened form of title may be used instead of *ibid.*, following the author's family name. Even so *ibid.* should be used instead of the shortened form for an immediately following citation of the same work. If a work is to be cited frequently, the short form to be used thereafter should be explained in the first footnote citing the work.[97]

8. A short form should contain the key words of the title. This requires a little thought. The title of the present Manual could not appropriately be shortened to Hockett, *Historical Writing*, although both of these words are in it. *Critical Method in Historical Research* would be better, or even *Critical Method.* Hockett, *op. cit.*, would also be acceptable if the rules stated below are observed. If no other work by the same writer was cited the reference could be reduced to Hockett, followed by the page citation. The form chosen should be adhered to.

When a work has once been cited and other references have intervened before it is referred to again, *op. cit.* (Latin *opere citato—in the work cited*) may be used instead of the title. The author's name must be repeated in this case, since without it the "work cited" could not be identified. Do not use *op. cit.* where *ibid.* should be employed.

[97] For examples see pp. 29, note 21; 35, note 32; 37, note 36.

One should not use a short title for a work at one time and *op. cit.* for the same work at another time. One form or the other should be used consistently. However, the frequent use of *op. cit.* smacks of pedantry, especially if the same work is constantly referred to. Shortened titles are generally preferable; indeed, some writers think that it is sufficient to use merely the author's name in all citations after the first. But neither this informal practice nor *op. cit.* has the flexibility of the shortened form. An author may have written more than one book, and if more than one of them is referred to, neither *op. cit.* nor the author's name, or both, will indicate which is intended in a particular citation.

9. If a writer's name is introduced into the text it need not be repeated in the note. Likewise if the title of a book is given in the text it need not be repeated in the note.[98] However, the frequent use of names of authors and titles of books in the text is to be deprecated. Citations belong in the notes, unless the name of the author or the title is an essential part of the discussion. If the identity of the authority is of no particular consequence to the reader it may be better to use a vague phrase in the text, such as "one author holds," or "according to a prominent authority," thus emphasizing the thought which is being presented to the reader and avoiding distracting his attention by the introduction of what is for him an irrelevant fact. It is better still, as far as possible, to tell the story in the text without intruding the thought of authorities, leaving that matter for the footnotes.

10. When a passage is quoted in a footnote the citation for it should be placed after the quoted words.[99] When a work not listed in the bibliography is cited in a footnote with bibliographical data included, such data should be interpolated in parentheses between the title of the volume and the page figures.[100] If the footnote is purely bibliographical and is without volume or page references, the marks of parenthesis may be omitted.[101] The form is then substantially what it would be in a bibliography except that the author's given name precedes the family name.[102]

11. The name of an author should not be used in the possessive case when preceding the title in a footnote. This rule does not hold for the text.[103]

12. A citation of an article followed immediately by a second

[98] See pages 102, note 15; 109, note 42; 110, note 45.
[99] See p. 27, note 16.
[100] See *ibid.* [101] See p. 150, paragraph 6. [102] See *ibid.*
[103] See p. 88, note 1; *cf.* 102. Larned's *Literature*.

citation of the same article calls for the use of *ibid.* in the second citation. If other citations intervene, *loc. cit.* (Latin *loco citato, in the place cited*) is used instead of *op. cit.* when the article is again mentioned. This usage makes a convenient distinction between the form for citing magazine articles and that for citing books. The writer's name must be repeated when *loc. cit.* is used.[104]

13. Some usages of which the text and notes of the Manual do not afford examples remain to be explained. If a writer uses information which another author has drawn from a newspaper which he cites, the note of the former gives credit to his secondary authority, but may mention the latter's source of information, thus:

> Dewey, op. cit., 307, citing Public Opinion, issue of October 17, 1895.

The form of this note may be reversed so that it will read: *Public Opinion*, October 17, 1895, cited by Dewey, *op. cit.*, 307. These forms should not be regarded as interchangeable; that is, the writer should adopt one or the other and adhere to it. Either means that he has not examined the issue of *Public Opinion*, but has relied on Dewey. If the newspaper is consulted the secondary reference drops out. Page and column references are useful in citing newspapers but are commonly omitted. Editorials or other special classes of items in newspapers should be distinguished thus:

> Editorial in New York Evening Post, Jan. 17, 1907.
> Associated Press Dispatch, Chicago Tribune, Aug. 11, 1914.

If a statement rests upon a document contained in a collection, the document should be cited, not merely the collection. A subsequent citation follows the form for a periodical article, *ibid.* or *loc. cit.* being used depending on whether there has been an intermediate citation:

> Letter of George Washington to Alexander Hamilton, July 10, 1787, in Farrand, Records, III, 56–57.
> Hamilton to King, Aug. 28, 1787, Ibid., 75.
> Washington, loc. cit.

If the name of the letter writer is brought into the text it need not be repeated in the note. Thus if the text reads: "'Influence is no

[104] See p. 35, note 32, and *cf.* p. 37, note 37; below, references to Washington's letter.

government,' said Washington, commenting on the failure of the Articles of Confederation," the footnote should read:

> Letter to Henry Lee, October 31, 1786. W. C. Ford, *The Writings of George Washington*, XI, 76 *et seq.*

References to books which belong in series should cite the particular volume used, but its place in the series should be indicated:

> J. H. Latané, *America as a World Power, 1897–1907* (volume XXV of *The American Nation*, ed. by A. B. Hart), 232.

An essay in a composite volume is cited like a periodical article.[a] A decision of the Supreme Court should be cited by name of the case and its location in the reports.[bc] Proceedings in Congress are cited by giving the title of the series, as *Annals, Globe,* or *Record*; the number of the Congress and session; and the page or column numbers.[d] Examples:

> [a] Carl Becker, "Kansas." *Turner Essays in American History*, 85–111. (A comma may be used instead of the period after "Kansas," followed by the word in.)
>
> [b] Marbury *v.* Madison, 1 Cranch 137.
>
> [c] De Lima *v.* Bidwell, 182 U.S. 1.
>
> [d] *Annals of Congress*, 5 Cong., 1 sess., 75–140. (In subsequent references the title may be abbreviated to *Annals*, or *Ann. of Cong.*)

The statutes are cited without name of editor or compiler.[a] Government documents are designated in various ways. In some cases they have titles and bear the names of authors, editors, or compilers.[bc] Sometimes they carry the name of a commission, committee, department, or bureau which is in a sense the author or at least the sponsor for them. Data of these kinds should be included in the citations, just as in the case of books. In the case of well-known and much-used compilations it is not necessary to include documentary description. Some of them have plain titles. Examples:

> [a] *U. S. Stat. at Large*, I, 76–84.
>
> [b] Joseph F. Johnson, *The Canadian Banking System.* U. S. National Monetary Commission Publications, 61 Cong., 2 sess., *Sen. Doc. 583.*
>
> [c] Kappler, *Indian Affairs*, I, 45.

The underscoring for italics in the title of the study of *The Canadian Banking System* indicates that it fills a whole volume in the documents. Some documents are like composite books, containing several items. If that were the case here the title of the part—"The Canadian Banking System"—would be enclosed in quotation marks as shown, and only the title of the document (*Sen. Doc.* 583) would be in italics. References to essays or articles in reports, annuals, and studies issued by learned organizations follow the same rules (see page 133 f.).

Logan Esarey, "The Organization of the Jacksonian Party in Indiana." Miss. Valley Histl. Assn. *Proceedings* for 1913–1914, pp. 220–243; W. F. Gephart, *Transportation and Industrial Development in the Middle West.* Columbia University *Studies*, XXXIV.

The citing of government publications is beset by difficulties. The first example below is a typical student effort; the second form is the correct one:

1. Brandeis Nomination, 64th Congress, 1st Session, #409 Sen. Doc., Vols. XVI–XVII, 234 (1916).
2. Subcommittee of the Committee on the Judiciary, United States Senate, *Nomination of Louis D. Brandeis.* . . . 2 vols. 64 Cong., 1 sess., *Sen. Doc. 409.*

iii. BIBLIOGRAPHY: CLASSIFICATION, FUNCTION, AND USAGE

A bibliography is a formal list of materials relating to a particular subject. In a typical treatise it is a list of the authorities, both source and secondary, cited in the footnotes. Sometimes it is extended to embrace materials not used in the treatise, in order that it may be complete for the subject. In certain kinds of writing, on the other hand, it may not include all works cited in the footnotes, but may be restricted to a particular class. (*Cf.* the present Manual.)

In a scholarly work the bibliography is often annotated; that is, each entry is followed by a comment evaluating the item with relation to the subject of the study. Annotated bibliographies are often required in the case of doctoral dissertations or essays submitted in prize competitions such as those of the American Historical Association.

The items in every bibliography should be classified; that is, they should be arranged in groups according to their character. The broad distinction between sources and secondary writings, or primary and secondary sources, as they are sometimes called, although often used as the basis of classification, is not entirely satisfactory, if there is no further segregation of items. Probably no two bibliographies can be classified on exactly the same plan, because the character of the materials and their grouping varies with the subject and purpose. The form here submitted may be taken as a model in a general way, subject to such modification as may be needed to adapt it to each specific study:

1. Manuscript Materials.
2. Government Publications:
    a. Federal.
    b. State.
    c. Local.
3. Newspapers.
4. Biographies, Memoirs, and Writings of Public Men.
5. Other Primary Sources.
6. General Histories.
7. Special Monographs.
8. Articles and Essays in Periodicals, Annuals, and Publications of Learned Societies.
9. Miscellaneous.

The function of the bibliography, as has already been explained in part, should be clearly distinguished from that of the footnotes. The latter are for citing the authority or source for specific statements; they designate the exact place where the utterance is to be found. The former *describes the works* in which the data cited in footnotes are to be found. Thus a footnote tells the reader that a particular statement by Thomas Jefferson was made in a letter written to John Adams on a certain day, and that this letter is published in a certain volume of a certain edition of Jefferson's writings, and on a certain page. A bibliography is not concerned with this letter, nor with any particular page or volume of Jefferson's works, even though there be but one citation of his works in the entire essay. Its purpose is to inform the reader that the edition of the works of Jefferson which has been cited was edited by So-and-so, and published in so many volumes, by such and such a publisher, in such and such a place, in certain years.

The footnotes and bibliography are thus supplementary; the reader who desires to look up a reference which he finds in a footnote must turn to the bibliography to find the full description of the work in which the letter or document is printed.

The relations between footnotes and bibliography, and the importance of the information which each supplies, may be perceived more clearly when it is realized that there is often more than one edition of a work—there are, for example, several editions of the writings of Jefferson. If a footnote merely mentioned a letter of Jefferson to Adams under a certain date, without referring to the edition in which the version used is printed, the reader would have difficulty in finding the letter. It might not be included at all in the edition first examined; or if found there, might not be in the identical form used by the person citing it. If the footnote specifies the edition, however, the reader can readily determine what text of a document or letter has been used. Editors of former days sometimes took liberties with the text of documents. Jared Sparks, for instance, corrected Washington's spelling and grammar in editing his works, so that the same documents often have somewhat different readings in the editions of Washington's writings edited by him and by Worthington C. Ford at a later time.

The data needed for each entry in the bibliography are presumed to have been gathered during the early stages of work as advised on preceding pages of this Manual, where it has also been said that some of the data needed for books are not required for that part of the bibliography which lists periodical literature.[105] This is because the publishers and places of publication of current journals are supposed to be generally known or at least easily ascertainable; and also because each article is in a sense a separate work. A bibliography accordingly should list each article separately, under the author's name, with an indication of the issue of the publication in which it is printed. To enter in the bibliography, in lieu of separate article entries, such a description of a magazine as is given of a book, effectually conceals the authorities really used, so far as they are contained in the issues of that journal. Only by thumbing through footnotes in such a case could the reader ascertain the authors and titles of the articles and the issues in which they are to be found. One main purpose of a bibliography is to obviate the necessity of such labor. In such an essay as we are considering the bibliography entry for an article practically duplicates the footnote giving the first citation of it, both in form and substance.

It is not easy to avoid this repetition in writings of this class, but in some other types it is possible to evade these complications by inserting at the outset a footnote reading to the following effect: In the footnotes throughout this volume the titles of books are printed

[105] See *ante*, pp. 130–134.

in *italics*, while titles of articles and essays in magazines and composite books are placed in quotation marks. To avoid repetition the place and date of publication of books and the volumes and pages of magazines, etc., in which articles and essays are to be found, as well as full titles, are given only in the bibliography at the end of the volume. All entries in this bibliography are arranged alphabetically under the names of authors or editors.[106]

The reasoning which calls for the listing of articles separately does not require separate listing of documents in a collection, such as Farrand's *Records of the Federal Convention.* The proper place for specifying particular documents is the footnotes.

Bibliographical entries of essays in annuals, university studies, composite books, and similar volumes resemble book entries in some ways and article entries in others. Titles are italicized or quoted according to the principles which have been explained, and volume citations are required (page citations also, where the study does not fill the volume), as for periodical articles.[107] In addition, since such volumes have definite places and dates of publication which are not so likely to be known as those of journals, they must be given as in book entries.

Volumes forming part of a series are handled in various ways. In both footnotes and bibliography the volume cited should be described in its relation to the series.[108] If the volumes of a series taken together form a whole, as in *The American Nation,* the bibliography should contain in addition a description of the series.[109] If, on the other hand, a single volume is an independent study published in a series like the *Harvard Historical Studies,* there need be no series entry in the bibliography, but the place and date of publication and publisher's name should be given for the individual volume, as well as its series identification.[110]

Unlike periodical articles, newspaper items are not listed separately in the bibliography, but are treated like individual items in a collection of documents. That is, the newspaper file is described, either *in toto* or for the years for which it proved useful. Often the division of the bibliography devoted to newspapers merely lists them by name with any necessary indications of the town or state where published. The same rule holds for speeches and other matter

[106] *Cf.* Hockett, *Constitutional History,* II, 3, f.n. 1.

[107] See *ante,* p. 131 f.

[108] For the form of the footnote see *ibid.*

[109] See *ibid.*

[110] For illustrations see p. 131.

in the records of the proceedings of Congress; that is, the separate items are not listed, but the works as a whole are described in the bibliography.

The proper forms to be used in the bibliography for Government publications is sometimes a perplexing question. There can hardly be said to be a generally accepted plan. The order of entry in the library catalogue may suggest a feasible arrangement; that is, the separate items may be entered under the department, bureau, or division which issues them. When the publication bears the name of an author, editor, compiler, commission, or committee, such name gives a basis for alphabetical arrangement within the special group of items. If the publication bears a document number, that is often included in the bibliography; but it is usually omitted in the case of much-used compilations; in these there are often Plain Title editions, apart from the documentary series.

Within each division of the bibliography the entries should be arranged alphabetically according to author, editor, or compiler. It is sometimes a puzzle to know whether the writings of a public man should be entered under his own name or that of the editor of the compilation. Should Jefferson's *Writings*, for instance, be placed under J or F (Worthington C. Ford being the editor)? One finds both forms used. It is perhaps wise in such cases to ask where a reader is most likely to look for the entry and place it there. Since the name of the editor is less likely to be known than that of the person whose writings are in question, the name of the latter should probably determine the position of the entry in most cases.

When more than one edition of the writings of a public man is listed in a bibliography the following form is one of the best: [111]

Under the names of the respective editors give the full bibliographical description of the edition.[112]

If the title of one edition was *Works of* instead of *Writings of*, the first entry should take the form: Johnson, John, *Works of*. See John Smith, editor; *Writings of*. See John Jones, editor.

If an author is listed more than once in the same division of the bibliography, the initial of the first significant word in the titles of his works determines the alphabetical precedence.[113]

[111] Jefferson, Thomas, *Writings of*. See P. L. Lord, editor, and H. A. Washington, editor.

[112] Ford, Paul Leicester, ed., *The Writings of Thomas Jefferson*. 10 vols. New York: 1892–1899.

[113] For an example see entries under Earl G. Swem (see Index for pages).

No very helpful suggestions can be given for arranging manuscript entries. They are best designated according to the manner in which they are stored or arranged in the depository which holds them. If one has occasion to use such collections, the depository's system of designations must be followed. This system may be described in some publication, or it may be illustrated in the bibliography of some monograph based on the collection. It is unlikely that the candidate for the master's degree will have much need to use manuscript collections.

d. *The Final Revision*

i. PARTS OF A FINISHED ESSAY

A completed study should include the following parts in the order given: (1) Title Page; (2) Preface; (3) Table of Contents; (4) Introduction; (5) Main Text in chapters or numbered subdivisions; (6) Bibliography. To these are often added a Dedication following the title page, and an Appendix and Index in the final pages.

The discussion of the making of a preliminary draft has centered around items (3), (5), and (6). In the process of drafting, the working outline has developed into a Table of Contents; the Main Text, including the footnotes, has been given rough form; and the Bibliography has been classified and perhaps annotated. Before the final revision is begun parts (1), (2), and (4) should be added, and possibly a Dedication, Appendix, and other parts. If the production is to have an Index it must be supplied last of all so that page numbers may be inserted.

If the study is the essay for a master's degree, Title Page and general make-up must conform to specifications, which may vary somewhat from school to school. They are obtainable from the graduate-school office.

A dedication is in doubtful taste; if used at all it should be modestly phrased and not expose the author to the suspicion of vanity or self-seeking. Especially it should avoid causing embarrassment to the person to whom it is addressed. Initials of the dedicatee are usually preferable to the full name unless his consent is first obtained. The dedication is a matter of personal relationships which do not much concern the public.

The function of the Preface is to enable the author to explain the purpose of the book, and if necessary, to justify the writing of it.

In olden times it was called the Author's Apology. If acknowledgments are due anyone for aid in the preparation of the study, the Preface is the proper place for making them.

The Table of Contents shows the location in the book of the parts composing it and especially the divisions of the text. The main divisions may be called chapters, or, as in this Manual, may be designated by numbered headings. Following this part of the Table there should be a list of the maps, diagrams, charts, or illustrations. Opposite each entry—part, division, or subdivision—near the right-hand margin of the page, should be placed the number of the page on which the item, or its beginning, is to be found. The list of Maps, Charts, or Illustrations is usually the last item in the Table, following the word Index.

The Introduction should define the objectives of the writer, give a summary view of the scope of the undertaking, indicate any special methods employed or bodies of material exploited, point out the place of the study in the literature of the subject, and state briefly or at least foreshadow any significant conclusions which have been reached.

Appendices are used for lengthy quotations, documentary matter, statistical tables, and other material to which the reader should have access but which would overload the text or make footnotes too cumbrous. Essential tables should not be relegated to an appendix, but only those of collateral significance which can be discussed just as well there as in the text. A brief extract from a document may be sufficient to quote in the text, but there are often cases where it may be desirable to have the entire document available for the reader without the trouble of seeking it in a library. Each item may be made a separate appendix and designated by a number or otherwise, or related items may be grouped in one appendix and distinguished by giving each its own number or letter.

The Index may be dispensed with in a brief treatise, if the Table of Contents is sufficiently analytical to be an adequate guide, but no extensive work can be easily consulted unless it is well indexed. An index may be prepared by going through the manuscript and listing each author's name, each title, and each important subject on separate slips as mention of them is found. Page numbers may be added each time the name, title, or subject is encountered, with cross references to call attention to cognate entries. The slips should be filed alphabetically so that they may be found easily for entering these additions. Book pages can be substituted for the manuscript paging when page proof is received from the printer.

An index should not merely list page numbers after an entry, but should indicate briefly what each page contains that relates to it. Such an analytical index enables one to turn directly to the page where he will find the information he wants. The *Harvard Guide* index, after the word "Senate," lists about 175 pages on which there is something about that body. If only the pages were given, one can imagine the state of mind of a person who found what he was seeking only after vainly looking over a hundred or more pages! [114]

ii. PUNCTUATION

Judging from what one may observe, most untrained writers use marks of punctuation subconsciously. There is seldom evidence of thoughtful use or familiarity with any system of rules. Periods at the end of sentences, a few commas dropped at random, mostly in the wrong places, promiscuous dashes and parentheses, seem to represent the resources of this kind at the command of the average college student. If spelling is a lost art, punctuation as an art was by many persons never recognized as such.

A textbook on punctuation cannot be interpolated here; but it is insisted that attention must be given to this phase of the technique of writing. The few comments offered are made in the hope of leading the student to pursue the subject for himself.

The tendency in recent years is to minimize the use of punctuation, dispensing with the marks where they do not serve to make statements clearer than they would be without them. To accomplish this they must be used with discretion. *That punctuation plays a significant part in determining meaning is the basic fact.* The lack of punctuation in medieval manuscripts was at the root of the difficulty in getting at the meaning of the passage in Seneca's letter, discussed in an earlier section. A recent writer, telling the story of Benedict Arnold, by the inadvertent insertion of a comma changed the meaning of his statement in a startling way. Intending to write "Washington, too just to ignore his merit, made him commander in Philadelphia," he actually wrote "Washington, too, just to ignore his merit, made him commander in Philadelphia"!

The Constitution of the United States might have become the

[114] There is an article on "Indexing" by Bertha Josephson, in *The American Archivist* for April, 1947.

basis of a quite different sort of government if the use of a semicolon instead of a comma had not been discovered before its final adoption. The Convention voted favorably on a provision reading:

> The Legislature shall have the power to lay and collect taxes, duties, imposts and excises, to pay the debts and provide for the common defence [*sic*] and general welfare of the United States.

When the Committee on Style reported the final draft, the comma after the word *excises* had been replaced by a semicolon. This made the power to promote the general welfare independent of the taxation clause, a reading which accorded with the desires of some members of the Committee, notably Gouverneur Morris, who made the draft. Through the vigilance of Roger Sherman, it seems, the original punctuation was restored before the Constitution was engrossed.[115]

It is said, although not on proved authority, that the change of a hyphen to a comma in a tariff act of June, 1872, cost the Government $3,000,000 before the error was corrected. The change of reading was in a provision for admitting certain imports free of duty. The intention was to admit duty-free "tropical fruit-plants, etc . . ."; the changed reading greatly enlarged the free list merely by omitting the hyphen, so that the phrase read as if the hyphen was a comma.

In punctuation as in other matters the attempt has been made in this Manual to follow approved usage so that it may be used as a model. In lieu of a set of rules, which may be found elsewhere,[116] stress is again laid on the importance of *thinking* about each phase of technique until the underlying reasons are discerned—of directing the *attention* to details so that they will not be unconsciously neglected—of *deliberately* studying proper procedures until they become habitual.

A few examples may enforce the need of this general attitude. Where the structure of a sentence requires a *pair* of commas to inclose a clause or phrase, the second one is often thoughtlessly omitted. If one writes "Smith, the president of the organization, was absent," it is clear that Smith is the president. A complete statement

[115] Max Farrand, *The Framing of the Constitution of the United States*, 177–179, 182. The charge against John Quincy Adams, mentioned on page 31, was that he had made a similar change in punctuation.

[116] A concise but comprehensive discussion of punctuation will be found in Spahr and Swenson, *op. cit.*, 304–314.

would remain if the words set off by commas were omitted. But if the second comma is omitted these words would become an inseparable part of the sentence, which would then apparently mean that *Smith* was addressed, and all that follows was information given him.

The use of punctuation in connection with parentheses is a stumbling block to many persons, yet one simple rule should dispel most of the difficulty: the parentheses should leave the punctuation just as it would stand if they were not there. Suppose a sentence reads: "The onslaught of the enemy was vicious, and threatened to throw the troops into confusion." If following the word "vicious," words were added in parentheses the whole sentence should read: "The onslaught of the enemy was vicious (it was a surprise attack), and threatened. . . ," etc. Here the comma follows the parentheses. If, however, a punctuation mark ended the inserted expression and was part of it, the comma should precede the parentheses and the form of the whole should be: "The onslaught of the enemy was vicious, (it was a surprise attack!) and threatened . . ." etc.

iii. THE LITERARY FINISH

a) *Paths to Good Writing*

Approaching the final stage in the production of an essay the candidate needs both encouragement and admonition. The famous Dr. Samuel Johnson wisely advised: "Do not exact from yourself at one effort of excogitation propriety of thought and elegance of expression. Invent first and then embellish." In line with this advice the student need pay little attention to literary style while making his preliminary draft. For the time being any form of expression that conveys the meaning reasonably well is all that need be sought. But instead of considering such a draft as final, one of the author's last acts should be to scrutinize the whole production with the object of improving it. Since attention cannot well be concentrated on both matter and literary excellence at the same time, it is well to go through the draft first on the lookout for misspelled words, erroneous punctuation, grammatical slips, and violations of the rules of rhetoric. He should remember that infinitives should not be split, that "a preposition should not be used to end a sentence with"—a rule which would lead to a stilted style if followed invariably—, and that there are many other rules which he memorized as a schoolboy and forgot forthwith. All that he knows of formal rhetoric is now put to the test.

The writer who habitually examines his work in this way is often surprised at the faults he discovers. Correction follows detection as a matter of course. There are some kinds of errors, however, which escape detection so easily that it is advisable to have a competent friend go over the manuscript. Two pairs of eyes are better than one in catching slips where the meaning is clear but the expression faulty. If one writes: "after encountering a few such references the necessity will occur to the writer of obtaining full information," one may read the sentence without noting its defects. Such errors slip into the work even of experienced writers and often go into print for want of adequate revision of copy by a second person. Clearly what the writer of the foregoing sentence intended to say was that "after encountering a few such references the writer will perceive the necessity of obtaining full information."

But the secret of a good style lies far deeper than the observance of the formal rules of rhetoric and grammar. It is sometimes said that poets are born, not made. The saying is probably just as true about good prose writers. Many persons who find themselves carried along by the writing of a master of style sense its charm without divining its secret. They may think of it as a gift of nature. It is true that people differ in natural gifts; but most intelligent persons are capable of becoming proficient writers if they will form the habit of thoughtfully recasting forms of expression until they say with exactitude what they are meant to say. In most cases good writing is the result of a combination in which talent is one-tenth and intelligent observation of good models combined with persistent effort are the other nine-tenths. By continual practice, far more than by any rule-of-thumb application of rules, a writer learns how to produce the effects he desires and to become a facile and versatile wielder of the pen. On the other hand *unconscious inattention* is the cause of much mediocre work; the chief cause of faults in writing, apart from sheer stupidity, is the *lack of the habit of looking for them.* The characteristic sin of the novice is neglect of the effort to achieve a good style.

The aspiring author must learn to observe, think, and experiment for himself. A cloud of witnesses testify to the necessity of doing just this; it is often painful but pays off in the end. Benjamin

Franklin tells us in his inimitable *Autobiography* that he trained himself by reading Addison's essays and writing out their substance in the best English he could command. With charming candor he says that he sometimes thought he improved on the style of this master of English prose writing. William James confessed that every page of his *Psychology*, an epoch-making book two generations ago, was rewritten on the average not less than six times! An admirer of Professor Ulrich B. Phillips, a noted writer of the history of the South, testifies that: "He would not leave a sentence until each word and the phrasing as an entity expressed exactly what he had in mind to say. He wrote paragraphs over and over and made a dozen or more drafts of a narrative. In time the result clearly justified the effort. Phillip's best writing had an insight, understanding, wit and sparkle, and over all a beauty of expression which made it outstanding." [117]

It is a rule of some translators never to be satisfied with their rendering into English of a foreign term until half a dozen synonyms have been rehearsed mentally, in order that the words finally chosen may preserve the shade of meaning of the original with the nicest accuracy. The rule is a good one to adapt to one's own writing. Nothing is more essential to good writing than a rich and varied vocabulary joined with a sensitive feeling for the right word in a given context. To develop this sense a good dictionary is one of a writer's best friends, especially when supplemented by a knowledge of the etymology of English words. For this some acquaintance with Latin is an excellent background. It is good practice to experiment with words, and also to make deliberate efforts to place words and phrases in the best order or position in sentences. Each paragraph should have a unity of its own and its successive sentences should lead to a thought climax. Likewise paragraphs should be arranged in a sequence culminating in a climax. By careful study of these devices, from the use of the word and sentence to the organization of the whole essay, bringing the subordinate portions into proper relations with the chief parts and the total work, the writer is more likely to make an effective appeal to the reader.

These are lessons learned and taught by men like Franklin, James, and others who by their literary attainments made them-

[117] Herbert A. Kellar, "The Historian and Life," in *MVHR* for June, 1947, p. 11.

selves models worthy of emulation. Their experience and that of others makes vivid the obstacles which have to be overcome. The author of this Manual carries in memory a cartoon which he saw many years ago. It touched his heart. It pictured a man seated at his desk beside an overflowing wastebasket, around which on the floor were numberless discarded sheets covered with writing. This man was saying *sotto voce*: "I've written and rewritten this chapter twenty times, and it still reads as if I had *labored* on it!" [118]

Robert van Gelder, editor of the *New York Times Book Review*, collected some years ago the reactions of about ninety authors to their work and published a summary of their responses. A reviewer of his book sums up his findings in these words: "Most writers find their work desperately difficult, no matter how long they have been at it, and regard the whole literary process as one part pleasure and nine parts drudgery." [119]

Arthur Frank Burns, chairman of President Eisenhower's Council of Economic Advisers and reputed ghostwriter of the President's economic report to Congress of February, 1954, "took the economic content as a professional matter of course; he expressed greater satisfaction in the report's style and readability. Says Burns: 'I've always considered writing important. I went through all the stages that economists go through, from jargon to lucidity, and on the way I passed through the sesquipedalian stage.'" [120]

To end this discussion of the trials and tribulations through which the successful writer must pass before he achieves his goal, it should be said for his comfort that whosoever persists until success crowns his efforts may look backward with satisfaction on the wreckage which lies strewn along his trail. Columnist Frank Colby writes: "One of my most treasured possessions is a notebook in which I have jotted down . . . literary blunders. . . . I call it my 'Chamber of Horrors.'"

[118] On one occasion a student of the present writer inquired why he had not been given a better grade on a theme he had written. When told that he had not used English well, he demanded "Are you a teacher of history or English"! Perhaps that question will arise in the minds of some readers of this portion of this Manual.

[119] Van Gelder's book: *Writers and Writing* (New York: Charles Scribner's Sons, 1946). The quotation is transcribed from *Time* for July 22, 1946.

[120] Quoted by *Time*, February 8, 1954, p. 14. (Sesquipedalian—a foot and a half in length; *i.e.*, given to the use of long words.)

b) *Changing Literary Fashions*

Literary style is a matter of taste, not of unvarying law. Like dress, writing that pleases one generation may be distasteful to another. Cultivated people of today often find what passed for excellent writing a century or so ago too florid. Washington Irving was one of the first American prose writers to command attention in England, yet he would now hardly be held up as a model by college teachers of composition. The following paragraph opened his *Astoria*, a book published a little more than a hundred years ago.

> Two leading objects of commercial gain have given birth to wide and daring enterprise in the early history of the Americas; the precious metals of the south, and the rich peltries of the north. While the fiery and magnificent Spaniard, inflamed with the mania for gold, has extended his discoveries and conquests over those brilliant countries scorched by the ardent sun of the tropics, the adroit and buoyant Frenchman, and the cool and calculating Briton, have pursued the less splendid, but no less lucrative, traffic in furs amidst the hyperborean regions of the Canadas, until they have advanced even within the Arctic circle.

There may be much to praise in this paragraph, but the modern reader notes a plethora of adjectives and a wordiness which contrasts with the more severe taste of our times. Before the end of the nineteenth century the change had affected even some of the writers of the earlier years who had outlived their generation. Thus the aged George Bancroft revised his *History of the United States* in the 1880's but confessed that the revision consisted chiefly in striking out superfluous adjectives. At long last he had discovered the merit of the maxim "the adjective is the enemy of the noun."

Yet in spite of inevitable change new fashions do not win favor unless they survive severe tests. Present ways gained acceptance just because they survived such tests. Only geniuses can afford to risk innovations; their powers transcend conventional rules and set the patterns which others may follow later. In the meantime the genius often suffers literary martyrdom. For most of us wisdom prescribes conformity to practices approved by time. Young writers should resist the youthful mania to innovate, and follow time-approved models even at the risk of being scorned as old-fashioned by their less cautious associates. Let their genius, if they have any, wait a while before it bursts confining bonds.

Unfortunately poor models often seem more attractive than the old ones. The young are fascinated by the smartness and novelty of style of feature writers in newspapers and magazines. Poor writing is not often acknowledged to be such by its authors; hence the following example is doubly valuable because it exhibits one unfortunate style in favor for the moment and at the same time naïvely acknowledges its dubious quality:

> Perhaps you may not like it . . . but when thoughts come hard . . . and subjects are not many . . . this is an easy way to write . . . lazy man's way of scrivening.

Even a greater threat to the young is the current slang to which they are prone to become slaves, for this manner of speaking or writing impoverishes the vocabulary and weakens the ability of the victim to develop and enrich his linguistic resources. The English language is a noble instrument and its use may be a fine art, perhaps the finest of all arts, for more than any other art it can express the whole range of human thought and feeling. Lending itself to the purposes of novelist, poet, scientist, philosopher, statesman, historian, or expositor of any area of knowledge or endeavor, it deserves to be respected and defended by every one against whosoever would abuse it!

c) *Limitations and Possibilities of Style*

Confessedly the present writer is setting up a standard of perfection which few ever attain. It is not a standard to which a master's essay can conform perfectly. But it should be kept in view. At best the master's essay will be a good piece of prentice work, but it should and may be a long step in the right direction and a valuable part of one's education. The historian works under certain limitations which do not embarrass the poet or novelist. It is desirable for the novice to recall what was said earlier about the dangers of fictionalized history and the importance of maintaining a distinct boundary between the two types of writing. The historian has no entrée into the minds of his characters such as the novelist enjoys. Nor does the biographer have any more freedom. When therefore a poet poses as a biographer and portrays the thoughts, say of Lincoln's mother about her unborn babe, the poet is visible through the thin disguise.[121]

One's style must be suited to one's theme. One theme calls chiefly for skill in narration, another in description, a third in exposition or argumentation. Some writers need to utilize all of these ways of presenting matters as the character of their task varies. The historian belongs in this large class; but he must not forget that he may obscure his meaning, if not misrepresent the truth, by overindulgence in figures of speech or literary effects. The fact that the freedom exercised by others in these respects has caused him trouble in getting at the meaning or truth of their statements should warn him against making similar errors. The poet and novelist have much greater license than the historian, whose repertory of literary artifices is restricted by the nature of his subject.

The essential qualities in written history are lucidity, directness, conciseness. These are not beyond the reach of the beginner and his work should show them. Even so, his product may seem dull and unattractive to the general reader. The fault may lie in the technical nature of the subject. But the historian is by no means condemned to a bald, plain, unattractive way of writing. Enough has been said already about the correction of common faults as well as about ways of improving, especially by self-directed effort; but there are tricks of style which help to capture the interest of readers and are easily learned. It is not possible to discuss these at length here, but a few may be mentioned. The mere use of alternative terms to avoid constant repetition of the same words and phrases is a simple device which will go far to prevent a discussion from becoming a bore to the reader. A careful choice of words, an avoidance of unusual ones, a correct placing of them in sentences, a merciless excision of those not needed, especially superfluous adjectives, a logical development of the theme, a breaking of long sentences into two or more—these are hints at a few of these devices.

Lucidity—clarity—is in large part a matter of knowing how to marshal words to throw the main idea into prominence. An unskillful assemblage of phrase may drop the chief idea to a secondary position. If a writer wishes to say (1) that the *Cumulative*

[121] The *Harvard Guide* takes a less strict view of this matter, having a good word for historical fiction. See pp. 237, 238. Its statement nonetheless is subject to the comment that the values of historical fiction are attainable only by a competent critic.

Index was consolidated with the *Readers' Guide*, and (2) that the independent issues are still useful, he should decide whether these statements are of equal importance. If one is of lesser importance a form of expression should be chosen which will subordinate that one to the more important. The emphasis is not precisely the same in the following:

> The *Cumulative Index* is still useful because it covered some magazines which Poole did not index, but it was consolidated with the *Readers' Guide* in 1903.
>
> The *Cumulative Index* was consolidated with the *Readers' Guide* in 1903, but it is still useful because . . . etc.

A statement may contain no error and yet on second thought may be seen to need rearrangement to make it more pointed, elegant, or forceful. Most beginners would regard the first form of the following passage as good enough, yet would probably agree that the second is an improvement:

> While these processes are logically distinct they are often, as a matter of fact, carried on simultaneously. Nevertheless they demand separate discussion, since each has its own technique.
>
> These processes are, as a matter of fact, often carried on simultaneously, but they require separate discussion since they are logically distinct and each has its own technique.

It might be difficult for an unpracticed reader to explain the superiority of the second even if he felt it. One who is accustomed to careful analysis would see that the second throws into relief the *simultaneity* of the process; that the sequence of ideas in the first is poor, because the reasons why the processes require separate discussion are not well coordinated. While the results of painstaking attention to such details will not transform the tyro into a Phillips overnight, they will command the approval of persons engaged in related studies if they are capable of recognizing good work. Of particular importance is the fact that they will convince the supervisor that the candidate shows promise.

Finally it should be impressed on the writer that there is more than one way to say a thing without sacrificing accuracy or truthfulness or intelligibility. Many a textbook has described the Boston "Tea Party" in a narrative essentially like this: "About fifty men disguised as Indians went aboard the ships in the harbor during the night and emptied 342 chests of tea into the water." A scholar with a better feeling for style lifted his account of the incident to a higher level by writing: "The radicals boarded the ships disguised as Indians, and next morning tea lay strewn like seaweed along Dorchester beach."

These two statements, to be sure, do not relate precisely the same facts. The first is a factual account telling explicitly that the boarding party emptied the tea into the water and giving (presumably) the exact number of chests (a detail of no use to the reader even if he remembered it). It is a prosy account weighted with ineffectual details. The second is comparatively interesting; it leaves no doubt about the really important occurrence, and it challenges the imagination. Factual history is largely to blame for giving children a false sense of values and goes far toward explaining their dislike of history as a mere matter of memorizing facts or figures.

Challenging the imagination is a wholesome procedure; it is not like the appeal to fancy. A description of the thoughts of Lincoln's mother about the unborn Lincoln is fanciful; it is altogether detached from any ascertainable verity. On the other hand, imagination leads the reader to see, mentally, actual happenings without having them, as it were, catalogued for him. "During the rivalry for control of the fur trade in Canada in the early years of the eighteenth century the French and English clashed whenever they met." The statement in these words would be factual history. Another way of saying the same thing would be: "The dim forest glades witnessed many a dark encounter the story of which can never be told." Both statements are legitimate generalizations about specific facts that cannot be recovered, but there is a considerable contrast in the mental pictures they create in the reader's mind, and the appeal they make to him.[122]

Another legitimate device for enlivening style, if one is not adept at coining phrases, is to make a moderate use of spicy quotations. Conditions in the Illinois settlements on the eve of George Rogers Clark's attack on them during the Revolution may be prosaically described in terms of England's inability to maintain adequate garrisons on that remote frontier. Such a prosy narrative could be relieved by the introduction of a catchy phrase to stimulate the flagging interest of the reader. Thus of the situation at Kaskaskia one has written:

[122] See the paragraph on Imagination in History, in the section on History as a Literary Art in *Harvard Guide*, 44–49.

"Here, as at most of the posts, only the 'flicker of a red flag' showed that the land was British."

This is a far cry from the efforts various authors have made to excite interest by fanciful accounts. Some of these have falsely related how Clark misled the British by marching his men repeatedly past a point where they could be seen, thus giving the impression that his small company was a considerable force. Equally fanciful is the story that Clark entered the village while a dance was in progress, and that the first warning the inhabitants received of the presence of an enemy was the startled outcry of the lone Indian sentinel when Clark appeared at the door of the dance hall.

The monotony of a long recital of bare facts may be relieved if the opportunity comes to introduce a bit of color. For example, details of the peace terms and transfers of territory at the close of the French and Indian War may justifiably be followed by a description of the significance of the British victory in which the author spreads his wings a little:

> With their defeat the French Bourbons made their exit from the North American mainland and the curtain fell on the dramatic and colorful history of New France. The turbid waters of the Mississippi now marked the eastward limits of the dominions of decadent Spain, and half a continent spread its invitation before the feet of the sturdy race whose multiplying paths led westward from the margin of the Atlantic.

However, too many flourishes are to be avoided. Many readers will recall the "f. w." of the instructor in English in the margin of their freshman themes warning them against "fine writing" where the context does not warrant it. Too much of it is likely to become as boresome as a tale without adornment. Above all, embellishment should never become a principal aim, or be allowed to hide or distort the truth. Clio is an austere muse whose natural charms are not to be enhanced by overdressing.

7. Some Conditions That Must Be Faced

More time is needed for the preparation of a meritorious master's essay in history than is generally contemplated by university regulations or the student's anticipations. It seems to be assumed that standardized requirements bear equally on the candidate regardless of his field of specialization. In fact, however, the undergraduate's studies in one field may fit him to undertake a research problem immediately on graduation, while in another he may find it necessary to spend a considerable part of his first year in the graduate school in learning how to use the tools of his trade. The person whose major interest is chemistry, for example, begins with his first course to learn its technique of research. His technical progress goes hand in hand with the growth of his knowledge of subject matter; each can advance only when accompanied by the other. The history major on the contrary finds little opportunity to become acquainted with the problems and tools of research until, after graduation, he faces the necessity of using them. He must spend from one-fourth to one-third of his first year on the prerequisites of research in his field, and by the time he has covered them he begins to realize that the end of the academic year is too near to permit satisfactory completion of the essay in addition to the prescribed quota of subject-matter courses.

This actual inequality of time requirements in the several fields favors the candidate trained in a laboratory science; he may find one year sufficient for handling his project. That is no discredit to him or his subject; but some important facts are not brought into view if the graduate school announces that the minimum period for earning a master's degree is one academic year. The implication is that a year is sufficient. It is safe to say that few candidates in history can gain the degree in so short a time, especially if they come to the university from a four-year college. Some of the older universities in the East recognize this situation and frankly say that it will ordinarily require two years. In the state universities of the West the experience of students confirms the need of the longer period, and in effect the universities provide for it. A great many history candidates either spend an extra summer or two in residence devoting their time to the essay, or, having gathered all the needed data, are permitted to write *in absentia* and submit the results for approval when the work is finished.

The primary purpose of this explanation is to warn candidates in history that since they cannot expect to earn the degree in one academic year, they should plan accordingly. An additional purpose is to urge the importance of taking time to do the best work possible, in confidence that the result will be worth the extra effort. Looking backward at the sacrifice needed for the painstaking performance, it will not seem to have been an unmitigated hardship.

The goal having been reached and a teaching position obtained, the teacher will find that his student days are not over. He is fortunate if his experience has taught him how to go ahead under his own power. But he need not work altogether in isolation. Teachers in colleges and public schools are jointly and severally becoming more and more conscious of their responsibilities and opportunities. In print and in conference they are discussing ways and means of making their subject a vital influence for good in the world of today. No teacher can afford to miss the enlargement of view and the inspiration gained by sharing these group activities in some way, if only by reading about them.

In this connection mention should be made of the Mississippi Valley Historical Association and its journal, *The Mississippi Valley Historical Review*, articles in which have been repeatedly cited in the footnotes of this Manual. The *Review* is the chief periodical of national scope devoted wholly to American history, both on the local and national level. No organization or publication has done more than these to promote interest in the problems connected with the study and teaching of American history, and neither has ever received the support it deserves from public-school teachers. It has reported investigations showing high-school pupils' disturbing ignorance of our country's history to be due in part to its poverty of content and in part to poor teaching. Efforts of the Association to enlist the cooperation of school administrators in improving conditions have not been encouraging in their results, being on the whole less fruitful than attempts to advance research on the college level.

The author of this Manual urges readers engaged in teaching this subject to avail themselves of the benefits offered by the *Review*. Much instructive reading is to be found in it. Some of it may be mentioned here. Under the title "History in the School Curriculum," Professor Edgar B. Wesley of the University of Minnesota pointed out a decade ago that the quality of history teaching had been deteriorating for some time, and in challenging terms exposed the reasons for it.[123] Similar criticisms were being offered elsewhere, but this article led directly to the inception of a joint project by the American Historical Association, the Mississippi Valley Historical Association, and the National Council for Social Studies, financed by a grant of the Rockefeller Foundation, to investigate and report on the history and social science program in schools and colleges. A

[123] *MVHR* for March, 1943, pp. 563–574.

committee representing these organizations under Professor Wesley's direction reported the next year.[124] It called out much discussion, not all of it favorable to the committee's findings, but wholesome as evidence of a genuine desire for improvement. Articles appeared demanding reconsideration of the content of textbooks,[125] stressing the need of better teaching,[126] and pointing out values to be promoted through the teaching of history.[127] The discussion covered a wide range. A committee of the Harvard faculty reported on *General Education in a Free Society*; [128] Robert E. Keohane, of the University of Chicago City College, advocated the use of source material as a means of promoting a better understanding of United States history and stimulating critical thinking.[129]

Of course not all of this stir grew out of the Wesley article. At the same time conferences of teachers were taking on new importance, seeming to gain impetus during the war years of the early forties. A series of meetings at Stanford University during 1943 led to the appointment of a committee representing the colleges and public schools of California to look into the status of American history in both classes of institutions and report with recommendations. The report was issued by the Institute of American History at Stanford in a pamphlet entitled "What of American History in the Public High Schools of California. . . . ?" It declared that the entire social science program in the public schools should be overhauled, that teachers should be required to have special training for the tasks assigned them, that they should have a share in shaping the social science program, and that the importance of history in the curriculum should be re-emphasized.[130]

The California movement is paralleled more or less closely by the

[124] *American History in Schools and Colleges* . . . New York: The Macmillan Company, 1944. Reviewed in *MVHR* for June, 1944, pp. 107–111, and in many other journals.

[125] *MVHR* for June, 1944, p. 93 *et seq.*

[126] See citations, *ibid.*, March, 1944, p. 568.

[127] Lucile Gustafson, "Social and Personal Values of American History," in *MVHR* for September, 1945, p. 25 *et seq.* This article deals with the importance of making young people feel that history has something to do with their own lives, bringing the past into their world of experience and picturing their world to come. "Past experience may be a guide for action today."

[128] Harvard University Press, 1945.

[129] "The Use of Primary Sources in the Teaching of Local and State History in High Schools," in *MVHR* for December, 1946, p. 455 *et seq.*

[130] See *MVHR* for December, 1944. Professor Edgar E. Robinson's article on "The Institute of American History at Stanford," published on pages 431–437

Middle States Council for the Social Sciences and similar organizations elsewhere. In some states action has anticipated the agitation and in others has followed it. Illinois, for example, requires all public schools and other institutions engaged in teaching, if supported by public funds, to give instruction in United States history and the principles of representative government, including in the latter such practices as the use of the Australian ballot.

These details are hardly more than straws in the wind showing the direction in which it is blowing. It might be better to say that they are like weather vanes indicating the trend of the better teachers' thinking. The breeze has brought into view the importance of the relations between historical method and the methodology of cognate subjects, especially law. At the meeting of the Mississippi Valley Historical Association in Cincinnati in 1951 an interesting discussion took place in which a historian, a lawyer, and a scientist participated. Pendleton Herring, president of the Social Science Research Council, expounded the historian's use of evidence to establish facts in terms which need not be repeated to users of this Manual. The speaker on behalf of the law pointed out that its quest was for ways to settle disputes. The lawyer must omit or suppress some evidence which the historian would be bound to examine. The objectives of the two are so different that they cannot use evidence in the same way. (This amounts to a confession that the lawyer is a special pleader. The speaker might have added that the duty of a judge is much like that of the historian, as has been asserted in this Manual.) The remarks of the scientist were quite in line with the comments made in the earlier portion of this Manual.[131]

The methods of science and history are so similar that it is disappointing, almost startling, to find that the scientist does not necessarily apply the historian's rules of evidence to a question of social justice. A recent example of this phenomenon is to be found in connection with the trial of the Rosenbergs for espionage in 1951. Although the evidence as reported in the daily press clearly established their guilt, and accounts of the trial indicated that they were afforded every protection under democratic processes of justice, two able scientists, Dr. Harold Urey, a pioneer in the study of nuclear

---

of this issue, should be read by all history teachers on all levels as a tentative appraisal of the unsatisfactory status of teaching in colleges and high schools and an account of the efforts of California teachers to bring about improvement.

[131] The report of this discussion is in *MVHR* for September, 1951.

physics, and the famous Dr. Albert Einstein, nevertheless agreed that the trial and conviction of the Rosenbergs represented a miscarriage of justice. Neither scientist was a lawyer, and apparently neither was able to weigh the evidence after reading it. Urey wrote that he thought the Rosenbergs had been wrongly condemned, and Einstein endorsed Urey's views.[132]

The attitude of these two men is significant for several reasons: it shows that it is difficult for a scientist deeply moved by concern for human welfare to carry over his critical judgment into the field of social science; it illustrates a tendency of citizens of a country where every one has the legal right to hold and express an opinion on any subject whatsoever, to disregard the weight of authoritative opinion; and finally it is a striking illustration of the importance of a lesson which this Manual has sought to teach, *viz.*, that the ability of our Republic to meet the social, political, and economic problems of the present and future depends largely on the success of efforts to inculcate the kind of intellectual and moral rectitude which the critical method in history is designed to foster. The chief obstacle to be overcome is the tendency of the individual, a tendency inherent in our prized freedom, to reject evidence and hold that all who disagree with him are wrong. That deplorable attitude approaches the Communist's dogma that no deviation from the "party line" can be tolerated. Our national faith is that the freedom to think and speak not only permits ignorance, intolerance, and dogmatism, but offers the only effective means of combating them. Voltaire, living in an era of despotism, stated the democratic faith in a striking way when he said "I may not believe a word you say, but I'll give my life to defend your right to say it." Our own political philosopher, Thomas Jefferson, echoed the sentiment in his famous maxim that "truth has nothing to fear from error on a free rostrum." Within two generations Justice Oliver Wendell Holmes voiced the same faith in his characteristic manner by saying that the best test of truth is its ability to get itself accepted in a free market.

Yet it is just at this point that the teacher of today may encounter one of his chief problems. The present age is putting our concepts of freedom to severe tests. Within little more than a generation we

[132] As I write the papers report the death of Dr. Einstein, and in reviewing his career quote him as saying that he asked the President to commute the death sentence of the Rosenbergs because of "my passionate sense of social justice and social responsibilities."

have fought two dreadful wars. War, when the very existence of the nation is at stake, plays havoc with individual liberties, because they must be subjected to every degree of control necessary to secure national safety. Whatever justification there may be for war, this temporary loss of liberty tends toward a permanent degradation of human rights. War has brought us into contact with Nazism and Fascism, both of which were contemptuous of individual human values and used methods which it seemed we could meet only by adopting similar practices. The menace of Communism, even in time of peace, is well called "a cold war"; its policy of secret infiltration with intent to undermine our institutions by "boring from within" has done incalculable damage to our morale. These experiences add up to a state of general tension, a condition of jittery apprehension in which the charge of any irresponsible demagogue that a person may be a subversive casts doubt on that person's loyalty. There is a definite danger today that we may forget that evidence must be produced to substantiate a charge, and come to accept an accusation as sufficient proof of guilt.

This is the atmosphere in which public officials including teachers must do their work today. For the latter it sometimes means that what they say and do is observed suspiciously by the school's public clientele and leads to unfortunate restrictions on their freedom of teaching. Under such conditions some teachers live in fear that any expression of opinion may cost them their positions. Critical points are reached in the history courses when so-called controversial questions have to be dealt with. To evade or ignore them, if they are important, is to deprive history of its significance and even its life. Teaching then becomes a mere means of earning a livelihood, and most teachers could abandon the calling and fare better financially in some other occupation. That, however, is not the way out for one who sincerely believes in the values he deals with. How, then, shall he direct his course when navigation becomes hazardous?

No prescription that can be given will adequately answer this question. Granting his loyalty, the issue depends on the teacher's common sense and tact. Let him cling to his faith in the values of his subject. At the same time he may be reminded that it is not his function to insist that *his* opinions are right and that his pupils must accept them. While in reaching his own conclusions he weighs evidence like a judge, his function as a teacher is to try to impart respect for evidence so that his pupils' opinions may be well founded. As a simple and perhaps sufficient illustration, one may say that the teacher's reasons for being a Republican or a Democrat are his own affair, and in no way concern the pupil. Nor do his pupils' party leanings concern him; but he may help the young person to draw up a statement of what each party stands for and thus help him to decide which holds the greater appeal for him. The method is sound, and if wisely pursued may inculcate the disposition in the adolescent to reshape his judgments as he matures, gains wider knowledge, and faces changing issues.

The successful teacher is the one who can generalize wisely from this principle.

The master's degree marks a point at which roads diverge. Perhaps most students who have gone thus far have thought of this degree as the goal and terminous of their college years and have planned to step from the classroom to the teacher's desk. Under present conditions they should find a ready welcome in a good school, public or private. Success thereafter will depend largely on continued self-education; the teacher who does not feel an inner urge to increase his proficiency is likely to find himself under pressure of the school administration to "keep moving" or "move on."

Those who at this point turn to teaching should also realize that it will not be easy later to find a position in the faculty of a college or university. One can no longer count on obtaining such a position without the degree of Doctor of Philosophy, and to win it will require a total of at least three years in the graduate school. Time is also an important factor, for a long postponement of graduate study is likely to mean a serious handicap in the competition with younger persons.

The prospective teacher who has weighed these possibilities may go into the secondary schools convinced that there is no position of greater importance or potential social service. In that case we now bid him Godspeed in his noble calling and turn our attention to those who carry their graduate studies further.[133]

[133] United States Chief Justice Earl Warren, who spoke to the alumni of George Washington University on March 20, 1954, is reported to have said that teachers have received a "great deal of unjust criticism," when the truth is that they "stand for more of what this country stands for than any other group. . . ." —*Santa Barbara News-Press*, April 21, 1954.

PART III

Beyond the Master's Degree

PART III

Beyond the Master's Degree

1. The Doctoral Dissertation

a. *Requirements for the Doctorate*

Whatever the aims of the doctoral candidate in American history may be the requirements for the degree are the same. They vary in detail from university to university, but there is substantial agreement that the candidate must devote at least three years to graduate study. Under certain conditions the master's degree may be bypassed, but it goes without saying that the candidate will need training, however obtained, equivalent to that for the master's degree and additional qualifications. He will have to know how to find his material, which will be more varied than the other degree necessitated; he must be prepared to apply critical principles to the problems he encounters; he must be able to write effectively. He will usually be required to spend at least one year, ordinarily the last, as a registered student in the institution from which he expects to receive the degree. His choice of fields will be subject to regulations, and formal admission to candidacy will be conditional on passing a general examination on these fields a year or more before the degree is expected. This general test is partly written, partly oral, and includes a reading knowledge of two or more foreign languages, most often German and French, and any others which may be essential for research on the subject of the dissertation. The dissertation must be submitted to a committee of the faculty, found acceptable, and defended in a final examination under the questioning of a committee.

b. *Choosing a Subject*

One of the candidate's first tasks is to choose a suitable subject for his dissertation. This study must be broader than the master's essay. All needed material may be found in the student's university library, since it is often possible to use what scholars have already worked over in making a new synthesis or interpretation. However, the sources for the chosen study may be widely scattered; what they are and where they are the candidate must be able to discover. If scattered, it may be necessary to visit each depository to make a personal examination in order to extract the data pertinent to the subject. However, inexpensive reproductions are almost daily becoming more available, thus reducing the need of personal visits.

A dissertation must be prepared in conformity with the best current standards. Yet it cannot be maintained that if it falls short in some particulars it will be wholly without value. The failure to locate and use some obscure but important materials may be chargeable against a work which shows excellent critical ability, power of interpretation, and skill in presentation; its faults may be due to the lack of adequate guides. One of the exercises suggested in an earlier part of this book illustrates the difficulty a competent writer might have had in locating the evidence refuting the charge that Van Buren sought to control the choice of President in the House election of 1825. Mr. Douglas McMurtrie sought some years ago to prepare a bibliography of Louisiana imprints. The earliest item listed by Evans in his *American Bibliography* was dated 1797. McMurtrie's investigation uncovered a number of earlier pieces, one dated thirty-three years earlier. Quite as interesting was the discovery that others were located in such odd places that finding them could be credited to fortunate accident rather than systematic research. Dr. Wilberforce Eames, another bibliographer, supplied him with a clue to one item in the Bibliothèque Nationale in Paris; others were found in such widely scattered places as Berkeley, California and Seville, Spain.[1] The moral is that Evans's compilation, long a standard work of reference, needed not condemnation but supplementation. Similarly a dissertation, if it has any substantial merit, may at least blaze a trail for others who enjoy better facilities for

[1] Douglas C. McMurtrie, "Locating the Printed Source Materials for United States History," in *MVHR* for December, 1944, pp. 369–406.

research, and whose productions may bring our historical knowledge nearer to the goal sought.

Nor does the establishment of the truth of a proposition beyond reasonable doubt always require that every scintilla of evidence be adduced in its support. *Once demonstrated as true,* a statement does not call for an endless piling up of corroborative data.

The need of care in selecting a dissertation subject is now much greater than it was fifty years ago. Currently there are constantly about eighteen hundred candidates for the doctorate in history, a majority of whom are probably working in the American field. As the number of candidates grew it became evident that more than one was likely to select the same subject. To avoid duplication the Carnegie Institution of Washington initiated a publication some years ago entitled *List of Doctoral Dissertations in History Now in Progress at Universities in the United States . . . and Canada.* Subsequently the American Historical Association took over the project; it printed its first List as a Supplement to the issue of *The American Historical Review* for April, 1940. An Appendix to the Supplement reported other researches in progress. Since then the AHA list of candidates and subjects has appeared triennially. Candidates and supervisors should consult the latest of these lists before fixing on subjects. Even the older lists will be valuable as evidence of the kinds of studies that have been considered suitable for dissertations.

In the middle forties a committee of the Mississippi Valley Historical Association made a report on areas of investigation which had been overlooked or neglected. It significantly recognized that the scope of history is expanding and implied that it is to be viewed as embracing all phases of the life of a people, since they do not live in isolation but in communities forming parts of a nation-wide—even world-wide—society.[2]

It is advisable for candidates for the doctor's degree, in most cases, to select dissertation subjects which can be developed by the use of printed materials rather than collections of manuscripts or archival matter. Special techniques are necessary for using these collections,

[2] Louis Pelzer, chm., and six other members of the MVHA, "Projects in American History and Culture," in *MVHR* for March, 1945, pp. 499–522. *Cf.* the discussion of new trends which appears *post* p. 237. The broadening range of history writing is an influence tending to lessen the risk of duplicating studies.

and access to them is more or less restricted to scholars of proved ability.

This discussion of requirements for the doctorate will perhaps make clear why three years of graduate work are regarded as the minimum period for attaining it. Quite often the dissertation requires more time and arrangements may have to be made to finish it *in absentia.* Other factors may prolong the time spent in residence. Many candidates find their knowledge of the languages inadequate and must take time to prepare for the test on them. Some must earn a part of the money needed to meet expenses. One possibility for supplementing financial resources is to obtain a graduate assistantship. Most universities appoint several such assistants each year. Students who have had some successful experience in teaching are likely to be preferred for these appointments. This Manual has warned holders of the master's degree of the risk incurred in taking time to teach a while if they intend to return to the university as candidates for the doctorate; but a year or two in the classroom is an asset which may offset the risk of one who seeks an assistantship. The time it takes from his own graduate study may be regained during the summer session. Besides, if his record as assistant is good, it will add to his chances when after gaining the degree he seeks an appointment.

Fortunate is the able student who has ample means of his own, and next to him is the able but needy one who, aided by scholarships and fellowships, can devote his energies to his studies. Some of these fortunate ones may find three years sufficient to meet all the requirements for the doctorate.

c. *Employment Value of the Doctorate*

The candidate should be aware of certain other facts. Probably most persons seeking the doctorate in history hope to become members of the faculty of a college or university. As a means of obtaining such a position history and perhaps all the social sciences are at a disadvantage when compared with some other branches of learning. The number of advanced students of science who plan to teach is decreasing while the demand is increasing. The demand for engineers also exceeds the supply. But the number of doctors of philosophy in history is growing more rapidly than the need of them in institutions of higher learning. Such positions are going more and more to those who show most promise; many may have to be content with appointments in secondary schools or abandon teaching to enter other occupations.

Many candidates write dissertations only because they must do so if they are to obtain the degree, and once vested with the gown and hood vow never again to undertake such a grueling task. Studies have been made which show that a large percentage of the holders of the doctorate end their writing with the dissertation. Others have found the desire to write an ineradicable inward impulse, and hope that a position on the college or university level will enable them to devote a fair share of their time and talent to research and production. It is chiefly from this group that the ranks of the historians are filled. But they often find themselves under compulsion of another kind, for teaching and writing are not ready yokefellows. Institutions have been slow to recognize the degree of incompatibility of these two functions, and have sometimes pressed teachers to produce almost to the point of making it a condition for promotion, while at the same time imposing so heavy a teaching load that only a superman could perform both obligations acceptably. The roots of good teaching are, indeed, nourished in the soil of research, and an adjustment of their relations is imperative. It is probably safe to say that it is becoming customary to lighten the teaching load sufficiently to permit a successful teacher to demonstrate his ability in research and writing. The resources of the university are supplemented by various other foundations and institutions. Never before was financial aid so abundant and so easily obtained. Beginning with the promising freshman it extends to and includes the top-rank faculty man. Scholarships, fellowships, and assistantships are available for graduate students, and grants by numerous foundations are even more plentiful for faculty members engaged in worthy projects.

Some even of the ablest holders of the Ph.D. degree will not care to teach or write, and for these there are alternatives. All of them require special training, and the student who finds his bent in the direction of one of them may prefer to prepare for it instead of the doctorate, and make the master's degree the starting point. Among the alternatives are positions in the libraries of colleges, universities, cities, towns, historical societies, private foundations, etc. The growth of archives offers another attractive opportunity. Some are adjuncts of libraries or universities, some are associated with the

Federal and state governments, some with business organizations or other public and private establishments. Many universities offer training courses in library science, but formal courses in archival work have not as yet entered the curriculum of the universities to any great extent. Archives have found it necessary to employ untrained recruits and give them training as apprentices. The National Archives have played a leading part in providing such opportunities. In 1940 the National Archivist began to advocate "internships," and the next year, in cooperation with the American University in Washington, inaugurated service-in-training courses on the history and management of archives, with seminars on arrangement and description of materials. In the following years these educational activities were continued and extended.[3]

Editing and compiling, which are cognate activities, present occupations in which many scholars engage; their total output forms a large percentage of the historical matter published. Comparatively little of it is produced on a commercial basis, for its market is almost negligible, but it is indispensable if history proper is to be written. Editing and compiling have become important functions of libraries, archives, state historical societies, and to some extent of universities. It is a part of the work for which salaries are paid to members of the staff of these institutions.

d. *The Dissertation Seen in Proper Perspective*

When the average student receives his degree of Doctor of Philosophy in history, he is likely not yet to have gained great depth of knowledge outside of the fields of his intensive preparation, nor to have enough general knowledge of historiography to appreciate fully the setting of his subject in its relation thereto. This is natural, for he has been immersed in the task of meeting the requirements imposed on candidates for the degree. It is desirable for him to understand that his dissertation has a place in historiography as a unified body of knowledge—that it has a potential value beyond its immediate personal utility to him as a means of obtaining a degree and a position. A brief review of the history of historical writing in America may contribute to such an understanding of the importance of what he is attempting to do.

[3] See Solon J. Buck, "The Training of an Archivist," in *MVHR* for September, 1940, pp. 251 *et seq.* See also *MVHR* for March, 1941, p. 707; for March, 1945, p. 652; December, 1945, p. 466; *et passim.*

2. A Brief Survey of American Historiography

a. *The Seventeenth Century*

"April 26. About foure a clocke in the morning, wee descried the Land of Virginia. . . ." These words of George Percy's "Discourse" may well have been the first bit of American history written on the spot in an English colony. Gabriel Archer presently wrote "A Relatyon of the Discovery of our River," and the redoubtable adventurer John Smith the "True Relation" and "Map of Virginia." [4] Upon the founding of Plymouth Governor Bradford began the "History of Plimouth Plantation" which he carried to the year 1646. He also lent aid to Edward Winslow who set down in his "Journal" the story of the colony's fortunes during its first year. Next John Winthrop, governor of the Massachusetts Bay colony, kept a "Journal" of happenings from 1630 to 1649. In the meantime John Smith produced his *Generall Historie of Virginia, New-england and the Summer Isles* (1624), and William Wood, who had sojourned in New England for three years, published *New England's Prospect* (London, 1634).

These nine items formed, so far as the public knew, well-nigh the whole output of historical writing in English colonial America prior to 1650. Indeed Bradford's "History" and Winthrop's "Journal" were still in manuscript form and were not printed in full until the nineteenth century, yet were widely known, while it is a question whether Archer's "Relatyon" was known at all to contemporaries. All these writings were narrations, annals, or descriptions, these being the only styles of writing suitable for recording events and observations in which the authors had taken part. Some of the writers were evidently convinced that the events should be recorded in permanent form before they were forgotten, because they were of great import for the future. Such reasons were needed to lead Bradford and Winthrop to prepare their long-unpublished narratives. On the other hand, some of the descriptive pieces were designed to "sell" America at once to readers in England and perhaps elsewhere. This was true of Smith's "Map of Virginia," Winslow's *Journal* (published in London in 1622 under the title of *Mourt's Relation*, or *Journal of the Plantation at Plymouth*, and used by Smith in 1624 in his *Generall Historie*), and Wood's *New England's Prospect* (London, 1634). Wood's book might fittingly have been

[4] *Supra*, page 21 f.

called "The Emigrant's Guide." That it was widely read appears from the fact that it was reprinted several times, but whether or not it sent any emigrants to America is not determined.

About the middle of the century conditions in New England were leading to some modification of the style and type of history writing. To Massachusetts Bay and Plymouth had been added Connecticut, Rhode Island, and New Haven, and the formation of the New England Confederation in 1643 showed the dawning consciousness of a larger community. The situation suggested the need of a general history which would include all of them. Moreover the generation which had written of its own doings was passing from the scene, replaced by a younger one which could survey the past with a view to appraising and interpreting it.

Any attempt at interpretation was certain to reflect prevailing ideas, and a clue to what they were is to be found in Winthrop's *Journal*, in which he suggested that writers should take note of such "providences of God as were manifest for the good of these plantations." In this climate of opinion Edward Johnson wrote *The Wonder-Working Providence of Sion's Savior in New England.* It dealt with the events of the years from 1622 to 1651, and came out in the early 1650's. It fell short of a general history, being rather a history of Massachusetts Bay, the first to be published for that commonwealth. As the title shows, it interpreted events as seen through the refracting medium of the Puritan faith. It sheds light on social and economic conditions, but for later times is valuable chiefly for its revelation of the New England mind. Perhaps the modern reader may gather its nature by reading the prophecy of the Hebrew prophet Amos, written about 750 B.C. Like that prophet the seventeenth-century Puritan leaders saw in every calamitous natural event—drought, famine, pestilence—the Lord's punishment for the people's sins, while good fortune bespoke his favor. This Old Testament viewpoint appeared in New England also in the belief in witchcraft, shared indeed at that time by the whole Christian world, but taken too literally by the zealous Puritans who knew that the Bible commanded "thou shalt not suffer a witch to live" (Exodus xxii: 13. *Cf.* Deut. xviii: 10).

The two Mathers, Increase and Cotton, intellectual and spiritual leaders in the second half of the century, shared the belief in remarkable providences. Increase saw danger in the growing worldliness of the people and their disregard of clerical admonitions, and sought to combat the growing evils by marshalling the evidence that God had made them the special objects of his care. His *Essay for the Recording of Illustrious Providences* unfortunately alluded to alleged cases of witchcraft as signs of the devil's work and the prevalence of sin, and in the existing state of culture was the spark which lighted the tinder of the witchcraft persecution.

Cotton Mather, the son, wrote the *Magnalia* in the same atmosphere. The stupendous production, properly entitled the *Ecclesiastical History of New England,* was, according to his own statement, an account of the "wonderful displays of [God's] infinite Power . . . wherewith His Divine Providence hath irradiated an Indian Wilderness." Every subject he touched—which included about all that he considered worth writing concerning the Puritan colonies—is affected by this purpose. A chapter "Relating to the Wonders of the Invisible World" shows his cultural kinship to Johnson. He doubted whether any town in New England had been free from the intrusion of evil spirits. However, by the time the *Magnalia* was published in 1702 the delusion had passed its crisis. Mather belonged to the more humane group who, without disavowing the reality of witchcraft, agreed with the magistrates that punishment of the accused had probably gone beyond what the evidence warranted.

Meantime interest in a general history of New England had brought results. A coterie of intellectuals deriving their inspiration from Harvard College as the cultural center of New England, feeling the need of such a history, realized nevertheless that a prerequisite was the collection of a mass of local material and, probably, a first use of it by writers of additional local histories. The younger colonies still lacked histories of the narrative and descriptive type. These ideas filtered into the mind of the educated class chiefly through the Harvard-bred clergy, the men who did most of the writing of all kinds in the seventeenth century. Two ministers encouraged Nathaniel Morton, a nephew of Governor Bradford, to write a history as an example for others to follow, as a first step toward the desired general history. His production, finished in 1669, was *New England's Memorial.* The important part of it was little more than an abridgement of his uncle's manuscript, but it had considerable vogue until the publication of the latter pushed it aside. That Morton did not regard his book as a general history appears from his appeal to Increase Mather to encourage efforts to produce such a work, and in his own diligence in collecting manuscript materials needed for it.

Holding a relation to Winthrop's *Journal* similar to that of Morton's *Memorial* to Bradford's *History* was William Hubbard's *General History of New England.* Owing to its inclusion of matter relating to Plymouth and Rhode Island, Winthrop's work was sometimes called a "History of New England." This fact lent color to the use of the same broad title by Hubbard, but he added little of importance to what Winthrop had written. Like the latter's work, the Hubbard history long remained unpublished (till 1815). In a way the *Magnalia* was the culmination of the series of attempts to approximate a general history.

From the beginning, relations with the aborigines supplied a continuous theme for colonial writers. In his account of the day on which Newport and his companions entered Chesapeake Bay Percy wrote: . . . "We landed and discovered a little way . . . At night, when we were going aboard, there came the Savages creeping upon all foure, from the Hills, like Beares, . . . charged us very desperately. . . ." For the following seventy years reports from Virginia tell of successive Indian wars, culminating with one in the 1670's which involved many of the white settlements and seems to have been associated in some obscure way with the contemporary struggle in New England known as King Philip's War.

In that Northern region as in Virginia, the conflict of the 1670's was the culmination of a series of lesser interracial contests, about which much is told in the histories and journals already mentioned. Increase Mather wrote a *Brief History of King Philip's War* in 1676, and William Hubbard followed the next year with a *Narrative of the Troubles with the Indians in New England.* Captain John Mason's *History of the Pequot War,* published in the same year, was the account of an officer who had actively participated in it. The next generation was sufficiently removed in time from the horrors of Indian warfare to read with fascination Thomas Church's *Entertaining Passages Relating to Philip's War* . . . (1716) and Samuel Penhallow's *History of the Wars of New England with the Eastern Indians 1703–1725* (printed in 1726). These bloody narratives, the thrillers of the age, found readers in two continents whose sympathetic suffering with the victims were not too severe to prevent enjoyment of the accounts.

Most seventeenth-century writers about Indian relations entirely failed to get the Indian's point of view. Thus again the writings betray the character of contemporary culture. The Puritan's morality was that of the Children of Israel as they conquered the promised land. The natives were the Canaanites; the treatment of the Pequots whom they sought to exterminate parallels that enjoined by the prophet Samuel during the war with the Amalekites (I Samuel, xv: 3). Cotton Mather called the campaigns against the Indians the "Wars of the Lord." He maintained that the natives by failing to develop the resources of their country had forfeited their right to it. Yet nineteen years after King Philip's War he admitted that the English had shown "an evil spirit" in directing their wrath indiscriminately against all Indians. At the time, however, only Daniel Gookin protested against the treatment accorded the Indians who had not joined Philip; but his *Historical Account of the Doings and Sufferings of the Christian Indians* was one of the manuscripts which remained unpublished for a century and a half (till 1836).[5]

b. *The Eighteenth Century*

One should not expect to find sharp differences between the histories with which the seventeenth century ends and the eighteenth begins. The old themes are carried over; the Indian continues to be a favorite subject; colonial writers still seek to inform English readers about conditions in America; but the emphasis shifts. Theological concepts yield somewhat to secular ideas; Indian relations become an administrative problem; theories and practices in politics become increasingly important; the writing group, so pre-

[5] Professor Perry Miller has made a careful study of Puritan philosophical and theological thought, which is the background of so much of the historical writing of New Englanders in the seventeenth century, in *The New England Mind* (New York: The Macmillan Company, 1939). Kraus gives an excellent survey of the historiography of the century on pages 21–67. The present writer is indebted to the latter for much bibliographical and biographical information.

The Bradford *History of Plymouth*, so often drawn upon by later historians, has been reprinted several times since it was first published. The latest edition is the one prepared for modern readers by Professor Samuel Eliot Morison, under the title *Of Plymouth Plantation* (New York: Alfred A. Knopf, Inc., 1952). Many other valuable historical works written long ago have been reprinted in recent times. The student who wishes to use these recent editions will find most of them in the index of the *Harvard Guide*.

That tales of Indian captivity have not even now lost their appeal to readers is evidenced by the recent publication of a volume by Howard H. Peckham entitled *Captured by the Indians* (New Brunswick: Rutgers University Press). It contains "fourteen true tales of pioneer survivors selected and rewritten for modern readers."

dominantly clerical in the seventeenth century, becomes more inclusive and the materials used more abundant. But as always, the writings reveal the dominant interests and character of the writers and their times.

One notable change is that numbers of Southern writers make their appearance. Aside from Virginia and Maryland, the Southern provinces were too young and immature in the seventeenth century for historical work. John Lawson, who went to North Carolina in 1700, blamed the lack of knowledge about that proprietary province on the fact that only ignorant traders with the natives knew it from personal contact, and they were incapable of describing it. Lawson, who was a surveyor, therefore wrote from personal observation the description which he published in 1709 with a title beginning *A New Voyage to Carolina.* The book stressed the advantages the country had over England, evidently with the hope that settlers might be drawn thither.

A long interval separates Smith's *Generall Historie* from the next notable Virginia writers. By the opening of the eighteenth century, however, the Old Dominion possessed a developed plantation system and a well-to-do leisure class. The aristocrats at least were able to send their young men to England to profit by its educational facilities and contact with its best society. Such were the opportunities enjoyed by Robert Beverley. From early youth he had studied government as practiced in America, and especially Virginia. Going abroad he read John Oldmixon's *British Empire in America* when it came from the press in 1708. The purpose of that work by an Englishman was to stress the value for England of colonial empire. It was so full of errors and so unfair to America, thought Beverley, that he enlarged his own first effort at a history of Virginia. The result was *The History of Virginia in four Parts,* published in 1722.

Beverley's narrative was slight, but the book was strong in its description of both native and white culture. However, it exaggerated the merits of both. Like Lawson's book, it was comparable to Wood's *New England's Prospect* in its portrayal of the attractions of life in America, in this case Virginia in particular. Designed to counteract the misrepresentations of Oldmixon and others, it asserted that slaves worked no harder than the "common freeman," and "not . . . near so hard . . . as the Day-labourers in England."

"This may in Truth be term'd the best poor Man's Country in the World."

Another Virginia aristocrat, William Byrd II, brother-in-law of Beverley, wrote on a subject closer akin to Lawson's than to Beverley's. The boundary between Virginia and North Carolina, in dispute since the erection of the latter province, was drawn in 1728 by a joint commission of the two colonies. Byrd represented Virginia on this commission, and afterwards wrote two accounts of the survey. Publication of these accounts was long delayed, but both are now available in a publication of the North Carolina Historical Commission.[6] The *Dividing Line* has literary merit and historical value as one of the earliest descriptions of frontier life. In contrast with Beverley's praise of the Virginia yeoman, he represents the frontiersman of North Carolina as lacking law, religion, and thrift. It is possible that later historians have not made sufficient allowance for his Virginia bias.[7]

Cadwallader Colden was a physician and one-time lieutenant-governor of New York. In his writings the Indian theme takes on an eighteenth-century hue. His *History of the Five Nations* grew out of the rivalry between France and England in North America, and especially their contest for the favor of the Iroquois. It was Colden's concern that England draw these tribes into her orbit. Thus in this matter he touches questions of imperial policy which he was one of the first colonial writers to envisage. Part I of the *History* was published in New York in 1727. He had already in hand notes for a second part, but under the press of affairs had abandoned further pursuit of the subject. Encouraged, however, by an interested Englishman, Peter Collinson, he continued the story to the Peace of Ryswick (1698).

Colden found most of his material in the reports of the Indian commissioners and certain French writers, and presented details of Indian life in selections from these sources. The complete *History* was in print by 1747. A two-volume reprint appeared in 1922, and a continuation which had hitherto remained in manuscript was published in 1935 by the New York Historical Society.[8]

[6] William Byrd, *Histories of the Dividing Line*, William K. Boyd, ed., Raleigh: 1929.

[7] On the *Histories of the Dividing Line* see Kraus, 75–76.

[8] "Cadwallader Colden Papers," in *Collections*, IX, 283–355, 359–434.

Daniel Neal commands a few words because he was an Englishman who viewed America more sympathetically than Oldmixon. As a dissenting clergyman he wrote a two-volume *History of New England . . . to . . . 1700*, first published in 1720. Although somewhat subdued, it was in tune with the New England authors from whom he gleaned most of his data—Winslow, Morton, Wood, Hubbard, and the two Mathers. He thought that the treatment of the Quakers could be justified, if at all, only on the ground that they were disturbers of the peace, while the confessions of the alleged witches were "extorted from Persons to save their Lives." [9] With a glance at the future, he believed that New England was not likely to revolt because continued connection with the mother country was to her interest.

Neal's moderation in writing about Quakers and witches was a sign of a general trend. By the middle of the century the belief in special providences was waning rapidly. When in 1755 a Harvard professor explained earthquakes as natural phenomena and a minister protested that they evidenced God's wrath, another clergyman supported the professor by asserting that "an Error in Philosophy is neither Heresy nor Treason. . . ." [10]

The professor's critic was Thomas Prince, who although behind the times "philosophically," made a good name for himself historiographically. In early life he read the standard histories with avidity—Morton, Johnson, Hubbard, the Mathers—and longed to see the whole matter brought into an orderly general account. Later while in England he found the same desire strong there. The first volume of his *Chronological History of New England* appeared in 1736. Since it began with Adam it barely reached New England, ending with the year 1630. Annals of three more years were published later. In spite of its oddities, Prince's presentation was orderly, and the tests he applied to his materials were quite in line with modern critical method. "I would not take the least iota upon trust. . . . I cite my vouchers to every passage; I have done my utmost to find the truth. . . ." [11]

A collateral contribution by Prince of greater ultimate value was a mass of manuscripts forming a notable library of Americana. One of the items was the Bradford manuscript. Eventually the whole Prince collection passed into the possession of the Boston Public

[9] Quoted by Kraus, 84.
[10] Quoted by Kraus, 85.
[11] Quoted by Kraus, 87.

Library, as a result of the nineteenth-century diligence of collectors in gathering great quantities of materials within the safe fold of the great libraries.

As a Harvard graduate and resident of the colony founded by Roger Williams, John Callender derived some of his qualities from each of these sources. Like Morton's Harvard friends, he felt the need of histories of colonies other than Massachusetts; like the Harvardians including Prince he wished steps to be taken to collect documents, private as well as public; and like Roger Williams he believed in every man's right to freedom of worship. His book, *An Historical Discourse on the Civil and Religious Affairs of the Colony of Rhode Island and Providence Plantations*, published in 1739, although more of a discourse on liberty of conscience than a history, was one of the first attempts at a history of a New England community aside from Massachusetts. No account of Rhode Island supplanted it for more than a century.[12]

The Virginia clergyman, William Stith, was a contemporary of Prince, Callender, Beverley, and William Byrd II. In *The History of the First Discovery and Settlement of Virginia*, published at Williamsburg in 1747, he resumed the narrative style, following John Smith's various writings principally for events to 1624. For the remainder of his book he drew most of his matter from the records of the London Company. Smith had not used these, and it was due to the aid of Byrd that Stith gained access to them. Like Prince and Callender, he desired to preserve historical matter, and fortunately for later historians, some of his passages preserve information which would otherwise have been lost entirely, since the originals have disappeared. He was careful and painstaking and quite modern in his methods. He indicates his sources in his preface and promises that he will try "to give [an] exact History . . . ever regarding Truth as the first requisite and principal Virtue in an Historian . . . relating nothing without . . . sufficient . . . authority."[13] The *History* was intended to be an Essay Towards a General History of this Colony, but nothing further followed.

The name Smith recurs frequently among early writers of American history. William and Samuel Smith were contemporaries, but the former was a New York Tory lawyer and the latter a patriotic

[12] Reprinted in Rhode Island Historical Society *Collections*, IV, 1838. See footnote 23 in Kraus, page 92.

[13] Quoted by Kraus, 93.

Quaker resident of New Jersey. William wrote *The History of the late Province of New York,*[14] Samuel, the first *History of the Colony of Nova-Caesaria, or New Jersey.*[15]

In contrast with Colden, William Smith's emphasis is on a topic of rising interest in his era, his history being an account of the controversies between the royal governors and the representatives of the people; while Samuel's aim is to tell "what the settlers here have been doing," a matter previously little publicized. The New Yorker knew little of the Dutch period of his province, but appended valuable descriptive material regarding the country, the people, trade, religion, and government. The New Jerseyite also inserted many documents, and showed some acquaintance with Beverley's *Virginia.* The placid Quaker wrote of struggles with the governor and Indian relations with undisturbed equanimity.

The mid-century brought an attempt at the long-desired general history of the colonies. William Douglass the author, a resident of Boston, was, like Colden, a physician.[16] Professing to write objectively, he betrayed unmistakable partisanship. His composition is "like a mass of ill-digested notes,"[17] and the product is full of misinformation. He managed to include more economic and social history than other writers of his day; but it requires careful winnowing.

Many of the works thus far considered used little material except what came from earlier histories, although some of the authors attempted "general histories" by drawing on several of the local narratives. Even the writers of the so-called general histories knew that a work deserving the title would need to use much matter not yet brought together, and some of them made sizable collections which they did not succeed in using in their own writings. Morton and Prince were among these pioneer collectors, and Ebenezer Hazard was reputed to have gathered the most complete collection for a general history of America. It was coming to be understood that many writings which were not themselves history—acts of

[14] The original work, ending with the year 1732, was published in 1757. A continuation written by a son carried it to 1762. The latter remained in manuscript until 1829 when the whole was printed by the New York Historical Society.

[15] Burlington: 1765.

[16] *Summary, Historical and Political, of the First Planting, Progressive Improvements, and Present State of the British Settlements in North America.* 2 vols. 1747–1755.

[17] Quoting Kraus's words, p. 102.

legislation, debates of legislators, public documents of all kinds, tracts, leaflets, the literature of controversies, diaries, correspondence even of private persons, newspapers, almanacs, and what not—were the materials from which history would be written in the future. By the middle of the eighteenth century it was expected that historians would make use of such materials. There being as yet no great public depositories, writers were still compelled to search for the documents they needed. As late as 1784 Jeremy Belknap was hunting in "garrets and ratholes of old houses"[18] in the faint hope of finding an occasional private document which could be used for a history of New Hampshire. In his case as in others the mass of manuscript material he got together was an argument for the creation of a public organization whose business it would be to preserve and supplement what individuals gathered.

The half-century which saw the rise of the revolutionary movement and its successful issue was a prolific period in American historiography. The community of interest which the struggle engendered in the American communities heightened the old sense of the need of a history embracing all of them, at the same time that it stimulated the writing of more provincial and state histories. The productions of the period reveal a changing mood and maturing culture in agreeable contrast with that of the era of the Pequot Indian War and the witchcraft episode. The leading historians show distinct progress in objectivity and critical standards, approximating the best of our own times, although others are prejudiced and unskilled. At least two have been convicted by modern critics of plagiarism, and at least one—with financial profit—wrote fictionalized history. The close connection between the acts of public men and the events of their times began to make the line between biography and history difficult to draw.

In contrast with the seventeenth century, ministers who were also historians are fewer in proportion to the doctors, lawyers, and public officials engaged likewise.

In the years following the Revolution that struggle became the engrossing theme, intensifying the zeal in gathering historical materials and bringing above the horizon the necessity of consulting British records to make the story complete. Finally, the generally heightened sense of the value of the nation's history led to the creation of societies and libraries devoted to the acquisition and preser-

[18] Quoted by Kraus, 135.

vation of its materials. A first fruit of this awakening was the creation in 1791 of the Massachusetts Historical Society. For this forward step Jeremy Belknap deserves chief credit. A new note was the advocacy of teaching history to young people as a part of their education for citizenship.

The two outstanding historians of the revolutionary era were Thomas Hutchinson and this same Jeremy Belknap. Both were lovers of history from childhood, and both enjoyed all the educational advantages Harvard could give. In some way both became judicially critical and objective in handling historical material. Like many of their contemporaries and predecessors both found it necessary to collect much of the matter they needed. These other historians habitually published numerous documents in part or in whole, stringing them together with a slender thread of narrative or comment in their so-called histories; Hutchinson and Belknap assimilated their subject matter and presented the results in their own words.

Hutchinson, Belknap's senior by thirty-two years, with a background of old New England stock, was governor of Massachusetts when the controversy with England over colonial rights verged to its climax. In 1773 the governor, a conservative by tradition and a student of the imperial constitution by necessity, defended British authority in a debate with the legislature.[19] As a result of this friction with the representatives of the people, he spent the rest of his life in England, a virtual exile.

The first volume of *The History of the Colony and Province of Massachusetts Bay* came out in 1764, the second in 1767. The latter was in manuscript in 1765 when the Stamp Act mob sacked Hutchinson's home and threw the draft into the street. The story of its recovery is well known. The last volume, bringing the *History* to the year 1774, was finished in England in 1778 and published there fifty years later by his grandson.

Significant for our historiography is the evidence of Hutchinson's diligence in collecting material. It appears from the story of the destruction by the mob of 1765 that much of a large collection he had gathered was lost. What escaped or was collected later was published separately in 1769. Hutchinson also had access to other private collections and used besides most of the older printed histories. His critical alertness is shown by his distrust of Douglass, and his strictures on the treatment of the Quakers and the alleged

[19] Homer C. Hockett, *Constitutional History*, I, 94.

witches are given broad application by his condemnation of the cruelties which he says are always attendant on superstition. His analysis of the personality of his opponents and accounts of the episodes in which he had a part exhibit a detachment quite in contrast with the emotional temper of some of his detractors. In short, the qualities of this first history deserving to be called a general history of Massachusetts place the author distinctly above the level of most contemporary writers.[20] The lasting value of his works is attested by their republication.

Jeremy Belknap conceived the idea of writing a history of New Hampshire while serving as pastor of a church in Dover. No other historian had tried his hand at that undertaking, a fact which made the burden of gathering material unusually heavy. Belknap had, indeed, access to the historical collections of New Hampshire's Governor Wentworth and Thomas Prince, but he sought the additional documents which he believed to be scattered far and wide in private hands, with the greatest assiduity. His history combines the narrative and descriptive forms. Looking backward, he judges the seventeenth century, as does Hutchinson, from the vantage point of the late eighteenth. His descriptions portray the state's natural features, the ways of life of its people, and their government and laws. He is careful to cite his authorities; and instead of composing his history of documents strung together in chronological order, or assembling them in an appendix, he leaves them for a later generation to put in print.[21]

Belknap and his Philadelphia friend, Ebenezer Hazard, compiled a two-volume *American Biography* (1794–1798), the data for which were a by-product of the former's collection of historical matter. Thus is illustrated the truth that leaders of men make history, and that history is sometimes chiefly a record of their deeds.

By his hunt for additions to the collection of the Massachusetts Historical Society, by his contagious interest in historical work and study, by his own writings and his scholarly standards Belknap gave the cause of history writing in America a full measure of service.

[20] *The Collection of Original Papers Relative to the History of the Colony of Massachusetts-Bay*, originally published in 1769, was reprinted in two volumes in Albany, N. Y., in 1865. The three volumes of the *History* appeared in a new edition in 1936 (Cambridge).

[21] *The History of New Hampshire*, Vol. I, Philadelphia: 1784; II and III, Boston: 1791–1792; 2d edn., Boston: 1813. "Jeremy Belknap Papers," in Massachusetts Historical Society *Collections*, 5th series, II, III (1877).

George Chalmers, a Scottish lawyer, spent several years in Baltimore when the quarrel between England and the colonies was verging toward armed conflict. When the war began he returned to the British Isles and there wrote his comments on the controversy and its antecedents. Hutchinson, loyal as he was to Britain, had hoped to find a basis for peaceful agreement; Chalmers, writing during and after the war, insisted more strongly than Hutchinson that the Americans had misinterpreted the imperial constitution. Indeed he contended that they, especially the New Englanders, had aimed at independence since the early years of the seventeenth century. Using as his sources the acts of assemblies, state papers, records of the Board of Trade, and letters of crown officers in America, all of which he conscientiously cited, he made an able argument to support his theses. His judicial temper and evident honesty won the respect of later American historians, whose main criticism is that his judgments are too legalistic.[22]

No American attempted to write a history of the War of Independence while it was being fought. However, the London *Annual Register* carried a serial account of it, written by sympathizers with the American cause, and several American periodicals copied or abridged its articles. William Gordon and David Ramsay were the first residents of the States to exploit the subject of the war, which was of great interest to readers on both sides of the Atlantic, and the histories by these two men enjoyed a place of pre-eminence in historical literature for more than a hundred years.

Ramsay, a South Carolina physician and one-time member of Congress during the Confederation, professed to have collected materials for his *History of the American Revolution* during the years 1782 to 1786.[23] He claimed, for example, to have read and taken notes from "every letter written to Congress by General Washington." [24] Granting the truth of his statements, it does not appear that he made much use of his notes, for his two histories have been shown to be plagiarized to such an extent that they have little worth.[25]

As for Gordon, an Englishman sympathetic with the Americans

[22] *Political Annals of the Present United Colonies. . . .* 1780; Continuation, Albany: New York Historical Society, [date?]. *Introduction to the History of the Revolt of the American Colonies.* Privately printed, 1782. Reprint, Boston: 1845.

[23] 2 vols., 1789.

[24] Quoted by Kraus, 128.

[25] Ramsay had published in 1785 the two-volume *History of the Revolution of South Carolina from a British Province to an independent State.*

who sojourned in Massachusetts from 1770 to 1786, serving a church there, his four volumes on the Revolution share with Ramsay's books the odious reputation due to plagiarisms. He seems like Ramsay to have done more or less gathering of materials, but both drew heavily on the *Annual Register*.[26] Moreover, Gordon's work approaches fictionalized history, for he presented it in the form of letters, some from Massachusetts and others from Europe, which were faked from the plagiarized matter.

During the war several writers gathered matter for histories which were not published until some years later. Some of them dealt with the Revolution and some were histories of individual states. Between 1776 and 1780 Robert Proud wrote a history of Pennsylvania.[27] His work exemplifies the customary practice of stringing documents together on a thread of narrative, with an added description of the area treated. This part of Proud's history related to Pennsylvania for the decade 1760 to 1770, and is the most valuable portion of it. Proud, who came to Philadelphia in 1759, was associated with the Quakers in both England and America, and shared the loyalist views of many of that sect. Much of the *History* concerned the Quakers and the Indians. It is written with a loyalist bias, but the treatment of the Indians shows a superior critical sense. Proud was somewhat indebted to Samuel Smith, but brought together and printed many documents which he thus made available to others. They also served as the vouchers for his statements. His loyalist sentiments probably explain the delay in publishing his work.

No such inhibitions restrained Alexander Hewat, whose work on South Carolina and Georgia was one of the few histories that got into print while the war was in progress.[28] This was due to its character, for he aimed to inform England concerning the potentialities

[26] The exposé of both of these histories by Orin G. Libby has been cited already, *supra*, p. 28, note 19. Libby writes of other plagiarisms in "Some Pseudo-Histories," in Wisconsin Academy of Sciences, Arts, and Letters, *Transactions*, XIII, 419, cited by Kraus, 112, footnote 21. The full title of Gordon's work is *The History of the Rise, Progress and Establishment of the Independence of the United States of America; Including an Account of the late War, and of the Thirteen Colonies from their Origin to that Period*. London: 1788. American edn., 3 vols., 1789.

[27] *History of Pennsylvania from . . . 1681. . . .* 2 vols. Philadelphia: 1797–1798.

[28] *An Historical Account of the Rise and Progress of the Colonies of South Carolina and Georgia*. 2 vols., London: 1779.

of commerce with this part of America, and he kept close to his theme. He was a sojourner in Charleston while collecting his documents, which he quoted at length in his volumes. His history was the first for the region, antedating Ramsay's *History of South Carolina* by a decade, and his material, which was largely descriptive, was of considerable use to later historians.

In point of time, Belknap's *New Hampshire* came next. The only other state history produced before 1800 comparable to Belknap's is Benjamin Trumbull's *Connecticut*.[29] It was planned before the Revolution, and although publication was long delayed, it was the first history of that state to appear in print. The pastor of one church for sixty years, Trumbull saw the hand of God in all New England's history. He tried to write in a plain style; cited his sources, which he had collected with "incredible" pains; did not regard traditional accounts as acceptable authority; and made his book a virtual encyclopedia of Connecticut history.

One other state history originating in the eighteenth century although not printed until early in the next was John Daly Burk's three-volume *History of Virginia*. Burk, a lawyer, came to Virginia as a refugee from his native Ireland and in his new home became a devoted Jeffersonian. In addition to the writings of his predecessors from John Smith to Beverley, he used Jefferson's large library. But he neglected other important sources. His *History*, ending with 1781, was written in rhetorical style, and is not given high rating in the state's historiography.

Events during the Confederation period divided Americans into two main groups. Shays's Rebellion alarmed conservatives and spurred them to form a stronger central government. Following their success in the Constitutional Convention of 1787, that group became the Federalist party and its opponent the Jeffersonian Republican. The histories prepared or published during the last dozen years of the century switched partisanship from the Tories and Patriots as opposing groups to the bias arising from domestic issues.

Shays's Rebellion was scarcely quelled before George R. Minot, a lawyer, made its history his theme.[30] Contemporary newspapers con-

[29] *A Complete History of Connecticut: Civil and Ecclesiastical from the Emigration of Its First Planters, from England in the Year 1630, to the Year 1764; and to the Close of the Indian Wars*. Vol. I, 1797; 2 vol. edn., 1818; 3d edn., 2 cols., New London, Conn.: 1898.

[30] *The History of the Rebellions in Massachusetts in the Year 1786*, published in 1788.

tained articles which showed that the rebels' grievances were real, but Minot shared the inability of the conservatives to understand their discontent. His work gratified the Federalist party heads, and became for them the classic account of the disturbance. Not for a century and a half did the rebels' side receive fair treatment.[31] Minot, whose conservatism was akin to Hutchinson's, wrote also a continuation of the latter's *History of Massachusetts*, which served as a stopgap until Hutchinson's third volume appeared in 1828.[32]

In these last years of the century two women are found in the ranks of the historians. Hannah Adams, an impecunious maiden lady, published in 1799 a potboiler *Summary History of New England*, which, although it dipped into some manuscripts, was derived in the main from extant publications including Minot's account of Shays's Rebellion. It was of the textbook order, and in fact an abridgement of 1807 was put to that use.

Mercy Otis Warren's *History of the Revolution* was a more substantial production.[33] Work on it was begun twenty-five or thirty years before it was put in print. A sister of James Otis, Hutchinson was for Mrs. Warren a veritable *bête noire*, yet, oddly enough, much of her history was written in Hutchinson's former residence. Bias appears again in the author's treatment of military history, and finally, in the postwar years it shows in her liking for Jefferson's political philosophy. One of the earliest histories of the Revolution and broader in scope than most of the others written in her generation, this work of a woman is marred not only by bias, but by a fondness for rhetoric, and by discoursiveness. All histories, good or bad, have a value in revealing the times they deal with, and some critics think that Mrs. Warren's is of unusual importance as a mirror in which we may find a reflection of the generation which gave it birth.

John Marshall also turned historian even while Chief Justice of the United States. His life of Washington, like Miss Adams's book, was written under pressure of financial need.[34] It is a good example of the virtual identity, at times, of biography and history. To tell the

[31] Julian Aronson, "The 'Forgotten Man' of Yesterday." *Scholastic*, XXIV, 15–16 (Feb. 3, 1934).

[32] *Continuation of the History of the Province of Massachusetts Bay from the year 1748 to 1765*. 2 vols. I, Boston: 1798; II (posthumous), 1803.

[33] *History of the Rise, Progress and Termination of the American Revolution interspersed with Biographical, Political and Moral Reflections*. Boston: 1805.

[34] *The Life of George Washington . . . to which is prefixed an Introduction Containing a Compendious View of the Colonies Planted by the English in the Continent of North America*. 1804–1807; rev. edn., 2 vols., 1832.

story of Washington, Marshall thought it necessary to begin with the planting of the colonies. Washington appears and disappears time and again, so that history and biography are interwoven like the warp and woof of a fabric. The method did not win public approval, and the Republicans charged that the work was a Federalist history designed to influence voters to repudiate Jefferson in the election of 1804.

Bushrod Washington's collection of George Washington's papers was Marshall's main reliance for the biographical passages. His technique as a historian was faulty, but was that of his time, for he wrote when writers had not yet learned to use quotation marks. The introductory historical portion was based on the usual histories, but had the unusual merit of dealing with all the colonies and states as parts of the larger whole. Marshall himself was dissatisfied with the original production, and in 1832 presented a new edition in which the *History of the American Colonies* and the *Life of Washington* are given separate volumes.

Mason Locke Weems, better known as "Parson Weems," rates a paragraph in this survey for two reasons. The first is the astounding vogue of his *Life of Washington*, the keynote of which is struck in the story of the cherry tree. The second is the character of his *Life of General Francis Marion*, which is an even worse example of fictionalized biography. Weems probably sought to appeal to readers by vividly portraying the nobility of his characters; his fault was not intentional deception, but rather arose from his ignorance of correct standards and even of those held by some of his contemporaries. Nevertheless all his zeal as a crusader in the cause of temperance and against gambling and other evils, and even the passage of time, have failed as an antidote of the poison he disseminated among countless thousands of readers by means of his fanciful writing. Much harm would be avoided if fiction could always be stripped of its false label of history or biography.

c. *The Nineteenth Century*

During the early years of the new century the people most concerned about history writing, past and future, were elderly persons who had come on the stage before the Revolution. The number was small, but the personnel was impressive, including John Adams, Thomas Jefferson, John Jay, Elbridge Gerry, Jedediah Morse, and others. The comments they exchanged were rather pessimistic but showed an understanding of the prerequisites for satisfactory work. While deploring the fact that a good general history had not yet been written, nor even a satisfactory history of the Revolution, they recognized that such histories must await the appearance of those dealing with the separate colonies and states, and that these in turn depended on much ampler collections of documents than had been gathered. Dissatisfaction with the annalistic or narrative style was also becoming apparent. John Adams had said in 1815 that "A history of military operations . . . is not a history of the American Revolution. . . . The Revolution was in the minds and hearts of the people," [35] while in 1826 Jared Sparks wrote that the best of the state histories were "valuable chiefly as materials . . . for future use," "telling much of events, but little of causes and consequences." [36]

The type of history these men advocated had not yet been attempted, but the need of gathering materials had long been felt. Thomas Hutchinson had anticipated the procedure of George Chalmers by saying that no complete history of the colonies could be written without recourse to documents preserved in England, and John Adams had early reached that same conclusion.[37] During the war suggestions were made that the work of individuals be supplemented by public agencies. Gerry tried in vain to persuade Congress to recommend that each state take measures to preserve its war records.[38] Thirty years later Adams was doing what he could to encourage young men in the states to collect materials on the war, but agreed with Jefferson that the documents for a true history of the Revolution probably could never be recovered.[39]

The survivors of the Revolutionary era were none too sympathetic in their attitude toward earlier writers. While these critics made some allowance for the paucity of materials, Sparks was their spokesman when he said that the early writings were "valuable chiefly as materials." Scholars are now perhaps more appreciative of the value of spadework. It is more evident when looked at from our vantage point. Not one of the early writers was primarily a historian. In their ranks were clergymen, physicians, lawyers, public officials, planters, European sojourners, loyalists, and women. Not one had been

[35] Kraus, 165.

[36] *Ibid.*, 171, quoting from Sparks's essay on "Materials for American History."

[37] *Ibid.* [38] *Ibid.*, 166. [39] *Ibid.*

trained in historical method, for as yet such training was nowhere to be had; but they were a good cross section of the educated class. Some of the earlier writers were victims of the superstitions of their times; others were biased this way or that; what some wrote was badly organized; at worst the style was clumsy, diffuse, rhetorical; at best it was the expression of intelligent men busy with other duties who nonetheless wrote well and with an evident desire to discover the truth and relate it simply and impartially. The standards of these few were derived from their praiseworthy aims, and anticipated in simple ways the critical techniques of our own times. Good or bad, the early efforts are the basis of the later interpretative histories of the period at the same time that they reveal the pitfalls in the path of untrained writers. These pioneers differed from today's scholars, not in intelligence, but chiefly in lacking comparable resources and technical training. In the story of their efforts the present-day student may find reasons for thanking the writers of books on methodology.

Some of the men who found the old histories deficient also took a gloomy view of the future. Two years before Adams tried to interest young men in collecting memorials of the Revolution, he complained to correspondents that they were not only ignorant but strangely disinterested in their country's history.[40] Insofar as this opinion was correct, it may have been due to the utter neglect of history as a subject of study in the colleges. Notwithstanding the urging of prominent men since the 1780's that history should be taught to the young,[41] no college in the United States offered courses in American history for more than half a century after the country had won its independence. The Adams letters referred to were written in 1813, in the shadow, it would seem, of an old man's shattered hopes. During the Revolution he had cherished the plan of retiring early to write a history of the war, and did collect a good deal of material to be used for the purpose. When Gerry suggested that Adams, seventy-seven years old, should carry out his plan, the latter replied that if he were only thirty, he would expect the writing to require not less than twenty years.[42] Other old men, too, who had gathered materials with the same intent left them for others to use.

When Adams wrote his despondent letters about the young men, there were several whose future he could not foresee. One was a boy of thirteen, named George Bancroft; another, a child of six, bore

[40] Kraus, 163 *et passim*. [41] *Ibid.*, 109. [42] *Ibid.*, 164.

the name Richard Hildreth; the birth of Francis Parkman was quite beyond anticipation, being an event which occurred ten years after the date of the letters; nor is it probable that Adams knew much about John G. Palfrey, aged seventeen; even Jared Sparks, the oldest of this group of five, if not quite unknown, was an unpredictable quantity at age twenty-four. At least three of the five were still unknown to fame when Adams died in 1826. In the following quarter-century, however, all of them shone as stars of the first magnitude among the lesser lights of the American historical firmament.

The nineteenth century is notable in American historiography for a series of significant developments which would have more than fulfilled the hopes of the old guard, to wit: the vast amount of historical material collected; the multiplication of historical associations devoted to the collection, housing, and publication of such materials; the great increase in the number of libraries with allied functions; the publication of historical material by periodicals, and of government records and documents by private printers and governments; the advances in writing made possible by these increased facilities; the addition of history to the curriculum of the colleges and universities and its advance to a commanding place as a subject of study; the introduction and teaching of critical method by means of the seminar; the rise of the new problem of how best to present history in its entirety; and the place of the doctoral dissertation in the program as a whole.

i. COLLECTORS AND COLLECTIONS

By the time Sparks and his younger contemporaries reached their productive years it was well understood that historical materials included almost everything in writing. One great class was made up of the correspondence and diaries of prominent persons. Aside from business records and diaries of public men, later generations have produced less of this class of matter, and in consequence what may be called intimate history has suffered.[43] Also understood was the fact that collecting, preserving, editing, publishing, and writing history were interwoven processes. In fact they were inseparable; but for the sake of clarity they need to be examined one by one.

Most of the earlier historians had been collectors perforce, but some of the collectors had done little or no writing. Thomas Prince is a good example of the latter type. On the other hand, Jeremy

[43] *Cf. Harvard Guide*, 177–188.

Belknap represents the worker who not only collected the material for his own history, but also for the Massachusetts Historical Society. In the same year that the first volume of that society's *Collections* came out, Ebenezer Hazard, Belknap's Philadelphia friend, began to publish the material he had gathered.[44] Engaged in the same kind of work but years later were Peter Force and Matthew Clarke, clerk of the House of Representatives. In 1822 they began to inspect the records of the original states, collecting documents for a general history of the country from the beginning of colonization to the ratification of the Constitution. Aided by a Government subsidy they began to publish in 1837, under the title *American Archives*, a series which, brought to an end with the exhaustion of the Government fund in 1953, contained documents on the Revolution for the years 1774 to 1783. Within these same years (1836–1846) Force published four more volumes of *Tracts* relating to the colonial period.[45] Continuing his activities, he accumulated a collection of around fifty thousand titles, which the Library of Congress acquired in 1867.[46]

Jared Sparks was also a collector and editor rather than a writer of history. His nearest approach to the last kind of activity was in the field of biography. His initial project, dating from 1819, was a life of John Ledyard, some of the data for which he obtained from London. He seemed always to have several projects in mind at the same time. About 1823 he caught the fever which was prompting others to attempt a general history of America, and at the same time began to plan a life of George Washington. With this second project in view he visited the older states in 1826, making an inventory of their archives and other collections and taking notes. This tour of inspection gave him a knowledge of existing materials for American history probably not equaled by any one else at that time. The information gained was the basis of the essay mentioned above on "Materials for American History." In 1828 he visited France and England seeking documents relating to the Revolution, and in the same year published the *Life and Travels of John Ledyard*.[47]

[44] *Historical Collections; consisting of State Papers . . . intended for an History of the United States. . . .* 2 vols. Philadelphia: 1792–1794. Kraus, 108.

[45] Kraus, 173 f. The *Tracts* were reprinted in 1947 (*Harvard Guide*, 207).

[46] Kraus, 175.

[47] An excellent essay on Sparks is presented by John S. Bassett, in *The Middle Group of American Historians*, 57–137, 307–311. Kraus's sketch draws a good deal of data from Bassett's book.

The twelve volumes of the *Diplomatic Correspondence of the American Revolution,* which Sparks edited in 1829 and 1830 under contract with the Federal Government, were in keeping with his main interest, a history of the Revolution. So also was the *Life of Gouverneur Morris,* published in 1832. Between 1834 and 1837 (after Bushrod Washington's reluctant consent to the use of his Uncle George's papers) came the twelve volumes dealing with the central figure of the war and following years—*The Life and Writings of George Washington.* Even before the last volume of this work was published, the first of the ten on *The Works of Benjamin Franklin* appeared (1836–1840). All of these were virtually parts of the history of the Revolution. They contained much of the material for the history of the Revolution which Sparks had hoped to write but did not.

Another undertaking was *The Library of American Biography.* The two series totaling twenty-five volumes came out during a period of thirteen years (1834–1847). They contained sixty biographies of which Sparks wrote eight. As a sort of appendix to all the publications touching the Revolution came in 1853 the *Correspondence . . . being letters of Eminent Men to George Washington.*

That Sparks shared Marshall's belief that "history can be told through the biographies of leading men" is evident in almost all of his productions; he seeks to let their character and deeds speak through the records. The *Life of Washington* is composed chiefly of documents selected to illustrate the character of the man believed by Sparks and his generation to be the greatest of all Americans. This purposeful selection, the meticulous correction of errors in spelling and grammar, the substitution of dignified phraseology for inelegant or careless terms, gave in fact a distorted portrait. Now and then he analyzes Washington's traits with good judgment and without exaggeration. His characterization of Franklin was even better, and was needed to restore a reputation unjustly maligned at the time.

Sparks's editorial practices are also subject to criticism. A forgiveable defect is the failure to utilize documentary material not yet available; but, unlike Force, he did not follow the example of the best European editors. They held that historical materials should be printed without alteration or correction. These shortcomings caused most of his work to be superseded. In spite of all this, he ranks as our first great editor of historical material; he brought together and published a great mass of manuscript matter which had not previously been easily accessible.

Early in the year which brought publication of the last volume of *The Library of American Biography*, Peter Force received a letter from a young man who wrote that he hoped "to effect something for the biographical literature of our country." [48] Force's correspondent was Lyman Copeland Draper, aged thirty-two. In boyhood Draper had listened to veterans of the Revolution and found the tales of border warfare most fascinating. When he wrote the letter to Force he had already collected five thousand pages of material for biographies of the heroes of these conflicts. During the next seven years he increased his holdings to fifteen thousand items, including papers of Daniel Boone, Simon Kenton, George Rogers Clark, and other pioneers of the trans-Allegheny West. All had been gathered by personal visits to the holders.

In 1854 he became secretary of the recently organized Wisconsin State Historical Society, an organization almost as old as the state itself. At that time the Society's library consisted of fifty volumes housed in the office of the state governor. To these Draper added his own collection. When he retired in January, 1887, the library numbered more than 110,000 titles. It was not confined to material on the history of Wisconsin, or even for the region somewhat vaguely designated as the pioneer West, about which his interest centered. Most of the states contributed in some measure to the treasures of the Society.[49]

Great as Draper was as a collector, he accomplished little as a writer. He took to heart a warning given him by Jared Sparks that traditions and reminiscences should be handled cautiously. His critical sifting of documents in quest of facts seemed to exhaust his energies; the mass of his accumulated facts overwhelmed him. Nor could he interpret his characters; in his eyes they were all heroes to whom honor was due. He manfully prepared a great field; others gathered the harvest.

Draper chose as his successor a journalist, Reuben Gold Thwaites.

[48] Words quoted by Kraus, 175.

[49] An article on Draper was published in the Spring issue of the *Wisconsin Magazine of History* for 1952, pages 163–166, 231–234. From it most of the factual matter in this sketch was drawn. The writer was Professor William Best Hesseltine, author of a life of Draper entitled *Pioneer's Mission*. Madison: State Historical Society, 1953.

As a collector the new secretary proved to be Draper's worthy disciple. From the archives of Canada, London, and Paris he obtained transcripts of documents related to Wisconsin history; he secured as gifts the records of the old fur-trading companies, the early missions and industries, the beginnings of schools, and the personal papers of pioneers. He filled gaps in the Society's book collection to make it representative of all the great interests of historical scholars in the field of American history in general and the Middle West in particular. He systematized the files of newspapers and pamphlets, and took for his guiding principle the faith that the rubbish of one generation might become the indispensable means of understanding its civilization at a later time. In organization and program of publishing he made the Wisconsin Historical Society a model which other states followed. While he was secretary the library grew from 118,000 titles to 352,000. His editorial work was that of an expert, exemplifying the best standards of the opening twentieth century.[50]

Thwaites, the "builder of a new type of state historical society" and a great editor, was less successful as a writer. Trained as a journalist, he had neither the taste nor patience for the critical work necessary for writing good history. Always strong in him was the liking for the romantic and picturesque. Though fond of details—the fringe of the garment—he was not nicely accurate in dealing with them; he lacked originality in interpretation and was not gifted in developing a story. He seldom showed appreciation of hidden motives or the forces underlying events. He credulously included in his reprints of *Early Western Travels* a book that had been shown to be in part plagiarized, and thought all-sufficient George Rogers Clark's own account of the occupation of the Illinois country. Some successor or other has illuminated almost every subject he touched by a more critical examination of the sources.[51]

Hubert Howe Bancroft, a contemporary of Draper, migrated from Buffalo, New York, to San Francisco in 1852, and within fifteen years amassed wealth as a bookdealer. Out of this experience grew an interest in the history of the Pacific Coast states and their neighbors

[50] Sketch based on Frederick Jackson Turner's *Reuben Gold Thwaites, Memorial Address. Madison*: State Historical Society of Wisconsin, 1914.

[51] Clarence W. Alvord, "A Critical Analysis of the Work . . . of Thwaites," in MVHA *Proceedings* for 1914–1915, pp. 321–333.

which led him to turn his attention to the collection of materials for a comprehensive history of the pioneer period of the region. Bancroft was a business man with no training for historical writing. His methods, both in gathering and later using the materials for such a history were those with which business had made him familiar. His collection included all obtainable material bearing on the West Coast from Central America to Alaska. It contained some sixty thousand volumes, thousands of pamphlets, hundreds of files of newspapers, great quantities of original manuscripts, masses of copies of state records, mission archives, and recollections of early settlers. Agents were sent to Alaska to copy Russian government records and others to Spain and elsewhere for similar work. Bancroft thought it important to get every scrap leaving the weeding out of worthless stuff for a later time. The vast mass thus brought together at a cost of about half a million dollars was used by the owner and a large staff of assistants in preparing the *History of the Pacific Coast States of North America.*[52]

Following the publication of the *History* Bancroft offered the entire collection to the University of California at a price much below the cost of gathering it. The university invited Dr. Thwaites to inspect it and give his advice on the wisdom of accepting the offer. His report that to duplicate the collection, even if that were possible, would cost far more than the price asked, decided the question. So runs the story of one of the most remarkable collections of the nineteenth century—and of one of the great collectors.

Comparable activities were carried on by numerous collectors working like Draper and Thwaites on behalf of some library or like Bancroft and Parkman to forward their own projects. The brothers, Paul Leicester and Worthington C. Ford, obtained a great quantity of transcripts from the French records of foreign relations which they planned to use in writing on the diplomatic history of the United States during the formative years. The tragic death of Paul led his brother to abandon the project and turn the transcripts over to the New York Public Library. The American Historical Association decided to publish them on condition that Professor Frederick Jackson Turner do the necessary editorial work. Thus while the

[52] 39 vols. San Francisco: 1883–1890. In the last volume, entitled *Literary Industries,* Bancroft describes his activities. The method used in writing the volumes is discussed later. (For pages see Index under H. Bancroft.)

original transcripts remained a part of the collection of the New York library, the published edition made the matter widely available. It fills more than a thousand pages in the second volume of the Association's *Annual Report* for 1903. The editorial task was assigned to Turner because he was currently engaged in studying the diplomatic history of the United States during the first twenty years of independence, and for the purpose had himself obtained transcripts from foreign repositories.[53]

ii. THE INCREASE OF LIBRARIES AND HISTORICAL SOCIETIES

These cases are typical in showing that historians continued to collect documents for their own writings, and also that collections tended to gravitate to the libraries. By the close of the century much of the material gathered by such historians as Bancroft and Parkman had found its way into some great library, setting a pattern quite often followed. They exemplify the relations which became customary between collectors on the one hand and historical societies, libraries, and universities on the other, and resulted in the creation of great depositories of matter for the use of historians and students, and the many-fold increase of their resources. The century saw the snowballing from the small beginnings in the colonial period. Bradford's manuscripts were drawn on by many early writers; William Byrd's library was used by his friends. Most historians also gathered some new materials; and the demand for organizations to engage in collecting on a large scale was not new when Belknap and the Massachusetts Historical Society attempted to perform that service for Massachusetts. The American Philosophical Society was formed at Philadelphia twenty years earlier. Other states and associations folowed these leads, and in 1826 Jared Sparks praised their work. Between 1830 and 1850 about thirty-five societies were founded. Many were short-lived or soon became inactive. Among those which survived were the New York Historical Society and the similar one in New Hampshire. Within a few decades the former gathered a valuable collection of books and manuscripts on the history of New York State. The American Antiquarian Society of Worcester, despite a name which belied its character and purpose, accumulated in the course of years a collection of very great importance to historians. It included what is still the largest collection of American

[53] For Turner's use of his transcripts see *Harvard Guide* index under his name.

newspapers printed between 1690 and 1820, as well as a large library of state and local histories.[54]

The period of rapid increase of historical societies came after the Civil War; measures to preserve its records were a part of the aftermath. The success of the Wisconsin Historical Society was an incentive to new states to organize their own and a spur to the older states to renew their activity. By the end of the century, most states, and many regions, counties, and municipalities had some kind of historical organization. The coming of history into the curriculum of the colleges and universities gave added impulse to the movement. In 1884 the American Historical Association was chartered by Congress, and within a few years became the mother of other national associations representing political science, economics, sociology, and special subjects, such as agriculture and constitutional law. Important sectional associations came later; the Mississippi Valley Historical Association was formed in 1908.[55] At the turn of the century university-trained men and women were replacing the former presidents and secretaries who had controlled the older societies and whose interests had often been antiquarian or genealogical.

The growth of libraries followed a similar course. In the colonial period men of wealth occasionally accumulated private libraries of a few hundred volumes. William Byrd's 4,000 volumes are believed to have been the largest collection of his generation. Free public libraries supported by taxation were then unknown. A so-called public library was started in Boston in 1673, and may have served clergymen until fire destroyed it in 1747. (The present Boston Public Library dates from 1854.) A few towns formed library associations which purchased books to circulate among the members. Of these the Philadelphia Association founded in 1731 largely through Benjamin Franklin's efforts still exists. The Harvard library is reported to have contained "above five thousand volumes" in 1723, but most of them were lost in a fire in 1764. George Ticknor declared that be-

[54] *Harvard Guide*, 59. The first edition of Brigham's *Bibliography of American Newspapers* was printed in the Society's *Proceedings*, n.s., XXIII, Part 2, 247–402, and succeeding volumes. *Cf. supra*, p. 110. The *Harvard Guide*, 14 f.; cites several books and articles dealing with historical societies, among them J. F. Jameson's *History of Historical Societies.* (Savannah: 1914.)

[55] For the history of the formation of the MVHA see volume I of the *Proceedings, 1907–1908*, pages 9–34. See also presidential address of James L. Sellers, "Before We Were Members," in *MVHR* for June, 1953, pp. 3–24.

fore he studied in Europe (1815–1819) he thought the Harvard collection was a large one, but on his return "it seemed a closetful of books." [56] In 1818 Harvard had the good fortune to acquire the library of Christophe D. Ebeling, a German scholar who, as he said, had spent all his money collecting it; he had published two years before a seven-volume history of America.[57] Harvard's purchase of this library made it the chief holder of Americana. In 1823 Sparks, contemplating a history of the United States, commented that the best facilities for it were the Ebeling library, the books in the Boston Athenaeum and the Massachusetts Historical Society.[58] After his extensive survey of 1826 he could still count only seven libraries with more books on America than could be shelved "in the corner of a single case." [59] His own collection became at length a part of the Harvard library.[60]

Among the nineteenth-century builders of private libraries were men of wealth who took pride in the possession of books of all kinds. Others made their selections according to their special interests, or concerned themselves with the preservation of the records of their business enterprises. In the last group was John Jacob Astor, who had made a fortune in the fur trade of the Far West. At his instance Washington Irving wrote *Astoria*, using Astor's papers, which Irving described in the Introduction.[61] Contemporaneously John R. Bartlett, a New York bookseller, Obadiah Rich, who was a minor American diplomat in Europe, and Henry Stevens, Jr., working in the British Museum, were reporting their findings of Americana. Bartlett was helpful to John Carter Brown, who collected five thousand titles on America.[62] This library is now controlled by a group of Associates, and contains a notable collection of Americana.[63]

Some of the great libraries of the present were formed by the union

[56] Kraus, 172.
[57] *Ibid.*, 191 f.
[58] *Ibid.*, 202. The Boston Athenaeum was founded in 1807.
[59] *Ibid.*, 172. The statement may have been made before the survey of 1826.
[60] Bassett, *op. cit.*, 137, footnote, citing Library of Harvard University *Bibliographical Contributions*, No. 22 (1889). The inventory showed 193 bound volumes of manuscripts.
[61] Author's revised edition. New York: G. P. Putnam & Company, 1854. Original edition, 2 vols. Philadelphia: 1839.
[62] Kraus, 176.
[63] Lawrence C. Wroth, *The First Century of the John Carter Brown Library: A History with a Guide to the Collections*. Providence, R. I.: The Associates of the John Carter Brown Library, 1946. For a list of Library Histories and Guides see *Harvard Guide*, 61.

of important private collections. One of these private libraries was that of James Lenox, of New York. In 1893 Lenox purchased George Bancroft's materials. In 1895 the Lenox and the Astor libraries, with others, came into the possession of the New York Public Library, organized that year.[64]

This sketch assembles a few facts to illustrate the process by which many of the great American libraries were built. Eventually the Library of Congress outgrew all others. It was established by act of Congress in 1800, but for a century failed to become outstanding. In the early years it suffered repeated losses by fire. Farsighted men perceived its unique opportunity as early as 1829; in that year Jared Sparks urged that it should obtain "a copy of every book and manuscript in existence relating to America." Until after the Civil War it had only occasional opportunities to make notable accessions, as when it acquired the Peter Force collection in 1867.[65] In 1870 an act of Congress took a step toward the goal set by Sparks by requiring copies of every book copyrighted in the United States to be deposited with it. During the nineteenth century it obtained the papers of a few national statesmen, but its period of greatness began with the present century, under Herbert Putnam, who became librarian in 1899.

iii. PUBLICATION OF HISTORICAL MATERIAL

During all these years of gathering material, building libraries, and creating historical societies, the publishing of documents and writing of histories were going on. The old practice of printing documents as appendices to volumes gave way to publications containing only documentary material. Peter Force's *American Archives* and Ebenezer Hazard's *Historical Collections* were examples. The volumes published by Force were only a part of his holdings; the rest remained in manuscript for want of adequate government aid.[66] Other undertakings left to private enterprise were Elliot's *Debates*,[67] the *American State Papers*, and all records of the proceedings in Congress prior to 1873, when the Government began to publish the

[64] *Ibid.; Harvard Guide*, 58. [65] Kraus, 176. [66] Kraus, 292 f.

[67] Jonathan Elliot, ed., *Debates, Resolutions and other Proceedings in Convention on the Adoption of the Federal Constitution.* 4 vols. 1827–1834. 2d edn. entitled *Debates in the Several State Conventions on the Adoption of the Federal Constitution, . . . Together with the Journal of the Federal Convention. . . .* 5 vols. Philadelphia: 1851.

Congressional Record.[68] The only considerable expenditures by the Government for the publication of historical records before the Civil War were the subsidy granted to Force and the $30,300 paid to Sparks for editing the *Diplomatic Correspondence of the American Revolution,* a sum which apparently met the costs of publication and left a compensation of $4,800 for the editor.[69]

Some of the historical societies began to publish as soon as they were organized. The Massachusetts Society put out the first volume of its *Collections* in 1792. The title indicates the nature of the contents of the series, which has been continuous. A general index of all the Society's publications was issued in 1935.

The New York Historical Society published the first volume of its *Collections* in 1811. Similar societies were formed in New Hampshire, 1824; Pennsylvania, 1826; and Rhode Island, 1827.[70] Theoretically their function was to gather materials relating to their respective communities, great or small, and to publish documents from time to time in volumes usually called *Collections.* Most of them also printed volumes of *Proceedings* containing the record of meetings where business was transacted and papers read. This pattern applied to the national as well as the local associations. For many years—as long as the funds were available—the American Historical Association had a Historical Manuscripts Commission which printed matter of general interest in the Association's *Annual Reports. The Autobiography of Martin Van Buren,* about which the illustrative problem of Part I centered, was published in one of these *Reports.*

The historical societies shared their functions with other organizations and publishers. The upsurge of nationalism following the War of 1812–1815 quickened interest in history. Signs of this interest were: the purchase of the Ebeling library by Harvard; the printing of records by Niles' *Weekly Register*; the numerous articles on history in the *North American Review* and other periodicals. Under a succession of editors including William Tudor and Jared Sparks this *Review* became almost a national magazine of history. State governments began to show an interest in such work. In 1814, Governor De Witt Clinton, who was at the same time vice president of the New

[68] *Supra,* p. 114.

[69] Bassett, *op. cit.*

[70] *Harvard Guide,* pages 163–168, lists these and others organized later: national, regional, state, local, and miscellaneous, and gives the titles of their publications.

York Historical Society, served both state and society by persuading the legislature to finance the translation of the records of Dutch New Netherland which had lain untouched in the state archives. This beginning was followed by a search in Europe for documents bearing on the colonial history of the state. John Romeyn Broadhead, sent as agent of the state in 1841, returned in 1844 with eighty volumes of documents.[71] Many of them were useful to New York's neighbors. When printed they filled nineteen volumes.[72]

New York's activity aroused other states and they began to consider efforts to obtain materials from Europe, although they did little at the time.[73] Most of the old states had already published their laws and other official records, but in this period they began to reprint as well as revise and supplement. Massachusetts is a good example. William Lincoln prepared for publication the state's journals of the provincial congresses of the early years of the Revolution, and they were printed at Boston in 1838. The outline of the story of state publication of official records can be worked out from the data given in *Harvard Guide*.[74]

iv. PROGRESS IN WRITING HISTORY

Nineteenth-century historians worked under conditions which were better than those of the preceding two centuries: they had at their command far greater masses of material, and the technique of writing had appreciably improved. Several rules had emerged from the trial-and-error methods of the earlier writers, although they had not been codified. They prescribed the objective search for truth and proscribed partisanship; they warned against the ready acceptance of tradition and reminiscences; they called for the citation of documents and authorities relied on; they favored the transcription of quoted documents in the exact form of the original; but they lacked established forms for such matters as citations of authorities and distinguishing quotations from the author's text. Not until after the Civil War did critical procedure with its elaborate rules become a recognized part of the historian's training. Lacking this formal training, nineteenth-century writers wrote well or ill, depending on

[71] Kraus, 180.

[72] Edmund B. O'Callaghan, ed., *Documentary History of the State of New York*. 4 vols. Albany: 1849–1851.

———and Berthold Fernow, eds., *Documents Relating to the Colonial History of the State of New York*. 15 vols. Albany: 1856–1887.

[73] Kraus, 160.

[74] Pages 125–139.

their native good sense and their acquaintance with the practices evolved by their predecessors. However objective in intent, each had his point of view, which today's students do well to recognize. George Bancroft, for instance, thought that history should "prove something." In the first half of the century most Americans believed with Bancroft that the world, or at least the United States, was "progressing" in accordance with universal laws governing human society. At one time he asserted that "the selfishness of evil defeats itself." In an oration delivered in 1854 he declared "no tramp of a despot's foot ever trod out one idea. The world cannot retrograde." [75]

Bancroft's *History of the United States* seemed to the generation which received its first volumes to be the general history so long awaited.[76] The initial volume was published in 1834, the last in 1882, almost half a century later.[77] His friend, the German historian Heeren, under whom he studied while abroad, was right in telling him that his subject was the work of a lifetime.[78]

The first volume suited the mood of the time so well that it was in its tenth edition within a decade. Although the author's style was somewhat chastened before the work was completed, it failed to meet the standards of the 1880's. As an honor to the old man, the American Historical Association chose him as its first president, although with tongue in cheek.

Bancroft's research was exhaustive and praiseworthy. During diplomatic missions in Europe he collected masses of material. Nor did he neglect the collections which had been made by Force and others in the United States. His statement of aims was also admirable: to collect the truth from trustworthy contemporary sources; to give his statements authenticity by applying critical principles to his authorities; to examine the reports of opposing parties; to check contradictory statements; to bear in mind that memories and traditions nourish error, etc.[79] His application of these principles, probably imbibed in Germany as well as drawn from American examples, was faulty. Perhaps to avoid tedious detail and hold the reader's

[75] Gooch, *op cit.*, 403–408.

[76] Good studies of Bancroft as a historian are to be found in Bassett, 138–210, and Kraus, 215–239.

[77] The history filled ten volumes in the original edition. The volumes appeared at irregular intervals from 1834 to 1874. Two on the *History of the Formation of the Constitution* were published in 1882; they were included a few years later in the revised six-volume edition.

[78] Kraus, 228.

[79] Kraus, 222.

interest, he did not scruple to compile from separate reports and offer as continuous deliverances parts of different speeches.[80] Nor did he always cite his sources; "the wondrous . . . sources of information remain mysterious." [81]

Bancroft's method was faulty in part because of the limitations of his system of handling his notes, which threw too great a burden on his own memory,[82] and partly because of his preconceptions and over-rhetorical use of language. Some of his concepts were fertile: that the history of the Revolution included much of the history of mankind in that era (an idea which John Adams had also held); that the idea of continuity "gives vitality to history." His chief generalization is that "the force which brought all influences harmoniously together was the movement of intellectual freedom." [83] The entire history is imbued with the exuberant confidence, uncritical self-laudation, and optimism of Jacksonian democracy.[84] When the German historian Von Ranke told him that his history was the "best . . . ever written from the democratic point of view," he replied that if democracy is a historical fact, to deal with it as such is to be objective. His over-all conclusion, stated in the *History of the Formation of the Constitution*, is that "in America a new people had risen up without king, or princes, or nobles. . . . They were more sincerely religious, better educated, of serener minds, and of purer morals than the men of any former republic." [85] To the end of his life George Bancroft was the Fourth-of-July orator!

Before the fourth volume of Bancroft's *History* was published in 1852 Richard Hildreth's offering entered the field. His work overlapped Bancroft's first three volumes, which stopped with the midyears of the eighteenth century, but from that point he explored virgin areas.[86] He obviously had Bancroft in mind when he ex-

[80] Kraus, quoting Howe, *Life and Letters of George Bancroft.*

[81] Kraus, 237 f., quoting a paper by Sydney G. Fisher, in American Philosophical Society *Proceedings* for 1912.

[82] *Supra*, p. 139.

[83] Kraus, 222.

[84] Jameson, *History of Historical Writing*, 104.

[85] Kraus, 232, footnote 34, citing Howe; Gooch, 403 ff. quoting *Formation of the Constitution.*

[86] *History of the United States of America, from the Discovery of the Continent to . . . the End of the Sixteenth Congress* (1821). 6 vols. New York: 1849–1856. The work came out in two series of three volumes each, the first ending with the organization of the Government under the Constitution in 1789. A revision was published in 1880–1882.

plained that "of centennial sermons and Fourth-of-July orations . . . there are more than enough. . . . It is due to our fathers and ourselves . . . to present . . . the founders of our American nation unbedaubed with patriotic rouge." [87] To him the Salem witchcraft was "the irrefragible evidence of an almost savage society"; "the period before 1789 . . . largely the domain of myths." "His sceptical volumes, like a cold north wind, blew away many a patriotic legend." [88] He himself describes the effect of his effort to give his readers "undress portraits of our progenitors" in the preface to the second edition: "My presumption in bursting the bubble of a colonial golden age of fabulous purity and virtue has given very serious offense." [89]

In critical attitude Hildreth was ahead of his times. His history is acknowledged to be better than Bancroft's, but it has conspicuous faults. In place of footnotes or other means of citing authorities precisely, he substitutes a long list of works used. In the second trio of volumes he betrays a Federalist bias. Jefferson is a demagogue, Hamilton the statesman. He shares the latter's low opinion of the average man. His bias in these matters is like Bancroft's but from the opposite point of view. His style is direct, clear, and without irrelevancies, but devoid of imagination, emotion, or fervor; it is never graphic or picturesque, and at times is ungrammatical. But he is accurate in factual statements and his insights are often keen, anticipating the conclusions of later scholars: he sees in the exercise of power by Parliament in the eighteenth century a greater tyranny than that of the king; the Boston "Massacre" is not to him "an unprovoked assault by brutal soldiers," but an act necessary to control an irresponsible mob; Shays's Rebellion is one of the events leading to the formation of the Constitution, but economic cleavages motivated its framing; the only real difference between the first political parties was over the degree of democracy which could safely be permitted in the union under the Constitution.[90] Federalist though he was, he saw that Federalism lost its vitality as it moved westward. In this fact he finds one important clue to the overthrow of the party, and foreshadows one of F. J. Turner's theses, that the frontier was a democratizing influence in American life.

Among nineteenth-century American historians Francis Parkman is unique. No other was more careful to get the facts, and no other

[87] Kraus, page 243, quoting Hildreth.
[88] Gooch, 407. [89] Quoted *ibid.* [90] Kraus, 246.

quite equaled him in writing good history which was at the same time fine literature. Henry Adams, an excellent judge of both history and literature wrote: "of its style and narrative the highest praise is that they are on a level with its thoroughness of study." [91] Hildreth collected little or no new material, while Parkman left to the Massachusetts Historical Society some seventy volumes of manuscripts which he had gathered in the United States, Canada, and Europe. He visited Europe four times on such errands.[92] He differed from other historians in supplementing documentary material by his own observations made on the scene of important events. This habit enabled him to give his narrative the vividness of an eyewitness account. His talents were well adapted to his theme, which was the struggle of France and England for the mastery of North America. Each volume of his history appeared under a separate title, and most of them dealt in monographic fashion with a division of the whole story which formed a complete unit of it. Between the first and last of the volumes forty years elapsed, a period almost equal to that which Bancroft's work required.[93]

James Ford Rhodes thought that Parkman was "our most original historian"; "No man whose training had been gained wholly in the best schools of Germany, France, or England," he said, "could have written" these books.[94] Gooch adds: "He worked with exceptional accuracy. . . . His knowledge of the Indians was derived from life. . . . His style . . . gained in simplicity and power, and his descriptive passages are among the finest in American literature." [95]

Parkman wrote as an heir of British ideals and betrayed his bias in such expressions as "A happier calamity never befell a people than the conquest of Canada by the British arms"; and "New France could not grow with a priest on guard at the gate to let in none but such as pleased him." [96] He was not blind to the faults of his own people—"Puritanism was not an unmixed blessing," he admitted; but he rejected the French criticism that he magnified the defects and minimized the merits of the Canadian system.[97] Catholics also

[91] Quoted by Kraus, 287. [92] *Ibid.*, 289.

[93] *France and England in North America.* 9 vols. Boston: 1865–1892. Two volumes published in 1851, entitled *The Conspiracy of Pontiac,* were really a part of the history, but dealt with events following those narrated in the other nine. The whole series was reprinted in the Centenary Edition of Parkman's *Works* (11 vols. Boston: 1922).

[94] *Historical Essays*, 28; 102–103.

[95] *Op. cit.*, 419–421. [96] Quoted by Kraus, 284 f. [97] *Ibid.*, 285, 288.

thought he showed prejudice against them, when in fact he respected them and paid them high tribute in *The Jesuits in North America.*[98]

Parkman's work did much to arouse interest in the West as a field for historical study. He encouraged Pierre Margry to edit a collection of sources on French colonial history.[99] Theodore Roosevelt dedicated the *Winning of the West* to him. Reuben G. Thwaites reedited the *Jesuit Relations* from which Parkman had drawn much material for his volume on the *Jesuits in North America.*[100] His influence on Lyman Draper and Frederick J. Turner would make an interesting study.

Perhaps the final estimate of Parkman's performance may be that while it accomplished superbly what he set out to do, the restricted theme and the romantic handling keep it from ranking with the greatest histories. In answer one may say that an analytic treatment must be soberly factual, and requires genius to give it the quality of fine literature. Parkman's writing is a model of narrative, free from any taint of fictionalizing. Moreover, in the volume entitled *The Old Regime in Canada* he proved his ability to analyze a culture, although in doing so his style "necessarily has less of the glow that lights the pages of frontier battles." [101] The criticism that his central theme is restricted applies to all written history, for all of it is restricted either in time or topic. Thus Bancroft's *History of the United States* deserves that title only by courtesy, since it ends with the very beginning of constitutional government, that is, with events that took place about a century before the author's death. James Schouler bridged the gap between the adoption of the Constitution and the close of the era of Reconstruction with a chronological narrative arranged in a framework of presidential terms and sessions of Congress.[102] Hermann E. von Holst's *Constitutional and Political History of the United States* is a long essay on the influence of slavery in the life of the nation.[103] James Ford Rhodes's *History of the United States from the Compromise of 1850* was planned to

[98] *Ibid.*, 274; Gooch, *passim.*

[99] Kraus, 294, *Découvertes et établissements des Français dans l'ouest et dans le sud de l'Amerique Septentrionale 1614–1754. Mémoires et documents originaux* (6 vols., 1876–1886).

[100] John G. Shea had edited the *Jesuit Relations* in 1857–1866.

[101] Kraus, 284.

[102] *History of the United States under the Constitution.* 6 vols. 1880–1899. Rev. edn., 7 vols. New York: 1894–1913.

[103] J. J. Lalor and others, translators. 7 vols. Chicago: 1876–1892.

close with the election of Cleveland in 1885. The author would have ranked higher as a historian if he had not later added two volumes extending the narrative to 1909. The whole is essentially a political history, giving scant attention to other subjects.[104] Henry Adams wrote an excellent *History of the United States* which actually covered only the sixteen years of the Jefferson and Madison administrations, and utilizes materials in the Federal capital city.[105]

These examples should be enough to show that the hope of an American history covering all topics from the beginning to date is illusory. It appeared in embryo in the colonial dream that good histories of the several provinces could be made the basis of a general history which would include all of them. The idea was never realistic, but it was persistent, and gave way only slowly late in the nineteenth century before the cold logic of facts. Cumulating evidence pointed to the conclusion that the all-embracing history, if within the range of possibility, was not a one-man job. New standards were demanding the critical examination of the sources at the same time that accessible source material was increasing faster than scholars could master it. And the publication of sources continued, an example being Margry's documents on French colonization. The Civil War did much to stir the interest of the public in its past. By the close of the century concepts of history were bringing within its scope new subjects, such as the status, interests, and influence of classes of the population which historians had not previously stressed. John Bach McMaster's *History of the People* was the first to focus attention on the "forgotten man." [106] It was inevitable that writing would keep pace with economic and social developments, and that an unprecedented output of books would be devoted to the intensive treatment of some one subject. Such studies might be long or short; one might be an article in a periodical, another a volume or more. A good example of the first class was the series carried in the *Century Magazine* during 1885 and 1886, later published in four volumes under the title *Battles and Leaders of the Civil War*. One author made an extended study of the rhymes, pamphlets, and other types of literary output of the era of

[104] 7 vols. New York: 1893–1906. Vols. VIII and IX, New York: 1919–1922.

[105] 9 vols. New York: 1889–1891. Reprint in 4 vols., New York: 1930.

[106] *A History of the People of the United States from the Revolution to the Civil War*. 9 vols. New York: 1883–1913. An added volume, *The History of the People . . . during Lincoln's Administration* carried the story to 1865 (New York: 1927).

the American Revolution, and a second wrote a monograph dealing with the same period which marked the appearance of a revisionist opinion concerning the unfortunate class of Loyalists.[107]

Magazines devoted to American history increased in number during these years, contributing to the reawakening of interest. *The Historical Magazine* of 1856–1875 was a forerunner of *The American Historical Review*, launched in 1895 as the organ of the American Historical Association.

The postwar period saw the beginning of Joseph Sabin's *Dictionary of Books*,[108] and almost simultaneously Harrisse's *Description of Works relating to America.*[109]

If it was the present author's purpose to write a history of American history, he would have to include numerous works which he does not mention. What he is attempting is to illustrate by a few typical historians the growth of ideas as to what history should be and how it should be written. The multiplication in the postwar years of monographic writings evidences a realization that inexorable conditions limit the scope of the undertakings of individuals *The History of the United States* by Edward Channing may prove to be the last attempt of a single scholar to cover the whole, or even the major portion, of American history by integrating the results of innumerable contributory studies.[110] This work, begun by the author at the mature age of fifty with the intention of writing eight volumes to cover the country's history to the close of the nineteenth century, came to a sudden end with his death in 1931. Thus it fell short of the planned time coverage. It also proved unsatisfactory in other ways, due to characteristics of the author. Although interpretative, the books are the work of a New Englander who never outgrew his provincialism. Western scholars chuckled at his references to the region west of the mountains as "Transappalachia"; one reviewer residing in that section countered by substituting "Cisappalachia." Channing himself once wrote that "no historian can hope to live as can a poet . . . new facts will . . . invalidate his most careful con-

[107] Moses Coit Tyler, *Literary History of the American Revolution*, 2 vols. New York: 1897.

Lorenzo Sabine, *Biographical Sketches of Loyalists*. 2 vols. Original edn., 1847; rev. edn., 1864.

[108] *Supra*, p. 124.

[109] Henry Harrisse, *A Description of Books relating to America published between the Years 1492 and 1551*. 30 vols. 1866. *Additions*, 1 vol. 1872.

[110] Six vols. New York: The Macmillan Company, 1905–1925.

clusions."[111] Of course there were many facts that never came within the range of Channing's vision. Perhaps it would be charitable to regard his *History* as a regional study of unusual length.

Channing's failure to satisfy some of his critics together with the trend toward monograph writing did not mean that the long-lived hope of an all-embracing history was at last dead and buried. There still seemed to be an alternative path to the goal through cooperative effort. That plan also had limitations. Soon after Bancroft's monumental history of the Pacific Coast region had been produced by the methods of the entrepreneur, Professor Jameson commented on these methods. While recognizing the great value of the collection, he perceived that Bancroft's part in writing the history was merely that of revising the drafts of his staff members. Hence there could be no fixing of responsibility, no assurance of approved critical procedure, or even of correctness of detail. The adoption of industry's practice of dividing labor among hired clerks does not command the best intellects for writing history.[112] A critical investigation a few years later of the authorship of the history led to the conclusion that Bancroft wrote only sixty pages of the seven volumes on the history of California. The study also threw light on the competence of some of his associates.[113] The experiment was an interesting effort to produce history wholesale, and had its lessons for those who wished to pursue further the attempt to write cooperatively. Its chief values were making available a mass of material needing critical examination, and the guidance publication gave to the collection on which it rested. The collection has been a mine of information for the scholars who have worked in the Bancroft Library of the University of California at Berkeley.

Justin Winsor, for years librarian of Harvard University, was also a cartographer, bibliographer, and editor. In the capacity of editor he is noted as the leader in another effort to produce a comprehensive history by the cooperative method. The chapters of the *Narrative and Critical History of America*[114] were parceled out to leading scholars so that each might keep within his special field, and each chapter was accompanied by a critical essay on the sources

[111] Quoted by Kraus, 452.
[112] *History of Historical Writing*, 152–156.
[113] William A. Morris, "The Origin and Authorship of the Bancroft Pacific States Publications: a History of a History," in the *Quarterly* of the Oregon Historical Society for Dec., 1903. See also *AHR* IX, 882 (July, 1904).
[114] *Supra*, p. 103.

for its subject matter. It is still valuable for its bibliographical information as far as gathered when the volumes were published. Jameson thought that "it splendidly sums up the historical labors of a century." [115] The publishers were confident that "when the superiority of the cooperative method is fully understood," the individual historian will hardly venture forth.[116] William A. Dunning, however, writing later, commented that "its portentous tomes followed one another . . . in mastodonic and microtypographic majesty. . . . Winsor's vast and minute information and his unquestioned gifts as an editor did not save his masterpiece from a general verdict of failure except as a mass of material." [117] In spite of Jameson's praise, he was probably not surprised by the fate of the work, for in his comment he had said: "Many of the finer qualities of the individual mind are likely to evaporate in the [cooperative] process; much of what is most valuable in individual views and conceptions of history will find no place. . . ."

V. AMERICAN HISTORY IN THE COLLEGES: THE SEMINAR AND CRITICAL METHOD

An important part of this story of changing fashions and experimentation with new patterns is the coming of history into the curriculum of the colleges, followed closely by the seminar. Most of the men whose names are written highest on the roll of nineteenth-century American historians were college graduates, but previous to the Civil War the few who had received any scholastic training in history had got it in Europe. Remarkable changes in intellectual interests came in the course of the nineteenth century. When it opened the classics and theology held the favored position. The little that was known of science was called "natural history," and history as we know it was not taught in any college in the United States.

George Bancroft, aged seventeen, graduated from Harvard in 1817. A year later his unusual promise led the college corporation to award him what would now be called a traveling fellowship, with an annual stipend of $1700, for three years' study in Germany. According to President Kirkland, he was expected to become "an accomplished philologian [*sic*] and biblical critic, able to expound and defend the Revelation of God." [118] In Germany, however, theology as taught at the University of Göttingen repelled him,

[115] *Op. cit.*, 156–158. [116] Quoted *ibid.* [117] AHA *Report* for 1918, p. 353.
[118] Orie D. Long, *Literary Pioneers* (Cambridge: 1935), p. 108.

while history under Heeren and later at the University of Berlin, had the opposite effect. He returned to America hoping for an opportunity to teach the subject at his alma mater, but the time was not ripe. Harvard's first venture in that field came in 1838, when Sparks was given the first professorship in American history in the United States. As early as 1823 Sparks had planned to write a history of the Revolution and had collected documents with that intent. Diverted into editorial work, he used them in that occupation, gaining incidentally an excellent preparation for the lectures on the Revolution which he delivered during a decade of teaching. Then becoming president of the college he missed no opportunity to urge both the necessity of raising the standards of college education and introducing American history into the course of study. His advice on history was slow to bear fruit, for as late as 1872 Andrew D. White, the president of Cornell, reported that an American had to go to France or Germany to hear lectures on American history.[119]

During the first half of the century numbers of young Americans drew their inspiration from the founts of learning in those countries. To visiting students the contrast between the European and American universities was painfully apparent. To a group of them who studied abroad in the 1850's belongs the honor of introducing history into the universities of their homeland. Andrew D. White came back from Germany to give at the University of Michigan the first history courses taught in the United States in the modern way. Later as president of Cornell he opened its doors to the subject. Charles Kendall Adams, one of his students, introduced the seminar at the University of Michigan in 1869; Henry Adams did the same at Harvard in 1872; and Herbert Baxter Adams pioneered the method at Johns Hopkins in 1876. The latter two had studied in Germany.

At first none of these men taught American history. Except for Sparks's temporary professorship at Harvard, the first holder of a chair in that field was Moses Coit Tyler, at Cornell. His tenure began in 1881. Thereafter scholars in increasing numbers taught American history. In his last two years at Harvard Henry Adams taught a general course on the United States divided into two parts at the year 1789.

In the history of American history the coming of the seminar means that for the first time critical method in a well-defined form was recognized and adopted as an essential part of the historian's

[119] Kraus, 311.

training. For many years individual historians of intelligence and good judgment had been cumulating rules which were similar to those governing present practice, but they had not been reduced to a formal code. These young men who introduced the seminar imported a code which spared native historians the trouble of compiling their own, and by winning a place for it in the scholastic curriculum, gave a pledge to the future that its historians need not be novices.

Along with the seminar they introduced another German "institution," the degree of Doctor of Philosophy in history, and the requirement of a dissertation as one condition of its attainment. Under Henry Adams several men won in 1876 the first Ph.D.'s conferred by Harvard. Adams believed that they compared favorably with the scholars trained in European schools. In collaboration they produced a volume of *Essays in Anglo-Saxon Law* which was published that same year; Herbert B. Adams called it "the first original historical work ever accomplished by American university students working in a . . . thoroughly scientific way." [120] By 1887 he was ready to add, perhaps with undue enthusiasm, that a student need no longer go to Germany for historical instruction, because what Harvard gave was just as good.[121]

Between 1880 and 1900, besides Harvard and Johns Hopkins, Columbia, the University of Michigan, and many others began to train candidates for the doctorate in seminars or otherwise. In the Harvard group to whom the degree was given in 1876 were Henry Cabot Lodge, J. Laurence Laughlin, Henry Osborn Taylor, and Edward Channing, all men of distinction later. Others of similar caliber were members of H. B. Adams's seminar at Johns Hopkins, among them Frederick Jackson Turner, John Franklin Jameson, and James A. Woodburn. Men from these seminars went to the universities which were burgeoning during the last two decades of the century, to pass on the lamp of historical learning to a younger generation which in turn repeated the process. It was a progression of the geometrical order.

VI. THE PLACE OF THE DOCTORAL DISSERTATION IN HISTORIOGRAPHY

As the number of universities with graduate schools increased, a dissertation became an invariable requirement for the doctorate in

[120] Kraus, 308. [121] *Ibid.*, 312.

history. In origin and in theory it was intended to prove that the candidate was master both of his subject matter and the principles of criticism; it was also to be a real contribution to historical literature. At least in the background was the possibility that numerous scholarly dissertations might make possible a near-perfect synthesis. That such a synthesis transcended the capacity of the individual scholar became all too clear in the early years of the present century, and even before the nineteenth closed scholars were looking to cooperative history as the most promising substitute. In the actual stress and strain of graduate-school experience, the ideal of the dissertation suffered somewhat. The writers were in a situation roughly comparable to the old-school historians who collected and owned their materials, because masses of untouched documents awaited investigation. A candidate could attack them at almost any point assured that the data for a "contribution" could be found. The chief requirement was that the product be novel. Sympathetic examiners who found productions substandard often accepted them if they showed promise; with time and experience, they were prone to say, the candidate might be expected to do well as a teacher, and many did. Although some of the dissertations were amateurish some were excellent. It is safe to say that *in toto* the dissertations of the last two generations represent a range of research and an accumulation of knowledge which none of the older historians who as individuals wrote more voluminously were able to equal. The least that can be said of these essays is that they supplied matter for riper scholars to digest, interpret, and merge into a larger unity dressed in good literary form. Indeed the ripe scholars of the past generation were trained as candidates for the degree. The same is true of the leading historians of the present, and it is likely to be true of those to come. A dissertation or monograph can be at best only a fragment of history, but it attains a kind of immortality if it loses its identity in something greater than itself.

As a result of the requirement of a dissertation, the graduate schools soon saw the need of a medium for the publication of the best essays. Johns Hopkins embarked on this innovation in 1883 when it began to publish a series of *Studies in Historical and Political Science*. Others followed: Columbia in 1891 with its *Studies in History, Economics, and Public Law*; Harvard in 1896 with the *Harvard Historical Studies*. Dissertations which were a credit to the authors found a place in these series, sometimes along with studies by their preceptors. Other universities and colleges fell into line and there are now more than two score institutions and agencies which publish series of studies in the field of the social sciences, or are otherwise more or less engaged in promoting their production.[122]

3. Twentieth Century: Problems and Activities

a. *Turn-of-the-Century Conditions*

The new century opened without much change in the activities of historians, but with changes in their concepts. Fresh efforts were made in writing cooperative histories, one being *The American Nation* edited by Albert B. Hart. It was an improvement over previous attempts, but the publisher's announcement of it as "definitive" was unfortunate. The series was well received, and while the merit of the volumes varied, the best ones seemed to warrant the hope that the cooperative plan might be used even more successfully in future. Much the same comment applies to the *Chronicles of America,* edited by Allen Johnson, and other series.[123] The cooperative plan was followed also in biography, and there the problem of continuity was less exacting. (For cooperative biographies see *Harvard Guide,* 188–189.) Publication of sources continued under first-class editorship, an outstanding example being Max Farrand's edition of the *Records of the Federal Convention.*

The gathering of materials went on at accelerated pace. Every state now had one or more agencies engaged in collecting them. Each had its library, historical society, or commission; many cities also had their libraries and historical associations; and here and there were important collections in private hands or in the custody of specially created libraries, such as the Newberry Library in Chicago and the John Carter Brown Library in Providence. These, too, were diligent in adding to their resources. With so many organizations thus engaged, the accumulation of materials was becoming a positive embarrassment. The rapidly growing mass outran the capacity of historians, editors, and custodians to utilize or even arrange and house it, and the competition of collectors caused it to be illogically distributed. The chaotic situation impeded research.

[122] *Cf. Harvard Guide,* 168–173.

[123] Allen Johnson, ed., *The Chronicles of America.* 50 vols. New Haven: Yale University Press, 1918–1921.—Allan Nevins, ed., 6 supplementary vols., 1950–1951.

The competition of changing concepts was interesting but bewildering. Able thinkers sought for ideas which could be used to synthesize historical facts. Henry Adams decided that one was supplied by the laws of thermodynamics, which meant to him that eventually the universe would become dead and inert. Recoiling from this dismal notion, others believed that the historian should apply Darwinian evolution in tracing the course of human history. And while the philosophers spun their theories, the writers of monographs worked like squatters staking out tomahawk claims on the public domain before the lands were surveyed.

The Adams seminar at Johns Hopkins had followed as a thread of continuity the concept of Edward A. Freeman, the English historian, that English and American political institutions had evolved from the customs of the primitive Germans. Adams, an exponent of this theory, remarked one day in 1889 that few topics for investigation remained. At least one of his hearers inwardly dissented, rejecting the Freeman view as too narrow. His reaction was manifest in the choice of subject for his dissertation—"The Character and Influence of the Indian Trade in Wisconsin." [124] This approach to history was a far cry from that which began with the early German forest, for it rooted in conditions familiar to a native of the semifrontier state of Wisconsin in the middle of the nineteenth century.

This ferment—the theories of the Eastern historians, the uncoordinated treatises of monograph writers, and the challenging accumulation of material calling for examination and interpretation—all this evidenced the need of a master plan to integrate historical writing, to provide a framework into which fragments could be fitted. Frederick Jackson Turner, author of the study of the Indian trade in Wisconsin, perceived possibilities which had barely come within the vision of contemporary scholars. McMaster had come nearest to a realization of the significance of the mass movement westward, but had dealt with it merely in narrative form. Turner's quest of a concept to integrate American history bore fruit in an essay on "The Significance of the Frontier in American History," read at the meeting of the American Historical Association in Chicago in 1893. The ideas it suggested were expanded in class lectures and later writings, but were never formally codified by Turner himself. It would not have been like him to frame a code which might

[124] Johns Hopkins University *Studies*, IX, 74 *et seq.*

have prevented the further enlargement of his vision. His approach and principles must be inferred from what he said or wrote in his scanty output. Any attempt to distill from these sources the essence of his thinking must be made at the interpreter's risk. The following is offered with that understanding:

Beginning with the first settlers on the Atlantic coast of North America and affecting each wave of population as it spread into the hinterland was the influence of an environment which changed with each remove. Each time strong solvents leached out some, but not all, of the old culture, while at the same time the dynamics of changed conditions tended to create a new one. Thus in each wilderness area pioneer life tended toward the primitive at first. But some forces—old habits and renewed or maintained contacts—worked also in the opposite direction, causing a new process of social evolution with sectional variations. In the course of time—almost three centuries—a wilderness of continental extent was redeemed and supplanted by a modern civilization. But the new did not reproduce the old; the result was an America with distinctive characteristics.

This framework is no doubt oversimplified, but is ample enough to include a surprising portion of the intricate fabric of American history. Using some such apparently simple outline, Turner was able to demonstrate that fact. Indeed, it is easier to think of topics which fit into it than any which do not. Although Turner would be the last to make such a claim, others may maintain that his approach comes nearer to the needed master plan than any other that has as yet been suggested. It includes, in fact, topics which some critics have thought were omitted, such as the struggle between economic classes. Turner would consider such a framework as is outlined above, not as setting forth conclusions, but as suggestions of promising fields of research. His essays give the results of his own researches within the framework. Monographs by his students and advisees prove that a great diversity of topics fit into the pattern implicit in his belief in the integrating influence of progressive development in new areas. A few instances will illustrate the wide range of subjects which can be and have been brought within the general framework: Consolidation of the Indian Tribes West of the Mississippi; The Agrarian Revolt; Colonial Precedents of the Federal Land System; The Influence of the West on Political Parties;

The Expansion of New England; Physiographic Influences on American History; Mining Rushes into the Inland Empire.[125]

Many other writings bear witness to Turner's influence; indeed, a considerable body of historical literature reflects his point of view. It may be doubted whether any other scholar of the present century has equaled his influence on the writing of American history. Although he dealt with the subject of expansion only as it affected the United States, he was conscious that it was a world-wide phenomenon without geographical or even time limits. He recognized that it was a phase of the history of the expansion of the European stock. Australian scholars have visited this country seeking what light they can get on their own problems from his interpretation of our experiences.[126]

[125] A. H. Abel, "Indian Consolidation." AHA *Report*, 1906, I, chs. 1–4.

Solon J. Buck, *The Agrarian Revolt*, vol. 45 of *Chronicles of America.*

Amelia C. Ford, *Colonial Precedents of Our National Land System as It Existed in 1800.* Madison: University of Wisconsin Press, 1910.

Homer C. Hockett, *Western Influences on Political Parties to 1825.* Columbus: The Ohio State University, 1917.

Lois K. Mathews, *The Expansion of New England.* Boston: 1909.

Ellen Churchill Semple, *American History and Its Geographic Conditions.* Boston: Houghton, Mifflin and Company, c1903.

William J. Trimble, Jr., *The Mining Advance into the Inland Empire.* Madison: University of Wisconsin Press, 1914.

[126] The Turner concepts have been the subject of much discussion. Fulmer Mood traces their evolution in the "Development of Frederick Jackson Turner as a Historical Thinker" (Colonial Society of Massachusetts *Publications,* XXXIV, 283 *et seq.* 1939); Charles A. Beard (*The New Republic* of Feb. 16, 1921, pp. 349–350) and Benjamin F. Wright (*Yale Review,* winter issue, 1931) are among the dissenting critics. Turner's published writings include two volumes of collected essays: *The Frontier in American History* (New York: Henry Holt and Company, 1920), and *The Significance of Sections in American History* (same publishers, c1932); and one on *The Rise of the New West, 1819–1829* (vol. 14 of *The American Nation*), 1906. A fourth entitled *The United States 1830–1850,* came posthumously from the Holt press in 1935. One entitled *The Early Writings of Frederick Jackson Turner* reprints the dissertation on the Indian trade, the essay on "The Significance of the Frontier," and two still earlier pieces, introduced by Fulmer Mood's "Turner's Formative Period." All are helpful in affording an understanding of the Turner ideas. Noteworthy is Mood's comment that the first essay, on "The Significance of History," contains "passages of suggestive historical interpretation which Turner never . . . developed into completed essays." Commenting on the one entitled "Problems in American History" he adds: "It is striking that . . . the research possibilities of this program have not been exhausted."

The volume has an exhaustive bibliography of Turner's writings, compiled by Everett E. Edwards, which can be obtained from the publishers, the University of Wisconsin Press, Madison.

At this point the student will do well to read pages 3 to 20 in *Harvard Guide,*

b. *New Trends*

Professor Turner came close to the concept that history should cover all features of a nation's life. He stressed the importance of the westward movement because it served so well as a theme around which other topics could be organized into a unity. His writing was kinetic as well as narrative and descriptive. *The History of American Life,* published during the thirties and forties, exemplified the same trend toward history treating American life as a whole; but as a cooperative effort in which fourteen scholars shared, social dynamics and a consistent plan of integration were less easily handled. *The Rise of American Civilization,* by Charles A. and Mary R. Beard, was a meritorious effort to write the same kind of history.[127]

The broadened scope of history as conceived by these scholars indicated a dawning comprehension that subjects had been treated as if distinct when they were in fact parts of a larger whole. Even writers of doctoral dissertations should share this consciousness and think of their own product accordingly. During the second quarter of the century social scientists began to discuss the interrelations of their respective disciplines. The walls of separation began to crumble, and presently the expanding horizon brought even the natural sciences within the range of the historian's vision. He realized that it was within his province to write histories of medicine, science, language, or the arts, provided that, in addition to his training in historical method, he possessed the necessary specialized knowledge. By the middle of the century historians were writing in these various fields. One wrote a history of medicine, another a history of science, a third dealt with architecture, a fourth with science in early New England.[128] Here, then, was an almost un-

---

to review and supplement the foregoing sketch of American historiography. It will serve also as an introduction to what follows.

The competition of concepts is evident in the addresses of the presidents of the AHA. See H. Ausubel, *Historians and Their Craft*, in Bibliography, p. 266.

[127] 4 vols. New York: The Macmillan Company, 1927–1942.

[128] Richard Harrison Shryock, *The Development of Modern Medicine: An Interpretation of the Social and Scientific Factors Involved.* New York: Alfred A. Knopf, c1936.

H. Butterfield, *The Origins of Modern Science, 1300–1800.* London: G. Bell and Sons Ltd., 1949.

James Marston Fitch, *American Building: The Forces that Shape It.* Boston: Houghton, Mifflin Company, c1947, 1948.

Dirk J. Struik, *Yankee Science in the Making.* Boston: Little, Brown and Company, 1948.

bounded field for the historical monograph. But the problem of over-all coverage lurked always in the shadows.

i. LOCAL HISTORY

Not only new topics but new approaches to old ones are among the recent trends associated with the preception of larger unities. One concerns regional, state, and local history. Antiquarians had always found local history of a sort interesting, but the new approach was akin to Turner's views. One of his distinguished disciples described his influence by saying that the word "frontier" "was . . . intriguing . . . it epitomized the historical beginning of every American area. It gave significance to the history of every township, county, territory, or state. . . ."[129] In this connection attention is called to the fact that the titles listed in note 125, page 236 can be classified as regional studies. It is reasonable to anticipate that such studies will eventually show that local development followed patterns which when fitted together will reveal the variegated fabric of American life and confirm Turner's theory that it is a culture essentially different from all others. The study of any locality should examine both its typical and unique characteristics, and their relation to the total fabric, for as improved means of communication have drawn into contact communities which had been isolated, both similarities and diversities have become manifest. The contacts have influenced the development of the several communities and at the same time the common culture. As a part of that culture our general government is a unique system which uses the resources of all states and regions to promote the general welfare, and normally enables Americans to iron out differences by debate and compromise instead of armed conflict. The union of the parts has endowed the nation with attributes which make it greater than the sum of those parts.

Interest in a new approach to local and regional history mounted during the forties. It aimed at studies of the literature, sociology, art, and folklore of communities as well as their politics and industries, in short at all aspects of their life. Associations were formed to promote them; universities sought to become centers of such study for their regions; state historical societies heartily cooperated; libraries joined the effort and awarded research fellowships; foundations lent their support by liberal grants of money; and conferences

[129] Herbert Eugene Bolton, "Turner, As I Remember Him." *Mid-America*, XXVI: New Series, vol. XXV, No. 1.

of scholars discussed plans. Details can be gathered by any one who will take the pains to look up the references in the footnote.[130] Only a few highlights can be given here.

In 1940 the North Carolina Historical Commission created the American Association for State and Local History to assemble information in the United States and Canada and organize local branches.[131] In 1949 the Association began to publish *American Heritage,* a quarterly devoted to the teaching of community history. Its announced purpose was to give "a sense of direction to studies in the culture of the United States, past and present"; it aimed at interdisciplinary "reaction at a high level." [132]

In 1944 the Rockefeller Foundation made a grant to the Huntington Library for regional studies in the Southwest, with special reference to the extension of Anglo-American culture into that area. In that year with funds from the same source the Newberry Library appointed seven fellows for Midwestern studies of various kinds.[133]

In 1949 a conference at the University of Wisconsin brought out the views of historians, sociologists, students of linguistics, historians of art and architecture, and men engaged in the administration of regional programs. The fifteen papers published give a good indication of the spirit and aims of interdisciplinary discussions.[134] Following the conference the Wisconsin State Historical Society inaugurated an American History Research Center to promote the study of all aspects of local history throughout the United States. The project contemplates grants-in-aid to applicants whose previous work indicates that their undertakings will be worth while.

Folklore had been a subject of interest for some years, and the American Folk-Lore Society had published a *Journal of American Folk-Lore* since 1888. Its kinship with local history was obvious and tended to draw the two interests together. By the end of the forties the *Michigan Historical Magazine* had a folklore section; the Indiana

[130] *MVHR* March, 1943, p. 651; March, 1944, p. 622; Sept., 1944, pp. 267–273, 275; March, 1947, p. 698.

[131] *MVHR* for March, 1941, p. 710.

[132] The sponsors of *American Heritage*—the American Association for State and Local History and The Society of American Historians—announced that, in 1955, the periodical will be made a bi-monthly popular magazine of American history.

[133] *MVHR*, March, 1944, p. 622; *ibid.*, December, 1944, p. 480.

[134] Merrill Jensen, ed., *Regionalism in America.* Madison: University of Wisconsin Press, 1951. Reviewed by Arthur E. Bestor, Jr., in *MVHR* for June, 1952, pp. 112–115.

Historical Bureau was sponsoring the quarterly *Hoosier Folklore*; the Minnesota Historical Society had helped start the Minnesota Folk Arts Foundation and was encouraging the publication of articles on folklore in *Minnesota History*; and the departments of history at the University of Minnesota and Michigan State College were offering courses in that field. In 1953 a joint session of the American Folk-Lore Society and the Mississippi Valley Historical Association deliberated on the way for historians to make better use of folklore.[135]

The Social Science Research Council was organized for the express purpose of forwarding the mutual interests of the groups composing it. In recent years it has maintained a joint Committee on Historiography which has made reports from time to time. One of them explored the competing theories of historians.[136] The latest, published in July, 1954, explores *The Social Sciences in Historical Study*.[137]

The trend toward regional and local history has its dangers. The broadening scope of history may very well enlist the interest of faddists in trivialities, and so may the attempt to popularize history which appeals to a public by a miscellany without form or high purpose. Good work in the field calls for trained investigators who have indeed a "sense of direction." Almost every class of material is grist for those who know where they are going. There is hardly a newspaper or periodical which does not at one time or other publish usable matter. Old files of newspapers are valuable sources. General, state, and local histories; the studies published by universities; the output of historical societies and libraries, local, state, and national; books of travel; emigrant guides of early days; biographies, autobiographies, and writings of public men; the proceedings of legislative bodies, courts, and administrative officials; publications of governments at all levels and on all sorts of topics; local, state, and Federal documents; reports of officials, committees, and commissions; manuscripts in private hands, historical societies, archives, and county court houses; the great collections in the Library of Congress and the National Archives—this long list only hints at the classes of material of potential utility. An examination of the

[135] *MVHR* for September, 1953, p. 315.

[136] Charles A. Beard *et al.*, *Theory and Practice in Historical Study: A Report of the Committee on Historiography*. Social Science Research Council *Bulletin* 54. New York: Social Science Research Council, 1946.

[137] New York: Social Science Research Council, 230 Park Avenue.

bibliography of such a work as Hicks's *Populist Revolt* will illustrate the variety of material needed by workers in the local-history field.[138]

The historian who applies scientific methods of research to a subject in this field must confine it within definite limits of time, locality, or topic. Bibliographies and guides give general aid; they cite works in which the investigator *may* find some data; but his research is likely to be "spade work," and his bibliography may consist largely of what he digs up. After that comes the firsthand critical evaluation. There are helpful lists in the *Harvard Guide* under such captions as Guides to State Documents; Colonial, State and Local Public Records; Collections of Narratives and Travels; and Historical Journals and Society Publications.[139] A list of historical societies which would include approximately all of the organizations in the United States that publish historical matter has been compiled by C. C. Crittenden and Doris Godard.[140] There are also two treatises which every one working in the field should study. The first has been described as "covering every step in writing local history."[141] The second is a product of the Association for Local History mentioned above.[142]

Some of the works described in Part II are helpful guides for study in this field. There is a section in Larned's *Literature of American History* which lists the chief collections for state history in print at the close of the nineteenth century.[143] Childs's *Account of Government Documentary Bibliography* includes publications by states as well as the Federal Government. A. P. C. Griffin's *Bibliography of American Historical Societies*, and the *Writings on American History* should be mentioned in this connection, and the student should bear in mind that some of the magazine indexes cover important publications by historical societies. Many publications of the Federal Government, including the census reports, bear on such aspects of local history as settlement, economic and social development, population

[138] Minneapolis: The University of Minnesota Press, c1931.

[139] Pages 115, 125–139, 150–161.

[140] *Historical Societies in the United States and Canada.* Washington: 1944.

[141] Donald Parker, *Local History: How to Gather It, Write It, and Publish It. Revised and edited by Bertha E. Josephson for the Committee on Guide for Study of Local History of the Social Science Research Council.* New York: Social Science Research Council, 1944.

[142] M. W. Schlegel, "Writing Local History Articles," in American Association for State and Local History *Bulletin* No. 2, pp. 47 *et seq.*

[143] Pages 7–13.

growth, Indian relations, etc. Some bibliographies which cover certain classes of local material have unfortunately not been brought down to date. One of them, Bowker's *State Publications,* is a checklist of state documents to 1900. It is still of some value for materials antedating the issue of the successive volumes. The volume for the New England states appeared in 1899, but that for the states of the South did not come out until ten years later.[144] The work is incomplete even for the years covered, but is now supplemented and in part superseded by the checklists compiled by G. E. MacDonald and William S. Jenkins respectively.[145]

Much information about the archives of the states has been published from time to time in the *Annual Reports* of the American Historical Association. This knowledge must be sought by using the indexes of the separate volumes or the general indexes already described.[146] Another work by A. P. C. Griffin is an index of articles on local history, but, like Bowker's compilation, it lists nothing on the present century.[147] It is supplemented by the same compiler's *Index of the Literature of American Local History in Collections Published in 1890–1895.*[148]

Of different content is Bradford's *Bibliographer's Manual.*[149] For county history, however, it has been superseded by Peterson's *Bibliography.*[150] Older but more inclusive is the Catalogue of the Arthur H. Clark Company.[151] This is supplemented by the compilations of Hodgson and Manvel, one dealing with publications of counties, the other with municipal documents.[152]

Some special aspects of local history have been dealt with. Miss

[144] Richard R. Bowker, comp., *State Publications; a Provisional List of the Official Publications of the Several States from their Organization.* 4 vols. New York: Publishers' Weekly, 1899–1909.

[145] See *Harvard Guide,* 116.

[146] *Supra,* page 112.

[147] *Index of Articles upon American Local History in Historical Collections.* Boston: 1889.

[148] Boston: 1896.

[149] Thomas L. Bradford, ed., *Bibliographer's Manual of American History, Containing an Account of All State, Treasury, Town, and County Histories, Edited and Revised by S. V. Henkels.* 5 vols. Philadelphia: Henkels, 1908–1910.

[150] C. S. Peterson, ed., *Bibliography of County Histories of the 3111 Counties in the 48 States.* Baltimore: 1946.

[151] *The United States: a Catalogue of Books Relating to the History of Its Various States, Counties and Cities and Territories.* Cleveland: 1928.

[152] See *Harvard Guide,* p. 117.

Hasse has indexed much economic material.[153] Her index, which ends with the year 1904, includes volumes for the statehood years of all New England states except Connecticut; all middle states; Kentucky; Ohio; Illinois; and California. Its geographic range was thus rather restricted, hardly touching the South. Moreover its contents are limited to the principal reports of administrative officials, legislative committees, special commissions, and governors' messages.

Soon after Bowker's last volume appeared its functions were taken over by the National Government in a *Monthly* which records all state publications received by the Library of Congress. As in Bowker's case, the failure of states to cooperate has prevented the *Monthly* from being complete. Besides, it is not cumulative, which makes its use tedious.[154]

ii. BUSINESS HISTORY

By placing the motto *e pluribus unum* on our coins, the founders of the Republic memorialized the creation of one state by uniting several without destroying their identity. When historians recognized that a nation's history includes the whole of its life, they applied in effect the same concept of diversity in unity. Yet until lately that unity was obscured by the habit of leaving its diverse elements to be studied as distinct subjects. Business history might have been considered a part of local history if custom had not assigned it to economics. Although it has always been an important feature of American life, history has rarely touched it except as it affected politics or public policy. For instance, the historian was interested only incidentally in the Virginia tobacco plantation as a form of business enterprise; but when the debts of planters to British merchants became an issue in diplomacy, discussion of the issue by historians became imperative.

Similarly Alexander Hamilton's Report on Manufactures of December, 1791, analyzed an economic situation, but the historian's concern with the analysis was subsidiary to his interest in its bearing on Government policy and legislation. Until after the Civil War

[153] Adelaide R. Hasse, comp., *Index of Economic Material in Documents of States of the United States*. 13 vols. Washington: Carnegie Institution, 1907–1922.

[154] Library of Congress, Division of Documents, *Monthly Checklist of State Publications*. Washington: Government Printing Office, 1910–.

historians dealt with the tariff, public lands, taxation, currency and banking, in narratives with a minimum of economic analysis and a maximum of attention to the political causes and effects of the questions. From time to time books like Timothy Pitkin's *Statistical View*[155] were compiled, which were capable both of influencing public policy and giving industry helpful information. Eventually the Federal Government took over the compiling of statistics of general value, as a function chiefly of the Bureau of the Census.[156]

By the end of the century many industries were publishing journals devoted to their respective interests and problems, universities were setting up schools for the study of business administration, and business history societies were being organized. In the 1920's the Harvard Graduate School of Business Administration joined with the Business Historical Society in publishing the *Journal of Economic and Business History*.[157]

However, before the end of the nineteenth century the logic of events had demonstrated that the parceling out of related topics among the several social sciences was unrealistic. The "third party" movements of the last decades of the century converted economic grievances of minority groups into the very substance of politics. The influence of these parties of discontent was enhanced by an abundant "literature of exposure" criticizing the conduct of "big business." Although often prejudiced or at least biased, these writings raised questions which the major parties and political leaders could not ignore. They also made obligatory unbiased study by economists, political scientists, sociologists, social psychologists, historians, and members of other groups. Competent scholars in these groups wrote monographs on specific problems in their respective fields; but even more important was the recognition that their specialties were parts of a whole and should be dealt with accordingly. As for historians, they thought that the origin, development, and social significance of particular industries and business in general should be studied. In the twentieth century some of them, influenced by the Turner concepts, examined significant episodes, calling into service for the purpose as far as applicable the methods

[155] *A Statistical View of the Commerce of the United States of America; its connection with Agriculture and Manufactures. . . .* Hartford, Conn.: 1816. New edn. 1835.

[156] For the history and bibliography of statistics see *Harvard Guide,* 25–30.

[157] *Harvard Guide,* 164.

of all the social scientists. Typical of such efforts were books by Solon J. Buck[158] and John B. Hicks.[159]

As it dawned upon the several groups of social scientists that they had been dealing with different parts of the same subject, they began to suspect that each group had something to learn from and contribute to the procedure of all the others. The leaven of this belief spread and carried with it the spirit of scientific investigation. The attitudes and activities of universities, libraries, business societies, and business interests were also affected. During the 1940's two of the great railway systems of the Middle West (The Chicago, Burlington and Quincy, and the Illinois Central) deposited their records in the Newberry Library where they were to be open to the use of qualified scholars. (These records added some fifteen tons to the materials for business history.)[160] An inquiry addressed to other railroads brought indications of the willingness of almost all to permit scholars to study their records.

The Mississippi Valley Historical Association at its 1947 meeting discussed the objective to be sought in the study of railroad history, and concluded that it should be the clarification of the net contribution of the roads to the nation's development. This decision, while not ruling out recognition of the roads' misdeeds, seemed to promise that muckraking would not be allowed to obscure the indispensable service they had rendered.[161]

In 1944 New York University had taken steps to preserve the records of business organizations; the next year the Wisconsin State Historical Society began to collect the records of the early lumbering industry. At about the same time a Colorado ranchmen's organization began to seek material for a history of the range cattle industry.[162] Aided by a grant of the Rockefeller Foundation, the promoters sent an agent to England, to whom the Library of Congress entrusted the further task of looking up Western Americana while abroad.[163] During the 1940's an Indiana group decided to organize a Business Historical Society to promote the establishment of

[158] *The Granger Movement.* Cambridge: 1913; *The Agrarian Crusade.*
[159] *The Populist Revolt.* 1931.
[160] *MVHR* for September, 1943, pp. 310–313; *ibid.*, March, 1945, pp. 645 f.
[161] *Ibid.*, Sept., 1947, p. 243.
[162] The Preliminary Guide to Indexed Newspapers mentioned in footnote 47 on page 111 was a by-product of this enterprise. Now reprinted as *Guide*, etc.
[163] *Ibid.*, March, 1945, p. 649; Dec., 1946, p. 514.

archives by business firms of that state; the Newberry Library received as a gift the records of the Chicago *Daily News*; and the Ford Motor Company set up its own archives and engaged a staff of experts to arrange and catalogue the contents. A Standard Oil Company grant to the University of Oklahoma to assist in the preparation of a history of the oil industry in that state is an example of another kind of cooperation between business and the historians.

A joint meeting of the Mississippi Valley Historical Association and the Economic History Association in 1952 agreed that no definite objective had yet been adopted for business history in general; that attempts to define it had been vague or reticent about such matters as the social implications of such history; and that an interdisciplinary committee should attempt to formulate some principles to promote scholarly procedure and proper ethical standards. The scholastic interest in business history was shown by such books as Donham [164] and McKinney had written.[165] Other writers dealt with special topics; [166] and there is one book designed to direct the investigator.[167]

c. *Tasks Extraordinary*

i. WORKS PROGRESS ADMINISTRATION

Abnormal conditions caused by depression and war prevailed during the thirties and forties, and greatly affected historical activities. Out of the depression came the Works Progress Administration (WPA) to replace doles to the unemployed. To finance it Congress

[164] Wallace Brett Donham, *Education for Responsible Living. The Opportunity for Liberal Arts Colleges*. Cambridge, Mass.: Harvard University Press, 1945.

The author was a professor in the Graduate School of Business Administration at Harvard. He proposed a curriculum which a reviewer calls "moderately cultural and thoroughly functional." Donham thought the young should be trained "for the hard realities of the market place and public affairs." *MVHR*, September, 1946, p. 3 *et seq*.

[165] Loren C. McKinney, ed., *A State University Surveys the Humanities*. Chapel Hill, N. C.: University of North Carolina Press, 1945.

Compare "University Programs in American Studies," *MVHR*, Sept., 1953, p. 315, and *ibid.*, June, 1944, p. 99 f.

[166] Shepard B. Clough, *A Century of Life Insurance: A History of the Mutual Life Insurance Company of New York, 1843–1943*. New York: Columbia University Press, 1946.

Edward Dies, *Behind the Wall Street Curtain*. Washington: Public Affairs Press, 1952.

[167] H. M. Larson, ed., *Guide to Business History*. Cambridge, Mass.: 1948.

appropriated all told several billion dollars to pay workers for tasks suited to their abilities. Professor Robert C. Binkley, chairman of the Joint Committee on Materials for Research of the American Council of Learned Societies and the Social Science Research Council, saw in the Government's plan an opportunity to promote the objectives of his committee while giving jobs to thousands of white-collar workers. The WPA was easily persuaded, and instituted two projects for them. One was the Federal Writers' Project.[168] The Historical Records Survey undertook to examine local records of many kinds, and prepare calendars, guides, and inventories of them for publication.[169] Although the project came to an end in 1940, the Archives Publishing Company of Harrisburg, Pa., was still publishing in 1947 inventories of Pennsylvania county records begun by the Survey.[170]

In 1937 the WPA added a third project by adopting an undertaking begun in 1927 by Douglas C. McMurtrie. He had planned a bibliography to list all works printed in the United States before the initial date of the United States Catalog (1876). The WPA assigned two thousand workers to assist by listing the titles found in libraries throughout the country. The project was carried to 1941, and drew into cooperation the Library of Congress, the State Historical Society of Wisconsin, the Detroit Public Library, the Bibliographical Society of America, the Newberry Library, and the Rockefeller Foundation, which gave financial aid. The product was the American Imprints Inventory of some 16,000,000 titles.[171] In 1941 the inventory file was turned over to the Library of Congress and became the basis of a series of bibliographies of imprints under the general title *Bibliography of American Imprints.* As fast as titles are edited they are added to the Union Catalog of the Library of Con-

[168] For the Federal Writers' Project see *Harvard Guide* index under Works Progress Administration. M. E. Colby made a *Final Report* on the project which gives some additional information. (Washington: [1943].)

[169] The history of the Historical Records Survey is sketched by Herbert A. Kellar in "The Historian and Life," *MVHR* for June, 1947, p. 15 *et seq.* See also Binkley's description of the work done (*Cultural Program of the WPA*) and Kellar's appraisal of it, both cited *ibid.* For additional references and comments consult *Harvard Guide,* pages 81, 126, and index under Historical Records Survey.

[170] *MVHR* for March, 1947, p. 699.

[171] Kellar, *loc. cit.,* 19 f. See also Douglas McMurtrie, "Locating the Printed Source Materials for United States History," in *MVHR* for December, 1944, pp. 369–378.

Note accompanying Lists of Regional Imprints and Check Lists, pp. 379–406.

gress where they serve as a supplement to the compilations of Charles Evans, Joseph Sabin, Wilberforce Eames, and R. W. G. Vail.[172] By consulting the Union Catalog one can often double one's references obtained from the older catalogues. McMurtrie himself compiled and published unofficially a list of publications by the inventory in the years 1937–1942.[173]

ii. WAR, HISTORIANS, AND HISTORY

By the beginning of the twentieth century historians were not studying the past merely to recover facts. Facts were to be synthesized and their significance sought in relation to the present and future. War narrowed the scope of research to immediate objectives, and scientific method was subordinated to the selection of facts to support a point of view or a purpose. The first necessity was to collect documents bearing on the causes and issues of war. Materials were to be preserved for future use, but selections were needed at once to clarify war aims and efforts.

A National Board for Historical Service, composed of historians who volunteered to serve without official status, was active for thirty-two months during World War I. It assisted the official Committee on Public Information, encouraged states to establish boards or commissions on war history, and urged the historical sections set up by the State, War, and Navy departments to preserve records. During World War II the National Archives published a book containing bibliographies and describing the records and functions of more than 2300 agencies and international bodies in which the United States was represented in the first World War.[174]

Reaction came with peace and fostered isolationism. The war records were stored and neglected; state war commissions turned their efforts to erecting memorials to the war veterans, and pressure was brought on the schools to teach history in accord with the mood of the era. Pragmatic historians lent their influence to the theory that the important part of the past was that which "could be explained in terms of the present." The present was to be "the frame of

[172] *Supra*, p. 124.

[173] *A List of Publications Issued 1937–1942 by the American Imprints Inventory of the WPA's Historical Records Survey.* Evanston, Ill.: 1943.

[174] *Handbook of Federal World War Agencies and Their Records.* Washington: National Archives, 1943.

reference."[175] The trend threatened to crowd the past out of the discussions of the historical associations. The topic featured in the program of the American Historical Association in 1939 was What Can History Learn from Other Disciplines. While this interest manifested the current disposition to respect interdisciplinary relations, the neglect of the evolutionary theory due to concentration on the present tended to cut off existing institutions from their roots. The stress was given to the "functional view." That was the attitude which circumstances had forced historians to take in World War I and they carried it into World War II.

In the second war their service was given official status. During the prewar preparations Arthur M. Schlesinger, in September, 1941, suggested to the National Archivist that a historian or archivist be attached to every wartime agency to preserve its documents and current records. Soon afterwards the Priorities Division of the Office of Production Management created the Office of Historian and Recorder. Step by step Professor Schlesinger's suggestion was carried out. In March, 1942, President Roosevelt approved Bureau of the Budget plans to set up a unit which would stimulate war agencies to keep full records, by asking the Bureau director to appoint a "Committee on Records of War Administration" to help him plan the "main objective of preserving . . . an accurate and objective account of our present experience." The committee as appointed was headed by a director from the Harvard Graduate School of Public Administration. It sponsored some forty government agencies in setting up offices to write the history of their respective contributions to the war. Procedures varied, but in general the agencies aimed at early publication of accounts of a popular type to be followed eventually by works by competent scholars.

In September, 1943, the Social Science Research Council appointed a Committee on War Studies to supplement the Federal agencies by fostering activities of states, industries, and private agencies in collecting data on their wartime experiences for later use by

[175] *Cf. Theory and Practice in Historical Study, ante*, p. 240, footnote 136. This is a report written by a committee of historians representing the Social Science Research Council, Beard being the guiding spirit. It attempted to appraise the principles followed by two generations of historians, but was a revolt against the "scientific objective" history of the earlier years. It stressed the "practical recognition of the functional nature" of history and Beard's rejection of "causality."

scholarly writers. The North Carolina Historical Commission had already arranged with the state Office of Civilian Defense for county collectors, the state Committee on Conservation of Cultural Resources aiding with advice.[176] Comparable action was taken in Ohio (*MVHR*, Sept., 1942, p. 306); Pennsylvania's Historical Commission asked the State Council of Defense to collect records of the state's participation; it set up state and local war-history programs, and asked the Pennsylvania Federation of Labor, the Manufacturers Association, and Council of Churches to cooperate (*ibid.*); Minnesota's Historical Society supplied members for a War Historical Committee with headquarters in the Society's building (*ibid.*). By midyear 1945 many states and universities had historical commissions engaged in preserving war records, appealing to the communities to gather them, and making reports to higher authorities (*ibid.*, June, 1945, p. 153).

A liaison was effected between the Commission on Records of the War Administration and the Committee on War Studies of the Social Science Research Council by the creation of an Advisory Council on War History to oversee the program as a whole. Supplemented by the local work sponsored by the American Association for State and Local History, the program offered "the basis for a more complete appraisal of what war does to society than has ever before been possible."

In the meantime the historical sections of the War and Navy departments dating from World War I awoke. Early in 1942 the Navy Department invited officers to inspect the records of the previous war with a view to their use in writing a history of operations in accordance with plans of the Committee on Records of War Administration. On July 15 the War Department established historical sections with the Historical Branch of the Army War College as advisor and coordinator. All three branches of the Army—the service forces, the ground forces, and the air forces—drew professional historians from university faculties. Besides these organizations, there were in Washington by midyear 1944 some twenty-six emergency and permanent agencies doing historical work not within the scope of the army history activities.[177] At length the Historical Branch of the

[176] *MVHR* for March, 1943, p. 653; *ibid.*, Sept., p. 316.

[177] List of these agencies will be found in *MVHR* for June, 1944, pp. 166–167.

Intelligence Division of the War Department General Staff was created to supervise all of that department's historical work.[178]

The second World War intensified the utilitarian use of history. About half of the professional historians in the country between the ages of 25 and 40 were drawn into the greatest cooperative project of all time. They worked under orders to achieve specified ends. They centered their attention on recording and interpreting events without the usual perspective. Did they compromise the principles of historical scholarship? What influence would their performance have on future concepts of history and its functions? [179] Apprehension was evident in the discussions of these matters by educators. One of the earliest manifestations was the criticism directed against the work of the WPA. It is not to be expected, it was said, that historical workers will write like scholars just because they lack employment.[180] To this a comment in *The Mississippi Valley Historical Review* replied that the WPA surveys are not expected to be finished products; they are gathering material for the skilled historian, and thus serve a useful purpose.[181]

Discussions by educators who stood rather apart from the current of war utilitarianism were somewhat reassuring. A report by the history staff of the University of Chicago urged that undergraduates should study history at least four class hours per week for a school year of forty weeks. The course should be in United States history with emphasis on its relations to world history.[182]

From other quarters came renewed assertions that "History holds the key both to the past and to the future." It should be so taught that "facts learned about the past will shed light on problems facing us today and tomorrow. . . ." [183]

Colleges took up the same theme. Augustana College adopted a

[178] The preceding sketch is based on William C. Binkley's article entitled "Two World Wars and American Historical Scholarship," in *MVHR* for June, 1946, pp. 3–26. Footnotes give much bibliographical information.

[179] *Ibid.*, 25.

[180] *Indiana History Bulletin* for October, 1940.

[181] *MVHR* for March, 1941, p. 715.

[182] *Adjustment of the College Curriculum to Wartime Conditions.* Report prepared by the history staff of the University of Chicago and published by the Federal Security Agency of the United States Office of Education as Report No. 2—History.

[183] State Department of Education, *A Wartime Focus for Ohio's Elementary Schools.* Columbus: 1944.

new plan for majors in American history, designed to correct the "woeful ignorance of graduates," inculcate knowledge of American democratic ideals and their growth while avoiding isolationism, and to contain a leaven of the humanities to broaden culture.[184] Other colleges placed the same emphasis on United States history and culture, among them Greensboro College, City College of New York, the University of Kentucky, Transylvania University, the New Jersey College for Women, Emory University, and the University of Maryland.[185] The Middle States Council for the Social Studies published a study of current practice and proposed a revision of the public school curriculum.[186]

The cessation of hostilities in 1918 had been the signal for ending the war work of the historians; the outbreak of World War II had ended the WPA; but the output of war histories which began during the second war has continued to the present. Moreover, top historical authorities have taken on new tasks under sponsorship of the Federal Government.

The quality of the war histories has varied, but some of them are excellent.[187] Glimpses of the processes by which they have been turned out will give some idea of how the complicated task was handled. Thus the Army made a contract with the history department of the University of Pittsburgh to write the official account of the Military Planning Division of the Quartermaster Corps. The University supplied ten research assistants, supervised by a Chief Historian, stationed in Washington and Chicago. Two years were allowed for completion of the project. A second contract was given to the same university for a history of the work done by the several branches of the armed forces. In undertaking these assignments the history department held a conference on technology, in which historians from twelve universities and ten from the armed forces took part.[188] For other phases the American Association for State and Local History sponsored a guide for local workers, which was written

[184] O. Fritiof Ander, "The New Augustana Plan and an American History Major," in *MVHR* for June, 1945, pp. 95–100.

[185] *Ibid., passim.*

[186] *History in the High School and Social Studies in the Elementary Schools.* Vol. 41 of the Council's *Annual Proceedings.*

[187] There is a selected list of war books in the Bibliography of this Manual, and in some cases the entries are followed by brief appraisals. See Writings on war, 278, *et seq.*

[188] *MVHR* for December, 1945, p. 466 f.

by Marvin W. Schlegel.[189] Various agencies of the Federal Government prepared tentative narratives based on documents and personal interviews. By 1946 nearly one hundred such narratives had been typewritten for eventual use in a many-volume series projected by the War Department.[190]

Historical societies discussed these activities and their bearing on teaching. The Mississippi Valley Historical Association meeting of 1947, in a session devoted to war history, summarized the activities and plans of the War Department, the Air Force, and the Navy; gave some attention to the vast growth of materials; mentioned some of the valuable studies already produced and gave bibliographical data about them. In this discussion and others emphasis was laid on the need of re-examining objectives in teaching American history as a means of understanding world civilization rather than one country, and on proficiency in presentation as well as scholarship as a qualification for college teaching.[191]

By midyear, 1947, the Historical Reports on War Administration numbered twenty-five, and these had been distributed to six hundred depositories. Early in that year the first issue of the *Air University Quarterly* appeared. Finally, in 1951, the President of the American Historical Association appointed a special committee to advise the Government in writing a history of the defense effort in World War II. The committee included the United States Archivist and the executive secretary of the Association, *ex officio*.[192]

A new departure came in 1950 when President Truman urged the need of preserving the personal papers of prominent persons, and suggested a National Historical Publications Commission, with the United States Archivist as chairman, to study the matter of selecting the papers to be published. The composition of the Commission as finally established made it a good representative of the country's historical interests.[193]

The Commission promptly assumed responsibility for compiling

[189] *Writing Your Community's War History. Bulletin*, vol. I, No. 2. Raleigh: September, 1946. Cited in *MVHR* for March, 1947, p. 700.

[190] *Ibid.*, 698–699.

[191] *Ibid.*, September, 1947, 238, 255.

[192] *Ibid.*, March, 1951, p. 763.

[193] *Ibid.*, September, 1950, p. 375. The Commission's personnel was as follows: Wayne C. Grover, Archivist; George M. Elsey; Richard H. Shryock; Claude R. Hoey; Howard W. Smith; Felix Frankfurter; G. Bernard Noble; Rudolph A. Winnaker; Solon J. Buck; Guy Stanton Ford; and Julian P. Boyd. *Ibid.*, March, 1951, pp. 763–764.

the annual volumes of *Writings on American History.* It also planned a comprehensive edition of the materials on the ratification of the Constitution, the first ten amendments, and the records of the First Congress; and discussed projects of Virginia, South Carolina, and Kentucky for publishing the papers of Madison, Calhoun, and Clay. A little later it aided in the formation of a committee in Virginia, including representatives of the Institute of Early American History and Culture at Williamsburg, and the University of Virginia at Richmond, to consider plans for publishing Madison's papers.[194]

At the meeting of the Mississippi Valley Historical Association in December, 1951, Philip Hamer, executive director of the Commission, asked the Association's cooperation in its program of publication.[195] The April meeting in 1952 heard a paper by Hamer outlining the Commission's plans, and received a report listing persons whose papers it thought should be published.[196] And in March, 1953, it announced the completion of an arrangement for the publication of the Calhoun papers by the University of South Carolina in cooperation with Clemson College and the Commission.[197]

d. *Chief Depositories of Historical Material*

i. NATIONAL

At the head of the list of holders of American history materials stands the Library of Congress. It was established by Act of Congress in 1800, but lost most of its thousand volumes by fire when the British forces took Washington during the War of 1812–1815. In this extremity ex-President Jefferson probably saved it from extinction by depositing with it his private library of 6,000 volumes. Congressional appropriations were niggardly until after the Civil War; in 1853 the library contained only 35,000 volumes. In the postbellum period, it shared in the general growth of libraries, with the advantage of the federal law of 1870 requiring the deposit of two copies of each book copyrighted. The law made it automatically an almost complete collection of American books as they came from the press. The building it now occupies was erected in 1886, except the annex, which was added later.

Growth since the turn of the century has been rapid. Foreign pub-

[194] *Ibid.*, June, 1952, pp. 175–176, 177.
[195] *Ibid.*, September, 1952, p. 391.
[196] *Ibid.*, 397.
[197] *Ibid.*, March, 1953, p. 817.

lications have been added constantly by purchase, gift, or exchange. An important function is the acquisition of manuscripts. It has had many transcripts made of matter in foreign archives relating to American history, and has accumulated a vast volume of the papers of American statesmen and other prominent men. Its newspaper collection is more complete for many localities than those of the localities themselves. For the historian its total resources exceed those in any other depository, although some of these others excel in particular classes of matter. Counting all classes of material, the total of its items numbers more than 31,000,000. About 9,000,000 of these are books and pamphlets, and manuscript pieces number 13,000,000.

In his report for 1940, his first, Archibald MacLeish the librarian described the library and submitted a Statement of Objectives.[198] He had already set up an Experimental Division of Library Cooperation to promote a cooperative effort of libraries to aid those holding outstanding collections in particular fields to expand them, to put at end to the competitive buying which tended to scatter materials and duplicate holdings, and to redistribute items more logically by interlibrary exchanges. An extension of the plan would apportion among the libraries the task of acquiring foreign research titles with the purpose of having somewhere in the United States at least one copy of every book of foreign publication likely to be consulted even infrequently, and to have at strategic centers of research at least two copies of the more important research titles. It was estimated that United States libraries possessed about 30 per cent of the world's research titles. The proposal outlined aimed to bring to this country the remaining 70 per cent. This project if carried out would have become a complete union catalogue which as it progressed would approximate a catalogue of the world's research resources. Regional duplicates of the union catalogue supplemented by union catalogues for regional areas would bring close to every investigator a guide to all these resources.[199]

The Union Catalog of the Library of Congress continued. On cards it lists by authors or titles the holdings of some 800 North American libraries including those examined by the WPA. The

[198] *Ibid.*, June, 1941, p. 148.

[199] Herbert A. Kellar had been placed at the head of the Experimental Division, and the statement in the text is a summary of a paragraph about its plans which appears *ibid.*, June, 1941, p. 147 f.

entries indicate the libraries where books are to be found, and for the guidance of users *The Union Catalog of the Library of Congress* has been prepared.[200] This work must not be confused with the unprinted Union Catalog.

The proposed plan was endorsed by several interested groups, including the American Library Association, the Society of American Archivists, and the Association of College Reference Libraries,[201] but the degree of cooperation it elicited was on the whole disappointing. The competition of the larger libraries had brought documents of great importance for one region into the possession of institutions where they were not likely to be looked for, and often had scattered items which should have been kept together. More than intuition was needed to inform historians that many of the papers of Father Junipero Serra, founder of the California missions, are in the Newberry Library in Chicago. There was no very apparent reason why the transcripts of French documents obtained by the Ford brothers should have been placed in the New York Public Library rather than, say, the Library of Congress. The historian's gratitude is due collectors like Lyman Draper whose zeal preserved documents which might otherwise have been lost, but the illogical location of many creates a continuing danger that important items may be overlooked in spite of diligent research. It might seem to be a simple matter to sort and redistribute them to logical depositories and thus bring related items into one collection, as proposed by the Library of Congress, but there is little hope that such a rearrangement will ever be made on any large scale. The rivalries of holders, their vested rights, and the pride of possession will not permit such action. Hope lies in other measures: more adequate guides, catalogs, calendars, and union lists may be prepared to give comprehensive information about the location, content, character, and value of collections. The Library of Congress Union Catalog is a long step in the right direction. When once the author or title of a production is known it may not be very difficult to run it down. In many cases the resources of each depository may be shared by others by using one or other of the processes of reproduction. At present the favored method of reproduction is the microfilm process.

[200] Washington, 1942. See *Harvard Guide,* p. 110, for this and kindred works, and *cf. A Catalog of Books* described *ante*, p. 247 f.

[201] *MVHR* for June, 1941, pp. 147–148.

It remains true that most investigators will not find awaiting them a ready-made bibliography of a subject under study. There is, to illustrate, no general bibliography of the publications of the Library of Congress. What it has printed on any particular topic the student must ascertain for himself. He will find the *Harvard Guide* helpful, but its specific-item references are scattered through Parts III–VI under the topical divisions of the chronological periods of American history. The entries in the index under Library of Congress may cite bibliographies or other pertinent data. For instance, if the subject under investigation is Secession, the index will cite page 387, where there is an entry "Library of Congress, *List of Books on Secession* (1914)." *The Library of Congress Subject Catalogue* and related works, described on page 109 of the *Guide*, are probably the most helpful guides, when accessible.

Next to the Library of Congress as a depository of the materials for American history is the National Archives, the custodian of the official documents of the United States Government. Tardily created by Act of Congress in 1934, a century and a third later than the Library, it sprang Venus-like, into being full grown. Up to that time each department had been responsible for housing its own records and destroying at its discretion any adjudged to be no longer useful. They were so scattered that there was need of a guide for use by any one desiring to locate them. To the rescue came the Carnegie Institution in 1907, under whose sponsorship Claude Halstead van Tyne and Walter G. Leland compiled the *Guide to the Archives of the Government of the United States in Washington.* Guides to the Cuban and Spanish archives were prepared the same year under the same auspices, and by assigning different countries to different compilers, the preparation of other volumes was so hastened that in less than a decade sixteen had been published. The series covered the principal depositories in Great Britain, Germany, Austria, Switzerland, Russia, Italy, Spain, Canada, and Mexico, all listing materials in the archives of these countries which were related to the history of the United States. Additional volumes covered the Protestant Church archives, the territorial papers in Washington, and the transcripts of Spanish documents in American libraries, and a *List of Manuscripts Concerning American History Preserved in European Libraries and Noted in Their Published Catalogues and Similar Printed Lists.*[202]

[202] A complete list of these guides will be found in *Harvard Guide,* 87–88.

In 1937 the present archives building was ready for occupancy, and transfers of records from their old locations began. The governing principle was that noncurrent documents should be housed in the new edifice. By the end of 1942 the building held approximately 80 per cent of all Federal records more than fifty years old if they had been stored in the District of Columbia; [203] and by midyear 1944 war records constituted more than a third of all the documents in the archives. In 1939 Franklin D. Roosevelt while President placed the Roosevelt Library at Hyde Park, N. Y., under the care of the United States Archivist.[204] It was rich in materials for the years following 1934, and included the President's collection of naval manuscripts and personal correspondence while in office.[205] During the remainder of his life he made additions from time to time.

From the archives during the 1940's came several series of publications about accessions, the contents of various collections, and guides for their use. Many were of transient value, intended to aid wartime officials or to inform the public. Some were semipermanent. Any one now interested in these publications can list them by using the *Harvard Guide* in the way suggested for publications of the Library of Congress.[206] However, a list of archives publications to about midyear 1947 is included in *National Archives—What It Is and What It Does*—a nontechnical description. A work likely to be useful for a long time (not included in any of the series) is the *Federal Records of World War II.*[207]

Another feature of the activities of the National Archives was educational in character. At a meeting of the Mississippi Valley Historical Association in 1940, Solon J. Buck, at that time United States Archivist, discussed "The Training of an Archivist." Pointing out the growing interest in archives management, the need of special training, and the lack of provision for it by the universities, he suggested

[203] *MVHR* for December, 1942, p. 467.

[204] *Ibid.*, June, 1944, p. 163.

[205] *Ibid.*, June, 1943, p. 133; Sept., p. 314; and Sept., 1944, p. 316.

[206] Titles of series: *Preliminary Inventories* (forty-six of these had been issued by the end of 1952); *Bulletins* (No. 7 is Carter's *Historical Editing*); and *Special Lists* (see *Harvard Guide*, p. 81). A quarterly, *National Archives Accessions,* was begun in 1940. The *Guide to the Records in the National Archives,* published in 1948, was a revision of earlier guides of the same kind. The 1948 edition applies to everything in the archives to June, 1947. The briefer list printed in 1950 has the title *Your Government Records in the National Archives.*

[207] 2 vols. I: *Civilian Agencies*; II: *Military Agencies*. Washington: 1950.

the possibility of apprenticeships in the National Archives.[208] A few months later, in cooperation with the American University of Washington, D. C., a training program was planned to include classroom instruction, actual work in the National Archives, and discussion in seminars.[209] With the Maryland Hall of Records also cooperating, a short training course on preservation and administration of archives was offered at the American University to custodians of institutional and business archives.[210] This program was put into operation during several summers. In 1945 two archivists, one from Chile and one from Mexico, were working in the United States Archives on fellowships, a fact which seems to have led to the idea of bringing Latin-American archivists to the United States to observe our methods. The plan was part of a program to advance cultural and scientific cooperation between the United States and her neighbors to the southward.[211]

Finally, at a Mississippi Valley Historical Association meeting in 1947, members of the National Archives staff suggested that graduate students should be better trained in the use of published records before venturing to use the unpublished. They needed better training in critical evaluation of archival material, and greater precision in footnote citations and bibliographical annotations.[212]

Perhaps the chief difficulty encountered by the administration of the National Archives was the problem of space for the rapidly accumulating documents. The capacity of the building was 1,000,000 cubic feet. From the viewpoint of needs at the close of World War I that seemed ample. The entire mass of material in the War Department archives in 1917 filled only 81,391 cubic feet, but two years of war multiplied by four the space needed. Adding the transfers of records from other departments and agencies threatened an early overcrowding. Accessions due to World War II tripled the holdings during 1941–1942, and by the end of the war the Archivist reported space needs of 18,000,000 cubic feet, not including collections in the states and the local records unearthed by the Historical Records Survey.[213] The 1948 edition of the *Guide to the Records in the National Archives* described more than 800,000 cubic feet of them, and by 1951 only about 150,000 cubic feet of unfilled space remained.

[208] *MVHR* for September, 1940, p. 251.
[209] *Ibid.*, March, 1941, p. 707.
[210] *Ibid.*, March, 1945, p. 652.
[211] *Ibid.*, December, 1945, p. 466.
[212] *Ibid.*, September, 1947, 249–250.
[213] United States Archivist, *Annual Report* for 1944–1945.

Clearly more efficient methods of handling materials were imperative.

One way out was to destroy obsolete matter; but to guard against errors of judgment the safe procedure was to microfilm before destroying. Only eight cubic feet were required to house 482 rolls of film reproducing destroyed records which had filled "scores" of filing cases.[214] This plan was adopted in 1940, and by war's end 1,400 rolls had been made. A summary of their contents was printed in *The Mississippi Valley Historical Review*.[215]

The archives adopted a new plan of organization which went into effect with the year 1947.[216]

ii. LOCAL

While much material for local history is in the Library of Congress and some in the National Archives, there are also great quantities in the libraries of historical societies, universities, municipalities, and privately endowed institutions. Many of these have notable holdings of books, manuscripts, and papers. Examples are the Draper collection of the State Historical Society of Wisconsin, the Bancroft collection of the University of California at Berkeley, the Jared Sparks materials in the Harvard University Library, and the George Bancroft papers in the New York Public Library. The "Union Catalog" of the Library of Congress has an "Index to Special Collections" arranged by locality and subject, "which contains helpful descriptions of individual collections, giving numbers of volumes, pamphlets, and manuscript material wherever possible, comparisons with similar collections elsewhere, and the existence or otherwise of published catalogues and lists of the collections."[217] The *Harvard Guide* describes several of the larger libraries and their contents, mentions the fields in which their collections are especially important, and lists Library Histories and Guides.[218]

Regional, state, and local societies and libraries have also published lists affording additional bibliographical information about local materials. Instead of attempting to describe these in detail at this point, a representative selection is given in the Bibliography.[219] The search for the particular guide or item one needs may require correspondence with the appropriate official.

[214] *MVHR* for March, 1943, p. 656.
[215] *Ibid.*, March, 1946, p. 640 f.
[216] See *ibid.*, March, 1947, p. 706.
[217] Quoting *Harvard Guide*, 109.
[218] *Ibid.*, pp. 57–61.
[219] Pages 281–295.

e. *Microfilming and Microcopies*

The use of microfilms in reproducing documents in order to economize space is matched by their use as a time-and-labor-saving procedure for scholars. Use of the process began about 1940 and after the war spread rapidly. One of the early ventures came in 1940, when a Committee on Aids to Scientific Learning undertook to microfilm journals promotive of learning, on a nonprofit basis.[220] The same year marked the adoption of the procedure by the National Archives. The progress of the practice is shown by such random facts as the following:

The State Historical Society of Wisconsin began to use the films in 1944 to save storage space, following the example of the National Archives.[221] In 1945 the Kansas legislature made an appropriation to the State Historical Society to establish a Microfilm Division to prevent loss of valuable old materials threatened with disintegration.[222] The meeting of the Mississippi Valley Historical Association in April, 1947, considered many problems associated with microfilming, reviewed the progress of the practice, and favored a program to enable the Library of Congress to microfilm basic source materials in all countries and make them available to institutions and scholars.[223] In the same year historical societies in Ohio undertook to microfilm one of the oldest newspapers of the state because it contained much historical material.[224] The Institute of Early American History and Culture at Williamsburg, Va., already possessed the completest file of photostats of *The Virginia Gazette*, and the Historical Society of Pennsylvania and the Connecticut Historical Society respectively had made available microfilms of *The Pennsylvania Gazette* (1728–1789) and the *Connecticut Courant* (1764–1792).[225] In 1947 the Special Libraries Association published a *Directory of Microfilm Service in the United States and Canada,* which showed that many libraries were equipped for microfilming and supplying duplicates to others. The University of Michigan Library was ready to microfilm for others any work it contained.[226]

[220] *MVHR* for June, 1940, p. 165.
[221] *Ibid.*, March, 1944, p. 621.
[222] *Ibid.*, December, 1945, pp. 469–470.
[223] *Ibid.*, June, 1947, p. 30 *et seq.*; September, p. 238.
[224] *Ibid.*, December, 1947, p. 526.
[225] *AHR*, January, 1948, p. 347.
[226] Cited in *Harvard Guide*, 61.

A *Union List of Microfilms* revealed that as of 1949 about 200 institutions held 25,000 films.[227] A supplement published in 1953 contained 14,000 items added during 1949–1952.[228] In 1948 a movement was on foot for a program of microfilming by joint action of the American Historical Association and the Library of Congress.[229] In 1950 the National Archives published a *List of Film Microcopies of the National Archives.* It covered the accumulations of the closing decade, and made available microcopies for some of the records of the following: the State Department; Treasury; Navy; Interior; Agriculture; Commerce; the Judiciary; Veterans Administration; National Resources Planning Board; the War Production Board; the Office of Price Administration; the World War II collection of Seized Enemy Records; and the War Department Collection of Confederate Records.[230]

The Mississippi Valley Historical Review for December, 1953, announced a new Microfilm Section to keep readers informed about historical material available in that form. Notices in the same number included a second edition of *Newspapers on Microfilm;* [231] the readiness of the National Archives to supply films of Government records of high research value at a moderate cost; figures showing that the *List of File Microcopies* contains 3,478 rolls; and announced that the National Archives has started to microfilm the unpublished studies by civilian agencies of the Federal Government in World War II, now in the National Historical Publishing Commission's *List of World War II Historical Studies Made by Civilian Agencies of the Federal Government.*[232] Other notes in the same number describe *Microfilms of Negro Newspapers* by the Library of Congress, and the program of the State Historical Society of Wisconsin for filming labor union papers.[233] Issues of *The Mississippi Valley Historical Review* during 1954 have contained much news of microfilming of newspapers throughout the United States, with an occasional announcement of a significant publication. Thus under the title *List of National Archives Microfilm Publications* the National Archives has brought out a new and

[227] Ann Arbor: 1951. Cited by *Harvard Guide,* 60.
[228] *MVHR* for December, 1953, p. 593.
[229] *Ibid.,* September, 1948, p. 364.
[230] *Ibid.,* September, 1951, p. 362.
[231] Washington: Library of Congress, 1953.
[232] *MVHR* for December, 1953, p. 593 f.
[233] Consult also *Harvard Guide,* index.

enlarged edition of the *File Microcopies* of 1950, listing more than 4,600 rolls of microfilm reproductions of over 3,000,000 pages of records.[234] From the Department of State the National Archives received on deposit about 75,000 frames of microfilm of documents from the former German Foreign Ministry.[235] Finally, it is reported that the Pope plans a Pius XII memorial library containing microfilms of the 50,000 manuscript volumes in the Vatican, to be built on the campus of St. Louis University at a cost of four or five million dollars.[236]

This presentation of historical method as exemplified in writing American history omits much that could be said about other classes of material and other techniques which are related to those used by the historian. But I forbear, and end on the note with which I began: History is one of the many ways by which human beings seek to understand the world they live in and their place in it. Their experience is like the astronomer's; the larger the sphere of knowledge, the greater the number of points at which it touches the unknown. Sir Isaac Newton is reported to have likened himself to a child playing on the seashore, picking up now and then a pebble more beautiful than the rest, while the great ocean of truth lay all undiscovered before him. But Newton did not live in vain; without the foundations he laid modern science could not exist.

The philosopher faces infinite truth saying Were I offered truth in one hand and the quest of it with the other, I would unhesitatingly choose the latter.

[234] *Ibid.*, June, 1954, p. 187.
[235] *Ibid.*, September, 1954, p. 381.
[236] *Time,* Nov. 16, 1953.

BIBLIOGRAPHY

This Bibliography requires a few words of explanation. If the present work were a monograph, the bibliography should include in classified form every writing used by the author as the source of data. This work, however, is not a monograph, and cannot follow the rules which would apply if it were. The Bibliography does not contain every work cited in the text or footnotes, but the user will find entries for each in the index under author, title, and subject. In each case also the first entry under author and title will cite the page where the full bibliographical description of that work is given.

It should be borne in mind that the footnote forms follow two rules: some of the notes are given as they should appear in a monograph containing a bibliography; others illustrate the forms necessary if the footnotes must give the full bibliographical data for want of a separately appended bibliography. In both cases, however, the first citation in the footnote indicates the short form which will be used in subsequent citations.

The Bibliography for this Manual lists some writings which are nowhere referred to in the text or footnotes. These titles are included because of their general utility. Among them are some listed under Methodology, Writings on War, and Regional and Local History.

The Bibliography as a whole is intended to represent the form for a classified bibliography.

1. Works Relating to Historical Research, Writing, and Teaching

a. *Methodology*

Bernheim, Ernst, *Lehrbuch der Historischen Methode und der Geschichtsphilosophie*. . . . 6th edn. Leipzig: Duncker & Humblot, 1908.

Chicago University Press, *A Manual of Style, Containing Typographical Rules Governing the Publications of the University of Chicago*. . . . Chicago: University of Chicago Press, 1927.

Dow, Earle W., *Principles of a Note-System*. . . . New York: The Century Co., 1924.

Fling, Fred Morrow, *The Writing of History: An Introduction to Historical Method*. New Haven: Yale University Press, 1920.

Garraghan, Gilbert J., S. J., *A Guide to Historical Method.* Edited by Jean Delanglez, S. J., New York: Fordham University Press, 1946.
(Written from a Catholic Point of View.)

Gee, Wilson, ed., *Research in the Social Sciences: Its Fundamental Methods and Objectives.* New York: The Macmillan Company, 1929.

Gottschalk, Louis, *Understanding History: A Primer of Historical Method.* New York: Alfred A. Knopf, 1950.

Hutchins, Margaret, Alice Sarah Johnson, and Margaret Stuart Williams, *Guide to the Use of Libraries: A Manual for College and University Students.* 4th edn. New York: The H. W. Wilson Company, 1929.

Johnson, Allen, *The Historian and Historical Evidence.* New York: Charles Scribner's Sons, 1926.

Jusserand, Jean Jules, Wilbur Cortez Abbott, Charles W. Colby, and John Spencer Bassett, *The Writing of History.* New York: Charles Scribner's Sons, [c1926].

Langlois, Charles V., and Charles Seignobos, *Introduction to the Study of History.* Translated from the French by G. G. Berry. New York: Henry Holt and Company, 1912.

Leopold, Richard W., and Arthur S. Link, eds., *Problems in American History.* New York: Prentice-Hall, Inc., 1952.

Macmillan Company, *The Authors' Book.* New York: 1944.

Nevins, Allan, *The Gateway to History.* Boston: D. C. Heath and Company, 1938.

Odum, Howard Washington, and Kath, Jocher, *An Introduction to Social Research.* New York: Henry Holt and Company, 1929.

Rice, Stuart A., ed., *Methods in Social Science: A Case Book. Compiled under the Direction of the Committee on Scientific Method in the Social Sciences of the Social Science Research Council.* Chicago: University of Chicago Press, [c1931].

Spahr, Walter Earl, and Rinehart John Swenson, *Methods and Status of Scientific Research; with Particular Application to the Social Sciences.* New York: Harper & Brothers, 1930.

b. *Writing and Teaching*

i. BOOKS

Ausubel, Herman, *Historians and Their Craft; A Study of the Presidential Addresses of the American Historical Association, 1884–1945.* New York: Columbia University Press, 1950.

Beard, Charles, *et al., Theory and Practice in Historical Study: A Report of the Committee on Historiography. Social Science Research Bulletin 54.* New York: Social Science Research Council, 1946.
(Stresses "recognition of the functional nature of history"—a revolt against "scientific," "objective" history.)

Bourne, Henry E., *The Teaching of History and Civics.* New York: Longmans, Green and Company, 1903.

Donham, Wallace Brett, *The Opportunity for Liberal Arts Colleges.* Cambridge: Harvard University Press, 1945.
(Author seems to wish teaching of the humanities subordinated to training for the realities of modern life. Functional.)

Ellis, Elmer, *Teaching Critical Thinking in the Social Studies.* Thirteenth Yearbook of the National Council for the Social Studies, 1943.

Harvard Committee, *General Education in a Free Society. . . .* Cambridge: Harvard University Press, 1945.

McKinney, Loren C., ed., *A State University Surveys the Humanities.* Chapel Hill, N. C.: North Carolina University Press, 1945.

Van Gelder, Robert, *Writers and Writing.* New York: Charles Scribner's Sons, 1946.

Wesley, Edgar B., Director, *American History in Schools and Colleges.* The Report of the Committee . . . of the American Historical Association, the Mississippi Valley Historical Association, and the National Council for the Social Studies. New York: The Macmillan Company, 1944.

ii. ARTICLES

Curti, Merle, "The Democratic Theme in American Historical Literature." *MVHR*, XXXIX, 3–28 (June, 1952).

Ellis, Elmer, "The Profession of Historian." *MVHR*, XXXVIII, 3 *et seq.* (June, 1951).

Esterquest, Frank L., "History without Chronology or Geography." *MVHR*, XXXIII, 629–639 (March, 1947).
(On the basic ignorance of students.)

Gould, Clarence P., "History a Science." *MVHR*, XXXII, 375–388 (December, 1945).

Gustafson, Lucile, "Social and Personal Values of American History." *MVHR*, XXXII, 251 *et seq.* (September, 1945).

Jordan, Philip D., "Is American History on the Way Out?" *The Chronicles of Oklahoma*, XXI, 15 (1942).

Josephson, Bertha E., "Indexing." *The American Archivist* for April, 1947.

Kellar, Herbert A., "The Historian and Life." *MVHR*, XXXIV, 3–36 (June, 1947).

Keohane, Robert E., "The Use of Primary Sources in the Teaching of Local and State History." *MVHR*, XXXIII, 455 *et seq.* (December, 1946).

Robinson, Edgar E., "The Institute of American History at Stanford University." *MVHR*, XXXI, 431–437 (December, 1944).

Sellers, James L., "Before We Were Members." *MVHR*, XL, 3–24 (June, 1953).
(History of the Mississippi Valley Historical Association.)

Wirth, Fremont P., "History in the Liberal Arts Colleges." *MVHR*, XXXIII, 121–127 (June, 1946).
(Thinks all college students should have training in historical method.)

(See pages 278–281 for influence of war on writing and teaching history.)

2. Bibliographies

Cadden, Rev. John Paul, *The Historiography of the American Catholic Church.* The Catholic University of America *Studies in Sacred Theology, Number 82.* Washington: The Catholic University of America, 1944.

Coulter, Edith, and Melanie Gerstenfeld, eds., *Historical Bibliographies.* Berkeley: University of California Press, 1935.

Griffin, Appleton Prentiss Clark, comp., *Bibliography of American Historical Societies.* AHA *Report* for 1905, II. Washington: Government Printing Office, 1907.

Hart, Albert Bushnell, ed., *The American Nation: A History.* 28 vols. New York: Harper & Brothers, 1904–1918.
(Chapter bibliographies.)

Harvard Guide to American History. Compiled by Oscar Handlin, Arthur Meier Schlesinger, Sr., Samuel Eliot Morison, Frederick Merk, Arthur Meier Schlesinger, Jr., and Paul Herman Buck. Cambridge: Harvard University Press, 1954.

Schlesinger, Arthur M., and Dixon Ryan Fox, eds., *A History of American Life.* 13 vols. New York: The Macmillan Company, 1927–1948.
(Chapter bibliographies.)

Winsor, Justin, ed., *Narrative and Critical History of America.* 8 vols. Boston: Houghton Mifflin Company, 1884–1889.

Writings on American History:
- 1902: E. C. Richardson and A. E. Morse, comps. Princeton, N. J.: Library Book Store, 1904.
- 1903: A. C. McLaughlin *et al.*, comps. Washington: Carnegie Institution, 1905.
- 1904–1905: No volumes prepared.
- 1906–1940: Grace Gardner Griffin, ed.
  - 1906–1908: New York: The Macmillan Company;
  - 1909–1911: Washington: Government Printing Office;
  - 1912–1917: New Haven: Yale University Press;
  - 1918–1940: Washington: in the *Annual Reports* of the American Historical Association;
- 1941–1947: No volumes prepared.
- 1948–1950: James R. Masterson, ed., in AHA *Reports* for 1950–1952.

3. Helps in Appraising

a. *Writings*

Allison, William Henry, Sidney Bradshaw Fay, *et al., A Guide to Historical Literature.* New York: The Macmillan Company, 1949.
(The original edition of 1931 was brought out under the auspices of

the American Historical Association by a committee headed by Professor George M. Dutcher. It lists and appraises the chief historical writings of all types, all times, and all countries.)

Book Review Digest, 1905–. New York: The H. W. Wilson Company, 1905–.

Larned, Josephus Nelson, ed., *The Literature of American History*. Boston: Houghton Mifflin Company, 1902.

—— *Supplement* for 1900 and 1901, ed. by P. P. Wells (American Library Association *Annotated Lists*). Boston: American Library Association Publishing Board, 1902.

—— *Supplements* for 1902 and 1903, ed. by P. P. Wells (*Annotated Titles of Books on English and American History*). Boston: American Library Association Publishing Board, 1903–1904.

—— *Supplement* for 1904. Boston: American Library Association Publishing Board, 1905.

b. *Authors*

Cattell, Jacques, ed., *Dictionary of American Scholars*. 2d edn. Lancaster, Pa.: The Science Press, 1951.

Johnson, Allen, and Dumas Malone, eds., *Dictionary of American Biography*. 22 vols., New York: Charles Scribner's Sons, 1928–1944.

Who's Who in America. Chicago: Marquis-Who's Who, Inc., biennially since 1899. *Monthly Supplement*. 1939–.

Who Was Who. 2 vols. Chicago: Marquis, 1942–1950.

4. Guides to Reference Works

Winchell, Constance, ed., *Guide to Reference Books*. 7th edn. Chicago: American Library Association, 1951.

(Latest issue of a work begun in the 1920's and from 1930 to 1940 compiled by Isadore G. Mudge, Doris M. Reed, and Constance M. Winchell. Then taken over by the last named. Title has varied according to the period covered: *Reference Books of 1929* (1930); *Guide to Reference Books* (1936); *Reference Books of 1935–1937* (1939); *Reference Books of 1938–1940* (1941). Other issues may follow.)

5. Indexes of Periodical Literature

a. *General*

American Historical Review: Classified subject bibliography for the first fifty volumes. AHA *Report* for 1944, I, 77–285.

American Library Annual, 1911–. New York: Publishers' Weekly, 1912–.

Annual Library Index, 1905–1910. 6 vols. New York: Publishers' Weekly, 1906–1911.

Annual Literary Index, 1892–1904. 13 vols. New York: Publishers' Weekly,1893–1905.

Annual Magazine Subject Index, 1908–. Boston: Faxon, 1909–.

Canadian Periodical Index, 1928–1948. Windsor and Toronto; succeeded by *Canadian Index*, 1948–. Ottawa.

Cumulative Index to a Selected List of Periodicals, 1896–1903. 8 vols. Cleveland: Cumulative Index Company, 1897–1903.

Gregory, Winifred, comp., *American Newspapers 1821–1936: Union List of Serials in Libraries of the United States and Canada.* New York: H. W. Wilson Company, 1937.

International Index to Periodicals, 1920–. New York: H. W. Wilson Company, 1921–.

Magazine Subject-Index. Boston: Boston Book Company, 1908.

Matteson, David Maydole, comp., *General Index to Papers and Annual Reports of the American Historical Association, 1884–1914.* AHA *Report* for 1914, II.

Mississippi Valley Historical Review, Cumulative Index. Vols. I and II compiled by Bertha Josephson; Vol. III by James P. Gregory.

(Complete and detailed general index of volumes I–XXXV. Obtainable from secretary-treasurer of *MVHA*, 1500 R St., Lincoln, Nebraska.)

Poole's Index to Periodical Literature, 1802–1881. Rev. edn. 2 vols. Boston: Houghton Mifflin, 1891.

—— *Supplements*, January, 1882–January, 1907. 5 vols. Boston: Houghton Mifflin Company, 1887–1908.

—— *Abridgment.* Boston: Houghton Mifflin Company, 1901.

—— *Supplement to Abridgment, 1900–1904.* Boston: Houghton Mifflin Company, 1905.

Readers' Guide to Periodical Literature, 1900–. New York: H. W. Wilson Company, 1900.

—— *Supplement, 1907–1919.* 2 vols. New York: H. W. Wilson Company, 1916–1920.

b. *Law Periodicals*

Index to Legal Periodicals, 1908– (published in conjunction with the *Law Library Journal*). New York: H. W. Wilson Company, 1909–.

Jones, Leonard Augustus, comp., *Index to Legal Periodical Literature.* 3 vols. Boston: Boston Book Company, 1888–1919.

c. *Newspaper Indexes and Checklists*

Brayer, Herbert, *A Guide to Indexed Newspapers in the United States, 1850–1900.*

(Obtainable from secretary-treasurer of MVHA, 1500 R St., Lincoln, Nebr.)

Brigham, Clarence S., *History and Bibliography of American Newspapers, 1690–1820.* 2 vols. Worcester, Mass.: American Antiquarian Society, 1947.

California State Library, Index of Newspapers, 1846–. (Card catalogue.)

Chicago Daily Tribune Index, 1847–.

New York Herald Tribune Index, 1875–1906. 31 vols. New York: Tribune Association, 1876–1907.

New York Times Index. New York Times, 1913.

Slauson, A. B., comp., *Check-List of American Newspapers in the Library of Congress. . . .* Washington: Government Printing Office, 1901.

6. Government Publications and Records

a. *Guides, Indexes, and Catalogues*

Ames, John G., *Comprehensive Index to the Publications of the United States Government, 1881–1893*. 2 vols. Washington: Government Printing Office, 1905.

Bemis, Samuel Flagg, and Grace Gardner Griffin, *Guide to the Diplomatic History of the United States, 1775–1921*. Washington: Government Printing Office, 1935.

Brown, Everett S., *Manual of Government Publications, United States and Foreign*. New York: Appleton-Century-Crofts, Inc., 1950.

Carter, Clarence E., comp., *The Territorial Papers of the United States*. Washington: Government Printing Office. In progress.

Childs, James Bennett, *An Account of Government Document Bibliography in the United States and Elsewhere*. 3d edn. Washington: Government Printing Office, 1942.

Church, Alonzo Webster, and Henry H. Smith, *Tables Showing the Contents of the Several Volumes Comprising the Annals of Congress, Congressional Debates, Congressional Globe, Congressional Record, Statutes at Large, U. S. Supreme Court Reports, Arranged by Years and Congresses*. Washington: Government Printing Office, [1892].

Clarke, Edith E., *Guide to the Use of United States Government Documents*. Boston: The Boston Book Company, 1918.

Everhart, Elfrida, *A Handbook of United States Public Documents*. Minneapolis: H. W. Wilson Company, 1910.

Ford, Paul Leicester, *Some Materials for a Bibliography of the Official Publications of the Continental Congress*. Boston: 1890.

Greely, A. W., *Public Documents of the First Fourteen Congresses, 1789–1817*. 56 Cong., 1 sess., *Sen. Doc. 428*. Supplement in AHA *Report* for 1893, I, 343.

Hartwell, M. A., ed., *Checklist of United States Public Documents, 1789–1909. Congressional: to the Close of the Sixtieth Congress; Departmental: to the End of the Calendar Year 1909*. 3d edn., Washington: Government Printing Office, 1911.

Hasse, Adelaide R., comp., *Index to United States Documents Relating to Foreign Affairs, 1828–1861. Carnegie Institution Publication No. 185*. Washington: Carnegie Institution, 1914.

Hirshberg, H. S., and C. H. Melinat, eds., *Subject Guide to United States Government Publications*. Chicago: 1947.

Lowrie, Walter, *et al.*, eds., *American State Papers: Documents Legislative and Executive*. 38 vols. Washington: Gales and Seaton, 1833–1861.

Poore, Benjamin Perley, *Descriptive Catalogue of the Government Pub-*

lications of the United States, 1774–1881. Washington: Government Printing Office, 1885.

United States Superintendent of Documents, *Catalogue of the Public Documents of Congress and of All Departments of the Government, 1893–1940*. Washington: Government Printing Office, 1896–1940.

—— *Monthly Catalog of United States Public Documents, 1895–*. Washington: 1895–.

—— *Selected United States Publications*. Washington: 1928–. (Semi-monthly title list.)

—— *Tables of and Annotated Index to the Congressional Series of United States Public Documents*. Washington: 1902.

Winchell (see *Guides to Reference Works*) has a section on Government Publications.

b. *Congressional Debates (Chronological Order)*

Ford, Worthington C., and Gaillard Hunt, eds., *Journals of the Continental Congresses, 1774–1789*. 34 vols. Washington: 1904–1937.

Debates and Proceedings in the Congress of the United States, 1789–1824. Gales and Seaton, comps. 42 vols. Washington: Gales and Seaton, 1834–1856. (Commonly known as the *Annals of Congress*.)

Register of Debates in Congress, 1825–1837. 29 vols. Washington: Gales and Seaton, 1825–1837.

Congressional Globe, Containing the Debates and Proceedings, 1833–1873. 109 vols. Washington: Blair and Rives, *et al.*, editors and publishers, 1834–1873.

Congressional Record, Containing the Proceedings and Debates, 1873–. Washington: Government Printing Office, 1873–.

(For the Journals of the two houses and enactments see Index.)

Supplementary

Maclay, Edgar S., ed., *Journals of William Maclay, United States Senator from Pennsylvania, 1789–1791*. New York: 1890.

Brown, Everett Somerville, ed., *William Plumer's Memorandum of Proceedings in the United States Senate, 1803–1807*. New York: The Macmillan Company, 1923.

Niles' Weekly Register. Baltimore, 1811–1849.

Claussen, Martin P., and Herman R. Fries, comps., *Descriptive Catalogue of Maps Published by Congress, 1817–1843*. Washington: Government Printing Office, 1941 (?).

(Hitherto buried in the Congressional Series and not indexed. To be extended from 1789 to 1861.)

Donaldson, Thomas, *The Public Domain*. 47 Cong., 2 sess., *H. Misc. Doc. 45, Pt. 4*.

Hall, E. F., *et al.*, eds., *Official Opinions of the Attorneys-General of the United States, 1791–1948*. 40 vols. Washington: 1852–1949.

Kappler, C. J., comp., *Indian Affairs, Laws and Treaties.* 57 Cong., 1 sess., *Sen. Doc. 452.*

Richardson, James Daniel, comp., *Compilation of the Messages and Papers of the Presidents, 1789–1897.* 10 vols. Washington: Government Printing Office, 1896–1900. (53 Cong., 2 sess., *H. Misc. Doc. No. 210, parts* 1–10.)

State Department, Bureau of Rolls and Library, *Documentary History of the Constitution of the United States.* 5 vols. Washington: 1894–1905.

State Department, *United States Treaties and Other International Agreements.* Washington: 1950.

(First of a projected series of annual volumes containing matter previously printed in the *Statutes at Large.* For sale by the Government Printing Office.)

Statutes at Large of the United States . . . 1789–1873. 17 vols. Boston: Little and Brown (later Little, Brown and Company), 1845–1873.

Statutes at Large of the United States, 1873–. Vol. 18 *et seq.* Government Printing Office, 1875–.

7. Guides to Archives and Manuscripts

a. *Archives: General*

Hill, Roscoe R., *The National Archives of Latin America.* Cambridge: Harvard University Press, 1945.

Leland, Waldo G., *et al., Guide to the Materials for American History in the Libraries and Archives of Paris.* Vol. I, 1933; Vol. II, 1943; third volume planned. Washington: Carnegie Institution, 1933–.

(The Library of Congress has copies of much of this material. See Bemis and Griffin, *Guide to the Diplomatic History of the United States.*)

Stock, Leo Francis, *Proceedings and Debates of the British Parliament Respecting North America.* Vol. IX, 1739–1754. Washington: Carnegie Institution, 1941.

(Other volumes in the series are more important for American history.)

Van Tyne, Claude Halstead, and Walter G. Leland, comps., *Guide to the Archives of the Government of the United States in Washington.* Rev. edn. Washington: Carnegie Institution, 1907.

(Prepared years before the erection of the Archives Building, while each department cared for its own records. Utility is much reduced since many of the records have been transferred to the Archives.)

(For full list of Guides to Archives published by the Carnegie Institution see Winchell, *Guide to Reference Books.*)

b. *Archives: United States Guides and Publications*

Carter, Clarence E., *Historical Editing.* National Archives. *Bulletin No. 7.* Washington: 1952.

Hufford, Harold E., and Walter G. Caudill, comps., *Preliminary Inventory of the Records of the United States Senate.* Washington: 1950.

Leisinger, Albert H., *List of File Microcopies of the National Archives.* 1950.

National Archives, *Your Government's Records in the National Archives.* 1950.

c. *Guides to Manuscript Collections*

Billington, Ray A., "Guides to American History Manuscript Collections in Libraries of the United States." *MVHR* for December, 1951, pp. 467–496.

(By far the most comprehensive and useful publication of the kind. It is essentially a catalogue of bibliographical lists. It is "divided into two sections: (1) Guides to Manuscript Collections in Federal Depositories, including the National Archives and the Library of Congress, and (2) Guides to Manuscript Collections in Libraries of the Several States. The latter section consists of: (1) union guides which list collections in a wide number of depositories, and (2) guides to single depositories. These are arranged by states, with libraries listed alphabetically under each state and the guides arranged by date of publication when more than one has been published. Current accession lists are included for the few libraries that regularly publish this information."

(Copies of this publication can be obtained from Peter Smith, 321 Fifth Avenue, New York 16, N. Y.)

8. General Catalogues of Books

American Catalogue of Books, 1876–1910. New York: Publishers' Weekly, 1881–1911.

American Imprints Survey, *Bibliographies of American Imprints.* A compilation of the results of the work of the WPA in book form by the *Publishers' Weekly* and the Bibliographical Society of America. New York: Publishers' Weekly, 1944–.

(Each volume covers the records of one state to the middle of the nineteenth century, beginning with the Eastern states.)

Annual American Catalogue, 1886–1910. New York: Publishers' Weekly, 1887–1911.

Cumulative Book Index, 1898–. New York: H. W. Wilson Company, 1898–.

Evans, Charles, *American Bibliography . . . 1639–1820.* 12 vols. Chicago: Blakely Press, 1903–1934.

Kelly, James, *American Catalogue of Books Published in the United States from January, 1861, to January, 1871.* 2 vols. New York: Wiley, 1866–1871.

Publishers' Weekly, January, 1872–. New York: 1872–.

Roorbach, Orville Augustus, *Bibliotheca Americana, 1820–1861.* 4 vols. New York: Roorbach, 1852–1861.

Sabin, Joseph, *et al.*, *Dictionary of Books Relating to America from Its Discovery to the Present Time.* 29 vols. (1936). New York: J. Sabin, and Portland, Me.: 1868–1936.
United States Catalogue, 1900–. Marion E. Potter *et al.*, eds. New York: H. W. Wilson Company, 1900–.

9. Biographies, Memoirs, and Writings of Public Men

Adams, Charles Francis, ed., *Memoirs of John Quincy Adams.* 12 vols. Philadelphia: J. B. Lippincott & Co., 1874–1877.
Bok, Edward, *The Americanization of Edward Bok.* 8th edn. New York: Charles Scribner's Sons, 1921.
Calhoun, John C., *Works.* Richard K. Crallé, ed. 6 vols. New York: 1853–1855.
—— "Correspondence." John Franklin Jameson, ed. AHA *Report*, 1899, II, 71 *et seq*.
Chandler, William E., "Chester A. Arthur." See James G. Wilson, ed.
Farrand, Max, ed., *The Autobiography of Benjamin Franklin.* Berkeley and Los Angeles: University of California Press, 1949.
—— ed., *Memoirs of Benjamin Franklin.* Berkeley and Los Angeles: University of California Press, 1949.
Ford, Worthington C., ed., *The Writings of George Washington.* 14 vols. New York: G. P. Putnam's Sons, 1889–1893.
Franklin, Benjamin. See Max Farrand, ed.
Howe, George F., *Chester A. Arthur* (*American Political Leaders*). New York: 1934.
Madison, James, *Papers of James Madison, Being his Correspondence and Reports of Debates.* Henry D. Gilpin, ed., 3 vols. Washington: 1840.
Washington, George, *Writings.* See Worthington C. Ford, ed.
Wilson, James Grant, ed., *The Presidents of the United States, 1789–1914*, by John Fiske . . . and many others. 4 vols. New York: Charles Scribner's Sons, 1914.

10. Some Histories Referred to in the Text

Bancroft, George, *History of the United States of America from the Discovery of the Continent.* 6 vols. New York: D. Appleton and Company, 1891–1892.
Hammond, Jabez D., *The History of Political Parties in the State of New York from the Ratification of the Constitution to December, 1840.* 4th edn. Buffalo: Phinney & Co., 1850.
Hart, Albert Bushnell, ed., *The American Nation: A History.* 28 vols. New York: Harper and Brothers, 1904–1918.
McMaster, John Bach, *A History of the People of the United States.* 8 vols. and supplementary volume. New York: 1883–1913, 1927.
Schlesinger, Arthur M., and Dixon Ryan Fox, eds., *A History of American Life.* 13 vols. New York: The Macmillan Company, 1929–1948.

Sparks, Edwin Erle, *National Development, 1877–1885* (volume XXIII of *The American Nation*, edited by Albert Bushnell Hart).

Winsor, Justin, ed., *The Narrative and Critical History of America.* 8 vols. Boston: 1884–1889.

11. Special Monographs

Bernard, George S., *Civil Service Reform versus the Spoils System.* New York: J. B. Alden, 1885.

Civil Service Reform Association, *Bibliography of Civil Service Reform and Related Subjects.* Published for the Women's Auxiliary to the Civil Service Reform Association. New York: 1900.

Fish, Carl Russell, *The Civil Service and the Patronage* (*Harvard Historical Studies,* XI). New York: Longmans, Green and Company, 1905.

Lambert, Henry, *Progress of Civil Service Reform in the United States.* Boston: 1885.

Sageser, A. B., *The First Two Decades of the Pendleton Act* (University of Nebraska *Studies,* XXXIV–XXXV). Lincoln: 1935.

Stewart, F. M., *The National Civil Service Reform League.* Austin, Texas: 1929.

12. Critical Books and Articles

Anderson, Frank M., *The Mystery of "A Public Man": A Historical Detective Story.* Minneapolis: University of Minnesota Press, 1948.

Angle, Paul M., "The Minor Collection: A Criticism." *Atlantic Monthly,* CXLIII, 516–525 (April, 1929).

Beale, Howard K., "Is the Printed Diary of Gideon Welles Reliable?" *AHR,* XXX, 547–552 (April, 1925).

Dunning, William A., "More Light on Andrew Johnson." *AHR,* XI, 574–594 (April, 1906).

Gander, Olivia, *The Authorship of Washington's Farewell Address.* Master's essay. Columbus: The Ohio State University. (Typewritten.)

Jameson, John Franklin, "Studies in the History of the Federal Convention." AHA *Report* for 1902, I, 89–167.

Lewis, Montgomery, *Legends that Libel Lincoln.* New York: Rinehart & Company, 1946.

Libby, Orin Grant, "A Critical Examination of Gordon's *History of the American Revolution.*" *MVHR,* I, 365 *et seq.* (December, 1914).

Lokken, Roy N., "Has the Mystery of 'A Public Man' been Solved?" *MVHR,* XL, 419–440 (December, 1953).

Quaife, Milo M., "A Critical Evaluation of the Sources for Western History." *MVHR,* I, 167–184 (September, 1914).

Rayback, Joseph G., "Who Wrote the Allison Letters: A Study in Historical Detection." *MVHR,* XXXIV, 51–72 (June, 1949).

Woolfolk, George, *The Original Reading of the Randolph Resolutions.* Master's essay. Columbus: The Ohio State University. (Typewritten.)

13. Miscellaneous

a. *Books Mentioned in Text*

Bridenbaugh, Carl, *Cities in the Wilderness: The First Century of Urban Life in America, 1625–1742.* New York: [c1938].

Bruce, Philip Alexander, *Social Life in Virginia in the Seventeenth Century.* Richmond, Va.: Whittet and Shepperson, 1907.

Farrand, Max, ed., *The Records of the Federal Convention of 1787.* 4 vols. New Haven: Yale University Press, 1911–1937.

Finnegan, Jack, *Light from the Ancient Past.* Princeton: Princeton University Press, 1949.

Holand, H. R., *America, 1355–1364.* New York: Duell, Sloan and Pearce. 1946.

Jameson, John Franklin, ed., *Original Narratives of Early American History.* 19 vols. New York: Charles Scribner's Sons, 1906–1914. Recently reprinted by Barnes and Noble, New York.

Schlesinger, Arthur M., Jr., *The Age of Jackson.* Boston: Little, Brown and Company, 1945.

Tyler, Lyon Gardner, ed., *Narratives of Early Virginia* (volume V of *Original Narratives of Early American History,* edited by J. F. Jameson).

Wertenbaker, Thomas J., *Patrician and Plebeian in Virginia.* Charlottesville, Va.: 1910.

b. *Articles and Essays in Periodicals, Annuals, and Publications of Learned Societies*

Adams, Herbert Baxter, "Maryland's Influence upon Land Cessions." Johns Hopkins University *Studies in History and Political Science,* III, No. 1, Baltimore: Johns Hopkins University, 1885.

Anonymous, "A Relatyon of the Discovery of our River. . . ." *Archaeologia Americana,* IV, 40–65 (1860).

Becker, Carl Lotus, "Kansas," in *Essays in American History Dedicated to Frederick Jackson Turner,* 85–111. New York: Henry Holt and Company, 1910.

Gephart, William F., *Transportation and Industrial Development in the Middle West.* Columbia University *Studies in Economics, History, and Public Law,* XXXIV. New York: Columbia University, 1922.

Hockett, Homer C., "The Literary Motive in the Writing of History." *MVHR,* XII, 469–482 (March, 1926).

Houston, David Franklin, *A Critical Study of Nullification in South Carolina. Harvard Historical Studies,* III. New York: Longmans, Green and Company, 1898.

c. *Newspapers*

Baltimore Sun.

Chicago Daily Tribune.

Christian Science Monitor (Boston).

New York Herald Tribune.
New York Times.
Public Opinion (New York).
Springfield Republican (Mass.).
Time, The Weekly Newsmagazine (Chicago).

d. *Business History*

Clough, Shepard B., *A Century of American Life Insurance: A History of the Mutual Life Insurance Company of New York, 1843–1943.* New York: Columbia Press, 1946.

Larson, H. M., ed., *Guide to Business History.* Cambridge, Mass.: 1948.

14. Writings on War

a. *General*

Binkley, William C., "Two World Wars and American Historical Scholarship." *MVHR*, XXXIII, 3–26 (June, 1946).

Poole, Bernard L., *The Caribbean Commission; Background of Cooperation in the West Indies.* Columbia, S. C.: University of South Carolina Press, 1951.

Smith, Louis, *American Democracy and Military Power: A Study of Civil Control of the Military Power in the United States.* Chicago: University of Chicago Press, 1951.

(First survey of the subject for the whole period of American history. Shows that the respective powers of President and Congress were never closely defined. Continued war could lead people to regard democratic government as subordinate to military security.)

Trefousse, H. L., *Germany and American Neutrality, 1939–1941.* New York: Bookman Associates, 1951.

(Deals chiefly with Hitler's efforts to keep the United States neutral.)

Van Alstyne, Richard W., *American Crisis Diplomacy, The Quest for Collective Security, 1918–1952.* Stanford, Calif.: Stanford University Press, 1952.

(". . . Superb analysis of the rise of the Far East as a crisis area. . . .")

Wright, Chester W., ed., *Economic Problems of War and the Aftermath.* Chicago: University of Chicago Press, 1942.

b. *World War I*

Fine, Herbert, *Preliminary Inventory of Records of the National War Labor Board,* etc., prepared by Herbert Fine supervised by Chief of Division of Labor Department Archives. Washington: The National Archives, 1943.

(Records of 1918–1919. Other *Preliminary Inventories* deal with Records of the U. S. Food Administration, 1917–1920, etc., and a series of *Special Lists* have to do with other records of that period. For example, No. 5 gives information about the Records of the Bureau of Insular Affairs.)

Handbook of Federal World War Agencies and Their Records, 1917–1921. Washington: The National Archives, 1943.

The National Archives, *Preliminary Inventory of the Council of National Defense Records, 1916–1921 . . . No. 2.* Washington: 1942.

Paxson, Frederic L., *American Democracy and the World War.* 3 vols.: I, II, *America at War, 1917–1918.* Boston: 1939; III, Berkeley, Calif.: 1939.

Thomas, Robert S., and Inez V. Allen, *United States Army in the World War, 1917–1919.*

c. *World War II*

Cleveland, Reginald M., *Air Transport at War.* New York: Harper & Brothers, 1947.

Cline, Ray S., *The United States Army in World War II, The War Department, Washington Command Post: The Operation Division.* Washington: Government Printing Office, 1951.

Coleman, John M., *The Development of Tactical Services in the Army Air Forces.* New York: Columbia University Press, 1950.

(A study of the unreadiness of the U.S. forces to meet an emergency situation. Author was in the Historical Office of the Air Service Command, and completed his study as a doctoral dissertation. A real contribution.)

Connery, Robert H., *The Navy and the Industrial Mobilization in World War II.* Princeton: Princeton University Press, 1951.

(A study of administrative problems of material procurement. Author had access to official records. Praises Secretary Forrestal's organization. Experience means U.S. will be better prepared next time.)

Craven, Wesley Frank, and James Lee Cate, eds., *The Army Forces in World War II, Europe: Argument to V-E Day, January 1944 to May 1945.* Chicago: University of Chicago Press, 1951.

(A product of skilled craftsmen.)

Eckhoff, Mark G., and Alexander P. Morse, comps., *List of Foreign Service Post Records in the National Archives. Special List No. 9.* Washington: The National Archives, 1952.

(Goes through December, 1951.)

Edmonds, Walter D., *They Fought with What They Had: The Story of the Army Air Forces in the Southwest Pacific, 1941–1942.* Boston: Little, Brown and Company, 1951.

(Written at request of Personnel Narratives Office of Chief of Air Staff. Distinguished for both research and writing.)

Greenfield, Kent Roberts, "Forging the United States Army in World War II into a Combined Arms Team." *MVHR*, XXXIV, 443–452 (December, 1947).

(Army organization in two wars.)

Haines, C. Grove, and Ross J. S. Hoffman, *The Origin and Background of the Second World War.* New York: Oxford University Press, 1943.

Hall, Walter Phelps, *Iron out of Calvary: An Interpretative History of the Second World War.* New York: D. Appleton-Century Company, 1946.
(A good popular account by a skilled writer.)

Harrison, Gordon A., *Cross-Channel Attack. United States Army in World War II: The European Theater of Operations.* Washington: Office of Chief of Military History, Department of the Army, 1951.
(Carefully planned and documented. Author had access to all American records. First full account from the American point of view.)

Holmes, Oliver W., *et al., The Problem of Federal Field Office Records.* Washington: The National Archives, 1943.

Isely, Jeter, and Philip A. Crowl, *The U. S. Marines and Amphibious War; Its Theory and Its Practice in the Pacific.* Princeton: Princeton University Press, 1951.
(A product of the Princeton University Marine Corps History Project. The book shows careful research and is scholarly and timely. Both authors were service men: Isely held a Ph.D. from Johns Hopkins University; Crowl taught at the Naval War College.)

Kammerer, Gladys M., *Impact of War on Federal Administration.* Lexington, Ky.: University of Kentucky Press, 1951.
(A study of the reasons for lowering qualifications.)

Karig, Commander Walter, USNR, and Lieutenant Welbourn Kelley, USNR, *Battle Report to Coral Sea.* New York: Farrar & Rinehart, Inc., 1944.
(Good work. Semiofficial. Does not discuss controversial subjects.)

——, with Lieutenant Earl Burton, USNR, and Lieutenant Stephen L. Freeland, USNR, *Battle Report: The Atlantic War.* New York: Farrar & Rinehart, Inc., 1946.
(Semiofficial, for average citizen. Superior to many popular histories of the war.)

McInnis, Edgar, *The War: Sixth Year.* Toronto: Oxford University Press, 1946.

Miller, Francis Trevelyan, with Board of Historians and Military Authorities, *History of World War II.* Philadelphia: John C. Winston Co., 1945.
(First product: only highlights for use before official histories are published.)

Morison, Samuel Eliot, *History of the United States Naval Operations in World War II.* Vols. I–VII. Boston: Little, Brown and Company, 1947–1951.
("Joins to industrious research and literary artistry the realism that can come only from personal participation and firsthand observation." Morison knows naval warfare as no other historian knows it.)

Office of Chief of Military History, *Guide to the Writing of Military History.* Applied Studies Division of the Department of the Army, 1950.

Schlegel, Mason W., *Writing Your Community's War History.* American Association for State and Local History History *Bulletins,* II, No. 1. Raleigh, N. C., 1946.

Shugg, Lynn W., and Heber P. Walker, *Indiana in World War II*, vol. IV. *Indiana at War; Civilian Directory*. Bloomington: Indiana War History Commission, 1951.

Vann Woodward, C., *The Battle for Leyte Gulf*. New York: Macmillan, 1942.

d. *War Influences on Writing and Teaching History*

Ander, O. Fritiof, "The New Augustana Plan and an American Studies Major." *MVHR*, XXXII, 95–100 (June, 1945).

Davis, S. L., "The Writing and Teaching of History after the Present War." *MVHR*, XXXI, 99–101 (June, 1944).

Ohio State Department of Education, *A Wartime Focus for Ohio's Elementary Schools*. Columbus: State Department of Education, 1944.

Phillips, Burr W., "History Teaching and the War." *MVHR*, XXVIII, 593–596 (March, 1942).

Robinson, Edgar E., *Scholarship and Cataclysm: Teaching and Research in American History, 1939–1945*. Stanford, Calif.: Stanford University Press, 1947.

Todd, Lewis Paul, "Wartime Relations of the Federal Government and the Public Schools, 1917–1918." Columbia University Teachers' College, *Contributions to Education, No. 907*. New York: Bureau of Education, Teachers' College, Columbia University, 1946.

(The good and the harm done to the schools by the educational activities of the Federal Government during World War I.)

University of Chicago, History Staff, *Adjustment of the College Curriculum to Wartime Conditions and Trends*. Federal Security Agency of the United States Office of Education, *Report No. 2—History*.

15. Bibliographies for Regional and Local History

The items in this section are selected as examples of the kind of bibliographies in this field prepared by various agencies. Many histories of states and regions contain bibliographies which would add to those listed here. For such books consult *Harvard Guide*, 219 *et seq*. The *Guide* includes also many bibliographies proper. The present list is limited to these. An investigator interested in some part of this vast field will doubtless find it necessary to seek further guidance by correspondence with the state historian, librarian, or archivist, or some other local authority attached to the state historical society or library. This section duplicates some entries in the *Guide*, but the two lists are essentially supplementary.

a. *General*

Adams, Randolph G., "Fugitive Archives, a National Problem." *Michigan Alumnus Magazine*, XLVI, 217–226 (1940).

Angle, Paul M., "Regional and Local History in the Teaching of American History." *MVHR*, XXXI, 267–273 (September, 1944).

Billington, Ray A., "Guide to American History Manuscript Collections."
(See Bibliography, 7, c.)

Bowker, Richard R., *State Publications.* 4 vols. New York: Publishers' Weekly, 1899–1909.

Bradford, Thomas L., *Bibliographer's Manual of American History, Edited and Revised by* S. V. *Henkels.* 5 vols. Philadelphia: Henkels, 1907–1910.

Carnegie Institution, *Handbook of Learned Societies and Institutions: American.* Washington: Carnegie Institution, 1908.

Childs, James B., *An Account of Government Document Bibliography in the United States and Elsewhere.* Washington: Government Printing Office, 1927.

Clark, Arthur Henry, *The United States: A Catalogue of Books Relating to the History of Its Various States, Counties, and Cities and Territories.* Cleveland: A. H. Clark Company, 1928.

Hasse, Adelaide R., *Index of Economic Material in Documents of the States of the United States.* 13 vols. Washington: Carnegie Institution, 1907–1922.

Hoole, W. Stanley, comp., "Recent Acquisitions." *MVHR* XXXIV, 725–731 (March, 1948).

(A list of notable additions to libraries of the Mississippi Valley.)

Jenkins, William S., comp., edited by Lillian A. Hamrick, *Supplemental Checklist of Legislative Journals of the States of the United States of America.* Boston: The National Association of State Libraries, 1943.

—— *et al.*, comps., Lillian A. Hamrick, ed., *A Guide to the Microfilm Collections of Early State Records.* Prepared by the Library of Congress in Association with the University of North Carolina. Washington: Library of Congress Photoduplication Service, 1950.

Jensen, Merrill, ed., *Regionalism in America.* Madison: University of Wisconsin Press, 1951.

McMurtrie, Donald, "Locating the Printed Source Materials for United States History, with a Bibliography of Lists of Regional Imprints." *MVHR,* XXXI, 369–378 (December, 1944).

Parker, Donald, *Local History; How to Gather It, Write It, and Publish It.* Revised and edited by Bertha E. Josephson for the Committee on Guide for Study of Local History of the Social Science Research Council. New York: 1944.

(Covers every step in writing local history.)

United States, Library of Congress, Division of Documents, *Monthly Check List of State Publications, 1909–.* Washington: Government Printing Office.

b. *Regional*

Original States

Andrews, Charles M., "Lists of Reports and Representations of Plantation Councils . . . in the Public Record Office." AHA *Report* for 1913, I, 319–496.

Cross, Whitney R., Curator, *First Report . . . 1942–1945.* Ithaca: Cornell University, 1945.

(Describes the Collection of Regional History at Cornell: manuscripts, newspapers, periodicals, almanacs, broadsides, etc. Explanatory notes; index.)

Greene, Evarts B., and R. B. Morris, comps., *Guide to the Principal Sources for Early American History (1600–1800) in the City of New York*. New York: Columbia University Press, 1929.

Hasse, Adelaide R., "Materials for a Bibliography of the Public Archives of the Thirteen Original States, Covering the Colonial Period and the State Period to 1789." AHA *Report* for 1906, II, 239–561.

Jameson, John Franklin, "Colonial Assemblies and Their Legislative Journals." AHA *Report* for 1897, 405–453.

Vail, R. W. G., *The Voice of the Old Frontier*. Philadelphia: University of Pennsylvania Press, 1949.

(Bibliography of firsthand accounts in 150 libraries: 1300 titles, subject and author entries, and index.)

South

Beer, William, "Bibliographical Notes on Materials Relating to the History of the Gulf States." *Gulf States Historical Magazine*, I, 419–422 (May, 1903).

Boyd, William Kenneth, and Robert Preston Brooks, comps., *A Selected Bibliography and Syllabus of the History of the South, 1584–1876*. Athens, Ga.: The McGregor Company, 1918.

Freeman, Douglas Southall, *A Calendar of Confederate Papers, with a Bibliography of Some Confederate Publications*. Richmond, Va., Confederate Museum, 1908.

Morrison, Hugh A., "A Bibliography of the Official Publications of the Confederate States of America." Bibliographical Society of America *Proceedings and Papers*, III, 92–132 (1909).

Virginia State Library, "A List of the Official Publications of the Confederate States Government in the Virginia State Library, and the Library of the Confederate Memorial Literary Society." Virginia State Library *Bulletin*, IV, No. 1, 1–72 (January, 1911).

Prairie States

Ross, Earle D., "A Generation of Prairie Historiography." *MVHR*, XXXIII, 391–410 (December, 1946).

Mississippi Valley

Surrey, Nancy M., *Calendar of Manuscripts in Paris Archives and Libraries Relating to the History of the Mississippi Valley to 1803*. 2 vols. Washington: Carnegie Institution, 1926–1928.

Thwaites, Reuben G., *Descriptive List of Manuscript Collections of the Society, Together with Reports on other Collections of Manuscript Material for American History in Adjacent States*. Madison: Wisconsin Historical Society, 1906.

Great Plains and West

Briggs, Harold E., "An Appraisal of Historical Writings on the Great Plains Region since 1920." *MVHR* XXXIV, 83 *et seq.* (June, 1947).

Caughey, John Walton, "The Mosaic of Western History." *MVHR,* XXXIV, 595–605 (June, 1947).

(Useful as a guide to guides and contents of journals on Western history.)

Eberstadt, Edward E., "The William Robertson Coe Collection of Western Americana." New Haven: *Yale University Library Gazette,* XXIII, No. 2, 41–130 (October, 1948). See also Connecticut.

Jackson, W. Turrentine, "Materials for Western History in the Department of the Interior Archives." *MVHR,* XXXV, 61–76 (June, 1948).

Winther, Oscar O., *The Trans-Mississippi West: A Guide to Its Periodical Literature, 1811–1938. Indiana University Publications: Social Science Series,* No. 3. Bloomington: Indiana University, 1942.

(Lists 3,500 historical articles: diaries and documents in sixty magazines: *Niles' Weekly Register, Harper's, Atlantic Monthly,* and state and regional historical magazines of the Trans-Mississippi region. Author index. Table of Contents serves as a subject index.)

Withington, Mary C., comp., *A Catalogue of Manuscripts in the Collection of Western Americana. Founded by William G. Robertson Coe.* New Haven: Yale University Press, 1952.

Southwest

Dobie, J. Frank, *Guide to Life and Literature of the Southwest.* Rev. edn. Dallas: Southern Methodist University Press, 1952.

Rader, Jesse L., *South of Forty, from the Mississippi to the Rio Grande: A Bibliography.* Norman: University of Oklahoma Press, 1947.

(Selected list of 3793 titles, many containing bibliographies. No periodicals or newspapers included.)

Pacific Coast

Chapman, C. E., *Catalogue of Materials in the Archivo General de Indias for the History of the Pacific Coast and the American Southwest.* Berkeley: University of California Press, 1919.

Judson, K. B., *Subject Index to the History of the Pacific Northwest and Alaska.* Olympia: Washington State Library, 1913.

Powell, Lawrence C., "Resources of Western Libraries for Research in History." *Pacific Coast Historical Review* for September, 1942, pp. 263 *et. seq.*

Smith, Charles Wesley, *Pacific Northwest Americana.* 2d edn. New York: H. W. Wilson Company, 1921.

—— *A Union List of Manuscripts in Libraries of the Pacific Northwest.* Seattle: University of Washington Press, 1931.

Van Male, John, *Resources of Pacific Northwest Libraries: A Survey of Facilities for Study and Research.* Seattle: Pacific Northwest Library Association, 1943.

(Summarizes holdings of about one hundred libraries in British Columbia, Washington, Oregon, Idaho, and Montana. Well indexed.)

c. *Alphabetically by States*

Alabama

Owen, Thomas McAdory, "Bibliography of Alabama." AHA *Report* 1897, p. 777.

Arizona

Alliot, Hector, *Bibliography of Arizona: Being the Record of Literature Collected by Dr. J. A. Munk, and Donated by Him to the Southwest Museum.* Los Angeles: The Southwest Museum, 1914.

Lutrell, Estelle, *A Bibliographical List of Books, Pamphlets and Articles on Arizona in the University of Arizona Library.* University of Arizona *Record,* ser. VI, No. 10 (1913).

Arkansas

Herndon, Dallas T., Secretary Arkansas History Commission, "Bibliography of Historical and Literary Writings of Arkansas." History Commission *Bulletin of Information* No. 4. Little Rock: 1912.

Reynolds, John Hugh, "An Account of Books, Records, and Manuscripts Concerning Arkansas in Public Repositories within the State." Arkansas Historical Association *Publications,* I, 110–185.

—— "An Account of Books, Manuscripts, Documents, and Papers Concerning Arkansas in Private Hands." Arkansas Historical Association *Publications,* I, 230–273.

—— "An Account of Manuscripts, Papers, and Documents Concerning Arkansas in Public Repositories beyond the State." Arkansas Historical Association *Publications,* I, 43–109.

California

Baker, C. C., "A List of Newspapers in the Los Angeles City Library." Southern California Historical Society *Publications,* X, Parts 1 and 2, 80–85.

Bancroft, Hubert Howe, "Authorities Consulted on the History of California." In *Works,* XVIII, xxv–lxxxviii.

Blumann, Ethel, and Mabel W. Thomas, eds., *California Local History; A Centennial Bibliography.* Compiled by the California Library Association Commission on Local History. Stanford: Stanford University Press, 1950.

(More than a hundred local libraries cooperated in preparing this list of collections of all sizes.)

Cowan, Robert Ernest, *A Bibliography of the History of California and the Pacific West, 1510–1906.* San Francisco: Book Club of California, 1914. New edn. Columbus, Ohio: 1952.

Cuthbert, Norma B., comp., *American Manuscript Collections in the Huntington Library for the History of the Seventeenth and Eighteenth Centuries. List No. 5.* San Marino, Calif.: Huntington Library, 1941.

Huntington Library, *Bulletin No. 1,* containing a brief description of one hundred of the most important accessions. Cambridge: Harvard University Press, 1931.

Matthews, William, and Roy Harvey Pearce, comps., *American Diaries: An Annotated Bibliography of American Diaries Written Prior to 1861.* Berkeley and Los Angeles: University of California Press, 1945.

Colorado

Checklist of Territorial and State Documents, 1861–1947. Division of State Archives, 1948.

Paxson, Frederic Logan, "A Preliminary Bibliography of Colorado History." Colorado University *Studies,* III, No. 3, Part I, 101–114 (1906).

Connecticut

Connecticut Historical Society, *The Connecticut Courant* (1764–1792). Microfilm. Hartford: The Society.

Eberstadt, Edward E., "The William Robertson Coe Collection of Western Americana." (See Bibliography, Great Plains and West.)

(Presented to Yale University Library in 1943. More than 7000 items for Wyoming, Dakota, Colorado, Nevada, Utah, Montana, Idaho, California, Oregon, Washington, British Columbia, Alaska, Northwest Coast, and Louisiana Purchase Territory.)

Flagg, Charles A., *Reference List on Connecticut Local History.* Albany: University of the State of New York, 1900.

Trumbull, J. H., *List of Books Printed in Connecticut, 1709–1800.* [Hartford:] 1904.

Withington, Mary G. (See Bibliography, Great Plains and West.)

Yale University Library, "A List of Newspapers in the Yale University Library." *Yale Historical Publications, Miscellany,* II. New Haven: Yale University Press, 1916.

Delaware

Ryden, G. H., *Bibliography of Delaware History.* [Newark, 1927.]

District of Columbia

Library of Congress, Publications Section, *Libraries and Reference Facilities in the Area of the District of Columbia.* New edn. Washington: 1952.

Georgia

Brooks, Robert Preston, "A Preliminary Bibliography of Georgia History." University of Georgia *Bulletin,* X, No. 10. A. Athens: The McGregor Company, 1910.

Jack, T. H., "Historiography in Georgia." Georgia Historical Association *Proceedings,* 1917, p. 21.

Thornton, E. M., *Finding List of Books and Pamphlets Relating to Georgia and Georgians.* Atlanta: 1928.

Illinois

Angle, Paul M., and Richard L. Beyer, "A Handbook of Illinois History," in *Papers in Illinois History and Transactions for the Year 1941*, pp. 73–168.

Buck, Solon Justus, *Travel and Description, 1765–1865.* . . . Illinois State Historical Library *Collections,* IX, *Bibliographical Series,* II. Springfield: Illinois State Historical Library, 1914.

Jackson, Elizabeth Coleman, and Carolyn Custer, comps., *Guide to the Burlington Archives in the Newberry Library, 1851–1901*. Chicago: The Newberry Library, 1949.

James, Edmund J., and Milo J. Loveless, *A Bibliography of Newspapers Published in Illinois Prior to 1860*. Illinois State Historical Society *Publications,* No. 1. Springfield: 1899.

Mohr, Carolyn Curtis, comp., *Guide to the Illinois Central Archives in The Newberry Library, 1851–1906*. Chicago: The Newberry Library, 1951.

Monaghan, Jay, comp., *Lincoln Bibliography, 1839–1939. Collections of the Illinois State Historical Library, Bibliographical Series,* IV and V. Springfield: Illinois State Historical Library, 1945.
(Based on examination of every important collection in the United States.)

Osborne, Georgia L., *A List of the Genealogical Works in the Illinois State Historical Library*. Springfield: Illinois State Historical Library, 1914.

Indiana

Henley, Lillian E., "Bibliography of Indiana Local History," *History,* VI, 43 *et seq*. (June, 1910).

—— "Bibliography of Town and City Histories in the Indiana State Library." *Indiana Quarterly Magazine of History,* VI, 91–95 (June, 1910).

Indiana Historical Bureau, comp., *Encyclopedia of State History*. In progress.

Indiana Historical Society, *A Descriptive Catalogue of the Official Publications of the Territory and State of Indiana from 1800 to 1890. Pamphlet No. 5*. Indianapolis, 1890.

Indiana State Library, "Bibliography of Indiana Local History Contained in County Histories, Atlases, and Collected Biographies." *Bulletin No. V*, 3–8 (March, 1910).

Indiana State Library, "A List of Indiana Newspapers Available in the Indiana State Library, the Indianapolis Public Library, the Library of Indiana University, and the Library of Congress. . . ." *Bulletin No. XI*, 1–31 (December, 1916).

Indiana State Library, "A Select Bibliography of Indiana Historical Material in the Indiana State Library." *Bulletin No. X*, 2–16 (September, 1915).

Iowa

Brigham, Johnson, "A General Survey of the Literature of Iowa History." *Iowa Journal of History,* I, 77–104 (January, 1903).

Fitzpatrick, T. J., "Bibliography of the Iowa Territorial Documents." *Iowa Journal of History,* V, 234–269 (April, 1907).

Iowa Library Commission, *Checklist of the Publications of the State of Iowa, with an Index to the Iowa Documents.* Des Moines: Iowa Library Commission, 1904.

Petersen, William J., comp., *Iowa History Reference Guide. Bulletin of Information Series,* No. 17. Iowa City: State Historical Society of Iowa, 1952.

Kansas

Connelley, William E., *A List of Kansas Newspapers. From the Newspaper Section of the State Historical Society.* Topeka: State Printing Office, 1914.

Kansas State Historical Society, *A List of Books Indispensable to a Knowledge of Kansas History and Literature. . . .* Topeka: State Printing Plant, 1916.

Kansas State Library, "List of One Hundred Books by Kansas Authors or Authors Writing about Kansas." Twentieth Biennial *Report* of the State Librarian, 11–14. Topeka: 1916.

Kentucky

Coleman, J. W., Jr., *A Bibliography of Kentucky History.* Lexington: 1949.

Maine

Williamson, Joseph, *Bibliography of the State of Maine . . . to 1891.* 2 vols. Portland: 1896.

Maryland

The Michael Jenkins Collection of Works on the History of Maryland. Washington: Catholic University of America, 1913.

Massachusetts

Colburn, Jeremiah, *Bibliography of the Local History of Massachusetts.* Boston: 1871.

—— *Handbook of the Massachusetts Historical Society, 1791–1948.* Boston: The Society, 1949.

(First complete description: manuscripts, early newspapers, printed books.)

Flagg, Charles A., *A Guide to Massachusetts Local History; Being a Bibliographic Index to the Literature of the Towns, Cities, and Counties of the State, including Books, Pamphlets, Articles in Periodicals and Collected Works, Books in Preparation, Historical Manuscripts, Newspaper Clippings, etc.* Salem: Salem Press, 1907.

Michigan

Michigan State Library, *Genealogy and American Local History in the Michigan State Library.* 2d edn., rev. and enlarged. Lansing: 1915.

Streeter, F. B., *Michigan Bibliography. . . .* 2 vols. Lansing: 1921.

Minnesota

Jerabek, Esther, *A Bibliography of Minnesota Territorial Documents.* Minnesota Historical Society *Special Bulletin* III. St. Paul: 1936.

——— comp., *Check List of Minnesota Public Documents Issued from 1941 through 1950: Supplement, 1923 through 1940.* St. Paul: Minnesota Historical Society, 1952.

Mississippi

McMurtrie, Douglas C., *A Bibliography of Mississippi Imprints, 1798–1830. Hearstman's Historical Series, No. 69.* Beauvoir Community, Mississippi: The Book Farm, 1945.

Mississippi Historical Records Survey, *Preliminary Checklist of Mississippi Newspaper, 1805–1940.*

Mississippi Historical Society, "An Account of Manuscripts, Papers and Documents in the Public Repositories within the State of Mississippi." Mississippi Historical Society *Publications,* V, 49–117 (1902).

Mississippi Historical Society, "An Account of Manuscripts, Papers, and Documents Pertaining to Mississippi in Public Repositories beyond the State." Mississippi Historical Society *Publications,* V, 49–117 (1802).

Owen, Thomas McAdory, "A Bibliography of Mississippi." AHA *Report* for 1899, I, 633–828.

Robinson, Mary, "Mississippi Newspaper Files in the Library of the American Antiquarian Society, Worcester, Mass." (to 1868). *Gulf States Historical Magazine,* II, 50–53 (July, 1903).

Rowland, Dunbar, *Lists of Documents in England, France, and Spain, 1540–1798, of Value for Mississippi History. Fifth Annual Report* of the Director of the Mississippi Department of Archives and History. Nashville, Tenn.: Brandon Printing Co., 1907.

Missouri

Missouri State Historical Society, *List of Old Newspapers in the Library of the State Historical Society of Missouri.* Columbia: The Society, 1911.

Moody, Katherine T., "Genealogical Material in the St. Louis Public Library." St. Louis Public Library *Monthly Bulletin,* XIII, No. 8 (August, 1915).

Sampson, Francis Asbury, "Bibliography of Books of Travel in Missouri." *Missouri Historical Review,* VI, 64–81 (January, 1912).

New Hampshire

Hammond, O. G., *Dover Public Library Checklist of New Hampshire Local History.* Concord: 1925.

New Jersey

Angle, Paul M., *A Shelf of Lincoln Books: A Critical, Selective Bibliography of Lincolniana.* New Brunswick, N. J.: Rutgers University Press, in association with the Abraham Lincoln Association of Springfield, Ill., 1946.

Johnson, Maude E., "A Bibliography of New Jersey Bibliographies." New Jersey Historical Society *Proceedings*, 3d series, X, 61–62 (April, 1915).

New Mexico

Bandelier, A. F. and A. R., *Historical Documents . . . to 1773.* 3 vols. Washington: 1923.

New York

Buffalo Historical Society, "Rough List of Manuscripts in the Library of the Buffalo Historical Society." Buffalo Historical Society *Publications,* XIV, 421–485 (Appendix B) (1910).

Flagg, Charles A., and Judson T. Jennings, "Bibliography of New York Colonial History." New York State Library *Bulletin No. 56* (February, 1901).

Haskell, Daniel C., *Check-list of Newspapers and Official Gazettes in the New York Public Library.* New York: New York Public Library, 1915.

Hasse, Adelaide R., "Some Materials for a Bibliography of the Official Publications of the General Assembly of the Colony of New York, 1693–1775." New York Public Library *Bulletin*, VII, 51–79, 95–116, 129–151 (Feb., April, 1903).

Jewett, Alice Louise, *Official Publications of the State of New York Relating to its History as Colony and State.* New York State Library, *Bibliography Bulletin No. 59* (1917).

Mix, David E. E., *Catalogue of Maps and Surveys in the Offices of the Secretary of State, State Engineer and Surveyor, and Comptroller, and the New York State Library.* Rev. Printed by order of the Assembly, Albany: 1859.

New York State Library, *Annotated List of the Principal Manuscripts in the New York State Library. History Bulletin No. 3* (June, 1899).

—— *Descriptive List of French Manuscripts Copied for the New York State Library from the National Archives and National Library at Paris, 1888. History Bulletin No. 5* (1902).

Severance, Frank Hayward, "Contributions towards a Bibliography of the Niagara Region. Pamphlets and Books Printed in Buffalo prior to 1850." Buffalo Historical Society *Publications*, VI, Appendix (1903).

Yoshpe, Harry B., ed., *Guide to Ten Major Depositories of Manuscript Collections in New York State.* New York: Historical Records Survey, 1941.

(See Billington, Bibliography 7 c, for names of these depositories.)

North Carolina

Frier, Adelaide L., ed., *Records of the Moravian Church in North Carolina, 1793–1808.* North Carolina Historical Commission *Publications,* VI. Raleigh: 1943.

Historical Records Survey, *Guide to Depositories of Manuscript Collections in the United States: North Carolina.* Raleigh: 1940.

—— *The Historical Records of North Carolina, The County Records.* A WPA Program sponsored by the North Carolina Historical Commission. 3 vols. 1938–1939. Raleigh: 1942.

North Carolina Historical Commission, *Guide to Depositories of Manuscript Collections in North Carolina.* Raleigh: 1941.

—— *Forty Years of Public Service, 1903–1943.* Raleigh: The Commission, 1943.

(Includes lists of archival holdings, manuscript collections, publications, and programs.)

North Carolina State Library, *A Bibliography of North Carolina. . . . Biennial Report . . . for . . . Years Ending November 30, 1918,* pp. 23–80. Raleigh: 1919.

Weeks, Stephen Beauregard, *A Select Bibliography of North Carolina. List of Books for Schools, Libraries, and Amateurs.* Raleigh: North Carolina Library Commission, 1913.

—— *A Bibliography of the Historical Literature of North Carolina.* Harvard University Library, *Bibliographical Contributions, No. 48.* Cambridge: 1895.

See also Ray Allen Billington, *Guides to American History Manuscript Collections. . . . MVHR,* XXXVIII, 489 (December, 1951).

Ohio

Baldwin, Charles Candee, *Early Maps of Ohio and the West.* Cleveland: Western Reserve Historical Society, 1875.

Hayes, R. P., *Publications of the State of Ohio, 1803–1896, together with an Index to the Executive Documents.* Norwalk: The Laning Printing Company, 1897.

Historical and Philosophical Society of Ohio, *A Partial List of the Books in Its Library Relating to the State of Ohio.* Cincinnati: The Society, 1895.

Mink, Arthur D., *Title List of Ohio Newspapers Available in Ohio.* Columbus: Ohio State Archaeological and Historical Society, 1946. *Title List of Ohio Newspapers,* 1945.

(Both lists may be had from the Society.)

Overman, W. D., "Index to the Materials for the Study of Ohio History." *Ohio Archaeological and Historical Quarterly,* XLIV, 138 *et seq.* (1935).

Ryan, Daniel Joseph, *The Civil War Literature of Ohio; A Bibliography with Explanatory and Historical Notes.* Cleveland: Burrows Brothers Company, 1911.

State Supervisor of Public Printing, *Official List of Newspapers Published in Ohio*. Columbus: F. J. Heer Printing Company, 1916.

Stevenson, Richard Taylor, "A Preliminary Report on the Archives of Ohio." AHA *Report* for 1906, II, 165–196.

Thompson, Peter G., *A Bibliography of the State of Ohio*. Cincinnati: The Author, 1880.

—— *Catalogue of Books Relating to the State of Ohio, the West and Northwest*. Cincinnati: 1890.

Oklahoma

Dale, Edward E., and M. L. Wardell, *Outlines and References for Oklahoma History*. Norman: 1924.

Wright, Muriel H., *A Guide to the Indian Tribes of Oklahoma: Civilization of the American Indian Series*, XXXIII. Norman: University of Oklahoma Press, 1951.

Pennsylvania

Americana Germanica, Carl Schurz Memorial Foundation, Inc., of Philadelphia issues an annual bibliography and occasional bibliographies on special subjects.

Bining, Arthur C., *et al.*, comps., *Writings on Pennsylvania History: A Bibliography. A List of Secondary Materials Compiled under the Auspices of the Pennsylvania Historical Association*. Harrisburg: Pennsylvania Historical and Museum Commission, 1946.

(A cooperative production of the Pennsylvania Historical Association and the American Philosophical Society. (1) Subject classification of about 6,000 periodical articles and books; (2) 4,056 titles in chronological order; (3) local, religious, and military history; (4) author index;—subject index to follow. First of a projected series. Annual checklists planned for current writings and bibliographies of source material.)

Historical Society of Pennsylvania, *Guide to the Manuscript Collections of the Historical Society of Pennsylvania*. 2d edn. Philadelphia: The Society, 1949.

—— *The Pennsylvania Gazette (1728–1789)*. Microfilm. Philadelphia: The Society.

Inventories of County Archives. Harrisburg: Archives Publishing Company.

(This company is publishing the results of work begun by the Historical Records Survey.)

Pennsylvania State Library, *Check-List of Pennsylvania County, Town, and Township Histories, 1794–1892*. Harrisburg: 1892.

Rhode Island

Chapin, Howard M., *Bibliography of Rhode Island Bibliography*. Providence: Preston & Rounds, 1914.

Wroth, Lawrence C., *The First Century of the John Carter Brown Library: A History with a Guide to Its Collections.* Providence: The Associates of The Library, 1946.

South Carolina

Easterby, J. H., *Guide to the Study and Reading of South Carolina History: A General Classified Bibliography.* Columbia: The Historical Commission of South Carolina, 1950.

Whitney, Edson L., "Bibliography of South Carolina." AHA *Report* for 1894, 563–586.

South Dakota

Works Progress Administration, *South Dakota Place Names.* . . . 1942.

Tennessee

Works Progress Administration, Writers Project, The Historical Records Survey of Tennessee, *Check List of Tennessee Imprints, 1841–1850.*

Texas

Carroll, H. Bailey, *Texas County Histories: A Bibliography.* Austin: 1943.

Raines, C. W., *A Bibliography of Texas; . . . Descriptive List of Books, Pamphlets, and Documents . . . in Print and Manuscript since 1536.* Austin: 1896.

Texas State Library and Historical Commission, "Calendar of the Mirabeau Buonaparte Lamar Papers." State Library *Report,* 1911–1912, Part II, 7–315. Austin: 1914. "Check List of Transcripts from the Archives of Mexico," *ibid.,* 46–64. "List of Transcripts from the British Public Records Office," *ibid.,* appendices 2 and 3.

Winkler, Ernest W., ed., *Check List of Texas Imprints, 1846–1860.* Austin: Texas State Historical Association, 1949.

Vermont

Gilman, M. D., *Bibliography.* . . . Burlington: 1897.

Jones, M. B., *List of Additions to Gilman's Bibliography.* . . . Boston: 1926.

Virginia

Cappon, Lester Jesse, comp., *Virginia Newspapers, 1821–1935.* New York: Appleton-Century Company.

—— *Twelfth Annual Report on Historical Collections, University of Virginia Library, for the Year 1941–1942.*

(A general survey of archives acquisitions in the United States.)

——, and Stella F. Duff, comps., *Virginia Gazette Index, 1736–1780.* 2 vols. Williamsburg: The Institute of Early American History and Culture, 1950.

(Microfilm edn. Replaces photostat edn. in Massachusetts Historical Society and covers more issues. Has matter from other colonial papers.

The full index is the first for a colonial newspaper. Supplemented by photostat copies of *Gazette* located elsewhere and found later.)

"Check-List of Virginia State Publications, 1946." Virginia State Library *Bulletin*, XXII, No. 3, 149–243. Richmond: 1948.

(Thirteenth check list of the series.)

Minor, Mrs. Kate Pleasants, *et al.*, "A List of Newspapers in the Virginia State Library, Confederate Museum, and Valentine Museum." Virginia Library *Bulletin*, V, No. 4, 285–425 (October, 1912).

Swem, Earl G., "A Bibliography of the Conventions and Constitutions of Virginia, Including References to Essays, Letters, and Speeches in Virginia Newspapers." Virginia State Library *Bulletin*, III, No. 4, 355–441 (October, 1910).

—— "A Bibliography of Virginia." Part I in Virginia State Library *Bulletin*, VIII, Nos. 2–4, 31–767 (1915; Part II in *Bulletin*, X, Nos. 1–4 (January–October, 1917); Part III in *Bulletin*, XII, Nos. 1–2 (January–April, 1919).

Torrence, William Clayton, *A Trial Bibliography of Colonial Virginia.* In *Fifth-Sixth Annual Report* of the Library Board of the Virginia State Library. Richmond: 1908–1910.

University of Virginia, Alderman Library, Check Lists of Manuscripts for Virginia Colonial History in British Archives. Mimeographed. Also F. L. Berkeley, Jr., Check List of Virginia Manuscripts in Unofficial Archives of the British Isles.

Virginia Imprint Series, No. 1. *Preliminary Checklist for Abingdon, 1807–1876*. Richmond: Virginia State Library, 1946.

Wisconsin

Schlinkert, Leroy, comp., *Subject Bibliography of Wisconsin History.* Madison: State Historical Society, 1947.

(Popular accessible references.)

Smith, Alice E., ed., *Guide to the Manuscripts of the Wisconsin State Historical Society*. Madison: State Historical Society, 1944.

(Does not include Draper Collection, for which see *Descriptive List* below.)

Wisconsin State Historical Society, *Annotated Catalogue of Newspaper Files in the Library of the Wisconsin State Historical Society*. 2d edn. Madison: The Society, 1911.

—— *Supplementary Catalogue of Newspaper Files in the Wisconsin State Historical Society Library, Listing the Papers Acquired . . . 1911–1917. Bulletin of Information No.* 93. Madison: The Society, 1918.

—— *Catalogue of Books on the War of the Rebellion, and Slavery, in the Library*. Madison: The Society, 1887.

—— *Checklist of Publications of the Society, 1850–1913. Bulletin of Information* No. 67. Madison: The Society, 1913.

—— *Descriptive List of Manuscript Collections of the Society. . . .* Madison: 1906.

Wyoming

Homsher, Lola M., "Archives of the Wyoming Stock Growers Association." *MVHR*, XXXIII, 279–288 (September, 1946).

(The University of Wyoming created the position of archivist to care for the growing collection of Western Americana.)

Riley, Gladys F., *Index to the Annals of Wyoming and Miscellaneous Historical Publications.* c1943.

INDEX

For each book and article mentioned in the text or notes the Index includes (1) an entry under the author's name with title and, sometimes, bibliographical data; (2) a title entry with cross reference to the author's name; (3) often one or more subject entries for topics with which the work deals. Other subject entries are concerned with topics discussed in the text rather than with any writing covered by author or title entries. Examples are: Criticism; Master's essays; Degree of Ph.D. Works listed in the Bibliography are not indexed unless they are mentioned in text or footnotes, or supplement those which are. Some of these are grouped in classified lists and indexed under group titles instead of separately. Examples: Local history; Writings on War.

In addition to the abbreviations referred to in the first index item, the Index uses the following: the word footnote is abbreviated to n.; title entries may be shortened to the words necessary to identify them, and the words abbreviated to easily understood forms. Thus *American History* may be reduced to *Amer. Hist.* The articles a, an, the, are used in titles only where really needed. Contracted forms may be used for organizations, as Amer. Folk-Lore Soc. Cross reference to an author's name uses only the family name if it identifies him; *e.g.*, McMurtrie. In case of common names like Smith, Jones, Brown, a distinguishing initial is added. The Index lists eight Adamses identifying them by initials; and as three persons of this name have given names beginning with H (Hannah, Henry, Herbert Baxter), these replace initials.

Author entries are followed by the titles of the author's writings mentioned in text or footnote, with the pages for them. Statements made by or about them also appear in such entries. If full bibliographical data are not found in text or footnote, the Index may carry an entry in the Bibliography containing the information.

Names of reviewers are indexed only when text or footnote includes matter from their comments.